A volume in
also includes:

Robert Spencer, Earl of Sunderland (1958)
The Stuart Constitution (1966)

J. P. KENYON

The Stuarts

*A Study in
English Kingship*

FONTANA/COLLINS

First published by B. T. Batsford Ltd. 1958
First issued in Fontana 1966
Ninth Impression October 1972

© J. P. Kenyon 1958, 1970

Printed in Great Britain
Collins Clear-Type Press
London and Glasgow

FOR DANTE AND SELINA

CONTENTS

ILLUSTRATIONS

PREFACE TO NEW EDITION

This book was published in 1958 (and written the year before), and I have seriously considered whether it ought not to be re-written from beginning to end. However, the results of such revisions are rarely very happy, and after scrutinising the book as objectively as possible I can only find two or three minor instances in which my conclusions need to be amended in the light of subsequent research. So, I have added some notes at the end of this Preface commenting on these points, and on one or two others which seem in need of elucidation. Their presence is indicated by an asterisk (*) in the text. I have also taken the opportunity to correct one or two minor typographical errors and bring the 'Suggestions for Further Reading' up to date.

I have now suppressed the prefaces to the previous editions, but I would not like my debt to Christopher Morris and Jack Plumb to be forgotten.

J.P.K.
1 Jan. 1970

Notes to New Edition

p. 20, line 12. I regret to say that this is quite wrong. In fact, the net increase in the English peerage between 1603 and 1641 was 66, more than 100%. See Lawrence Stone, *Crisis of the Aristocracy*, p. 758, App. vi.

p. 23, line 15. Our whole picture of the Hampton Court Conference must be revised in the light of Professor Mark Curtis's article in *History*, xlvi (1961). The most important point he makes is that James was much less prejudiced in favour of the bishops than has been supposed.

p. 27, line 34. This chronic litigation, which died away in the 18th century, seems to have arisen in part from the difficulty of establishing title to land under Common Law, and in this connexion a useful book is A. W. B. Simpson's *Introduction to the History of Land Law* (1961). But Professor Thomas Barnes argues that it was also a recreation and a means of asserting social prestige (*American Journal of Legal History*, vi (1962), 337-9).

p. 30, line 23. It has been pointed out to me that this speech only survives in draft amongst Eliot's papers, and he may never have delivered it. This would invalidate the next sentence in the text, though my main point stands.

p. 37, line 9. I am now more convinced than ever that opposition in James's first parliament, as in Elizabeth's last, hinged on fiscal or financial grievances. Professor Elton has recently pointed out that even the 'Form of Apology' evolved out of a petition against wardship (G. R. Elton, 'A High Road to Civil War?' in *From the Renaissance to the Counter-Reformation*, ed. Charles H. Carter (1966), p. 325).

p. 37, last line. This mistake arose from a hasty reading of Gardiner (*History of England*, i, 191); see Kenyon, *Stuart Constitution*, pp. 39-42. It is significant that James did *not* mention the Form of Apology, even obliquely; it suggests that he had not received it, or perhaps even seen it.

p. 52, line 8. It has now been shown that Cranfield's origins were petty bourgeois at the worst, though this made little difference in a status-conscious society. Since *The Stuarts* was written two very good books have appeared on Cranfield: *Business and Politics under James I* (1958) by R. H. Tawney, and *Cranfield* (1966) by Menna Prestwich.

p. 60, line 30. As Vice-Admiral of Devon Eliot could also expect to make a large personal profit out of such a war.

p. 75, line 2. This statement needs to be modified slightly in the light of Robert Ashton's *The Crown and the Money Market 1603-1640* (1960). Charles's credit was particularly bad in 1640, but there was a community of interest between the established government and the London financial interests which obliged them to rally to him in 1641.

p. 82, line 32. See Hugh F. Kearney, *Strafford in Ireland 1633-41* (1959). Most of the articles of impeachment exhibited against Strafford in 1641 related to his rule in Ireland.

p. 88, line 29. In fact, the dispute over the king's right to appoint ministers of state and officers of the armed forces was probably as important as the dispute over the future of the Church.

p. 111, line 14. Here I am guilty of perpetuating an error contained in many standard histories, which refer to Charles's 'First Declaration of Indulgence'. All Charles did in December 1662 was to issue a general declaration dealing with a variety of topics, in which he expressed his regret at the failure to implement the promise of 'a liberty for tender consciences' contained in the Declaration of Breda, and remarked that he would gladly give his assent to a bill authorising his use of the dispensing power in individual cases. (See Kenyon, *Stuart Constitution*, pp. 404-5). Parliament could have ignored this overture, but it chose to reject it formally. There is no comparison between this and the Declaration of 1672, which suspended the penal statutes outright.

p. 118, line 22. It has been pointed out to me that this is wrong. Charles merely undertook to announce his own personal conversion; if this provoked a rebellion, then military assistance would be forthcoming from France.

p. 121, line 34. There is a tradition to the effect that Clifford betrayed the secret clauses of the Treaty of Dover to Shaftesbury, but I cannot find any reliable proof. It is difficult to see why Clifford should have done so, and Shaftesbury's subsequent conduct would surely have been very different if he had.

p. 179, line 36. Some reviewers expressed pious horror at the use of the word 'homosexual' in this context. It is surely possible to have a non-physical homosexual relationship, and this, I believe, was the case with William and Bentinck. I may, of course, be wrong.

J.P.K.

ACKNOWLEDGMENTS

The sketch of the Countess of Castlemaine and the portrait of Queen Catherine of Braganza from a miniature by Samuel Cooper are reproduced by gracious permission of Her Majesty the Queen, and the portrait of Charles I, at his trial, by gracious permission of Her Majesty Queen Elizabeth the Queen Mother. The portrait Mary II as Princess of Orange from a contemporary miniature is reproduced by gracious permission of Her Majesty Queen Juliana of the Netherlands.

The Author and the Publishers wish to thank the following for permission to reproduce the illustrations appearing in this book:

The Trustees of the British Museum, for the engravings of The Whitehall of Charles I, for the medals of William and Mary, Anne and James I; His Grace the Duke of Buccleuch and Queensberry, for the portraits of Mary Davis, Lucy Walter, The Duchess of Portsmouth and Queen Anne by Charles Boit; the Fitzwilliam Museum, Cambridge, for the pastel drawing of Charles II by Edward Lutterel; His Grace the Duke of Grafton, for the portrait of Charles II in exile; the National Maritime Museum, Greenwich, for the portrait of James I attributed to Jan de Critz; the National Portrait Gallery, for the portraits of Nell Gwyn after Sir Peter Lely and James II by Sir Godfrey Kneller; the National Galleries of Scotland, for the portrait of Charles II as Prince of Wales; Royal Academy of Arts, for the portraits of Charles I and Henrietta Maria by Van Dyck and Princess Anne by John Riley; the Right Hon. the Earl Spencer, for the portrait of Princess Anne by John Riley; Walker Art Gallery, Liverpool, and the National Trust, for the portrait of William III by Gottfried Schalcken.

CHAPTER I

THE TUDOR SUNSET

Elizabeth I was a great woman and a great queen, but in the decade straddling her death her popularity was at its nadir. The reign closed in an atmosphere of depression, with war abroad, pestilence and rising prices at home, the government wracked by faction and bitterly unpopular, and parliament sunk in discontented apathy. The Tudor polity was running down, and men awaited the first king to sit on the English throne for half a century in expectation of some decisive change.

The first two Tudors had created a state as absolute as any in Europe. The ruler appointed, and dismissed at will, the judges of common law, whose efforts were supplemented by the prerogative courts of Star Chamber and High Commission under his direct command. A highly efficient Council not only superintended every branch of administration but also controlled the local justices of the peace, who were also appointed by the king, through his Lord Chancellor. The will of the King in Parliament, expressed through statute, knew no limitations or boundaries whatsoever, except the vague prescription of "natural", "moral" or "higher" law. But the King in Council, or the king acting alone, also possessed wide and ill-defined powers. When the Stuarts formally tested these powers the results were alarming; in 1627, for instance, the judges discovered, somewhat to their uneasiness, that no precedent limited the king's powers of arbitrary arrest and imprisonment. The formidable oath of supremacy, taken by all officials, declared that Elizabeth was "the only Supreme Governor of this realm and of all other her highness's dominions and countries, as well in all spiritual or ecclesiastical things or causes as temporal".

But the appearance of power was not the reality. Government was still the monarch's personal concern, and the administration of justice, diplomacy and the secret services, as well as the upkeep of the royal household, palaces and guards, were all supported on the revenue from his private estate (the Crown Lands), the profits of justice, in fines and forfeitures, such perquisites as came his way in his capacity as feudal overlord, and tunnage and poundage, the great mediaeval customs duties on wine and wool, granted by Tudor parliaments for life. This budget left little room for expansion, and since there was no regular direct taxation there could be no standing army or navy of any size. In war the monarch used the shire levies, or militia, and called upon parliament for extra taxation to support more seasoned forces; naval warfare was conducted on an amateur, piratic basis. Similarly, the crown could never finance a paid local bureaucracy; the provincial administration was handled mainly by justices of the peace in their alternative capacity as fiscal and administrative officials. Even the central government was not based on a salary system; officials relied mainly on fees, or perquisites in kind—though these could be considerable.

Not surprisingly, then, the Tudor state was only approximately efficient, and never even approximately honest. Graft and corruption were inherent in the system, even in the provinces, and at times reached stupefying proportions. The discovery that the Ordnance Office was running guns to Vigo at the height of the war against Spain caused a petulant stir, but not the comprehensive upheaval that might have been expected.[1] Similarly, the much-lauded justices of the peace administered what laws or regulations were convenient to them; the rest they ignored. Their formidable powers of obstruction and inertia are evident in the almost total failure of the many Tudor Enclosure Acts, but even the administration of the recusancy laws and the acts against Puritan preachers varied in its efficiency according to the sympathies or prejudices of the local bench. The outparts—Wales and the Marches, Yorkshire, Lancashire and parts north—were virtually ruled by the local nobility

[1] David Mathew, *The Celtic Peoples and Renaissance Europe*, ch. xvii.

and gentry; the Privy Council maintained an appearance of authority by agreeing with or anticipating their decisions. The conciliar courts set up in these semi-civilised regions—the Council of the North, and the Council of the Marches and Wales—were a leasing-out of central power in return for minimum good order. Except in cases of lower-class insurrection the Star Chamber was only called in when one side or another in a local feud was at its last gasp. Even then, public order was only sketchily maintained. Cornish piracy, organised by the local magnates, flourished in despite of the central government throughout Elizabeth's reign; and even in the 1630s the miners of the Forest of Dean remained to all intents and purposes outside the law.[2]

In fact, the Tudor system was a voluntary alliance between a central monarchy and a provincial landowning class. It was at its strongest in the reign of Henry VIII, when each partner had most to expect from the other. In carrying out his revolutionary break-away from Rome, the king had leaned heavily on his faithful Commons, and they were rewarded, whether intentionally or not, by the redistribution of monastic land. But this honeymoon did not last a generation, for the steep rise in prices soon overtook rents and forced land values down. Moreover, a new generation rose to question the assumptions on which the Henrican Reformation was based, and the gentry's anxious search for a New Interpretation bedevilled their relations with Elizabeth. The long war with Spain produced a relentless economic pressure that distorted a semi-molten social system as it set.

The economic condition of the Elizabethan and Stuart gentry has roused more controversy amongst English historians than any other question in recent years. The main difficulty lies in distinguishing between various types of gentry, or even defining the term " gentleman " at all. The technical qualifications of a gentleman were merely the possession of freehold land to the value of forty shillings a year,

[2] W. B. Willcox, *Gloucestershire 1590-1640* (Yale 1940), ch. vii, and D. G. C. Allan, " The Rising in the West, 1628-1631," *Economic History Review*, 2nd ser., v. 76.

and the right to bear arms (literally, as well as heraldically). Neither presented much of a stumbling-block to a man with money.

These technical qualifications, however, did little more than create a large county electorate of forty-shilling free-holders. Within each county was a much smaller class, whose supremacy is undeniable but not easily definable; resting partly on greater wealth (at least £500 a year), partly on tradition, but principally on action. In other words, a man who could sustain the rôle of a gentleman, was one. From this class exclusively were drawn the justices of the peace, the sheriffs, the deputy-lieutenants, the knights of the shires and most of the borough M.P.s. These were the county élite, what is most usually meant by " the gentry " at a national level, and what is known sometimes as " the parliamentary gentry ".

In support of this status they were expected to set standards in dress, patronage, hospitality and building far above the means of most small landowners, and if only for this reason they could never form a large class. In the period 1603-40 there were probably not more than four hundred families which attained a considerable position in the provinces and established a lien on a Commons seat in two successive parliaments. To achieve such a position required not merely wealth and estate—though that was, of course, essential—but also ability, personality and luck. For each county was uneasily divided between two or three, perhaps four or five leading families (depending on its area, wealth and parliamentary representation), and any new family had to crash this exclusive circle. Sometimes the intruder was repulsed in disorder; sometimes one of the reigning families fell, undermined in its court connexions, ruined by mercantile speculation or the excesses of a spendthrift heir, or eliminated by the failure of the male line (no uncommon thing in an age of high infant mortality). But, failing an immediate solution, the issue had to be decided in a struggle that could last generations; punctuated by sudden sallies on unguarded boroughs, thunderous attempts to swing county elections, acrimonious disputes over precedence on Grand

Juries and open quarrels at Quarter Sessions, which culminated in public insults or even fighting, especially amongst servants and retainers. It would peter out in a flicker of petty animosities, a rumble of Star Chamber suits over the horizon. But in many counties, where there was a large " establishment " of aspirant gentry and never enough spoils to go round, such warfare was endemic. Buckinghamshire was so overcrowded, with the Godwins, the Fleetwoods, the Verneys, the Dentons, the Bulstrodes and the Hampdens, that between 1603 and 1641 it secured six extra parliamentary seats—at Wendover, Amersham and Marlow—bringing its total representation up to fourteen. Even then, the recurrent disputes were not smothered until the Whartons from the North intermarried with the Godwins and seized a majority of the borough seats at the end of the century.

All this sounds anarchic, and was; but in this anarchy lay the gentry's peculiar strength. They were a class in perpetual motion, and the rise or fall of individual families scarcely affected their general stability. The ceaseless struggle for prestige, wealth and power, its achievement or retention, generation on generation, hardened and toughened those families that survived. They were proud, independent, acquisitive and able, breeding large families and marrying off their children with Hapsburg foresight. The social prestige attaching to ownership of land, and the rule of primogeniture, made county society an ideal organisation for the conservation of wealth, and whatever the vicissitudes of individuals or families in any given area the power complex within that area remained virtually unchanged. As one family fell, two others rose to take its place. So each county appeared to the outside world as a concentrated nexus of power, spinning, changing, but ever constant, and it is this that gave the gentry their tremendous impact and driving force. It enabled them to dominate the parliamentary representation of England in the period 1560 to 1690; even if they could not turn that domination to constructive ends.

The hard economic conditions of the late sixteenth century —particularly the price rise—were felt most keenly by the gentry just below the highest class: competing for the highest positions but not yet enjoying their fruits. But by the 1590s the depression in agriculture and trade, and the slow collapse of crown finances, had also begun to wittle away the marginal income that enabled the parliamentary gentleman to sustain the "port" appropriate to his station. Plague abounded; commerce was disrupted; wet summers brought poor harvests. The government, always the biggest customer of industry in wartime, was often a defaulting creditor, and already the decline of the staple English wool trade had begun to set in. Depression conditions forced the merchants into tighter rings, or cartels; government interference led them to take parliament more seriously, to seek self-expression as a class. They were less willing than before to distribute their wealth amongst the landed gentry by intermarriage. Similarly, the great self-made legal officers, their status rising with their fees, were now founding landed families of their own.

One of the principal sources of income remaining was the court. Court attendance was loyal as well as gentlemanly, fashionable as well as profitable. Sometimes decisively so, to families like the Cecils, Sydneys, Seymours and Russells; but many men who never aspired to an earldom materially improved their finances, and their status in the localities, by virtue of their connexions at court. The Tudors had encouraged this practice; the close-fisted Henry VII realised that the king must always outshine his greatest subjects in hospitality and display, and his son outshone most of the European monarchs of his time. From the circumstances of their youth Mary and Elizabeth both had particularly close relations with their gentry courtiers. All of them regarded Whitehall or Greenwich rather as the Bourbons regarded Versailles: properly used, it could attract a representative selection of the landowning classes and hold them in a position of dependence on, or obligation to, the crown.

Almost to the last the Tudors maintained the stream of pickings for their courtiers, high and low. The great flow of monastic lands soon died away to a trickle, but crown estates were still doled out in small lots, with timber rights and mining concessions. Ecclesiastical preferment, the income from vacant sees, the forfeited estates of papists, were the contributions of God to Mammon. For the rest, there were grants of customs duties and industrial monopolies, there were pensions and ceremonial offices, and all that profusion of sinecures left over from centuries of mediaeval experimentation in law and household government.

The institution of wardship was particularly valuable, because it worked both ways. By the foundation of the Court of Wards in 1540 Henry VIII consolidated his feudal rights over English landowners; widows, idiots, and heirs or heiresses who were minors fell in to the Court of Wards, which administered their estates and arranged their marriage or remarriage. By this means the crown always held part of the landowning classes *in terrorem* and at the same time provided another part with occasional gratuities, for the grant of a ward was a much-sought-after part of the king's bounty.

The Tudors have sometimes been criticised for their generosity to courtiers—particularly for the issue of monopolies and the alienation of Crown Lands. In fact, much of this generosity was calculated policy; they knew the danger in the dissipation of crown revenue at source, but they knew also that it was vital to have around them a strong, contented courtier class, recruited from among a satisfied gentry.

The system began to break down in the 1590s, when the steep rise in European prices, coupled with the Spanish war and revolt in Ireland, put the crown finances to an intolerable strain. The ineffectiveness and inequity of sixteenth-century taxation, the resistance of the gentry, who were themselves feeling the pinch, Elizabeth's reluctance to go against her father and grandfather's conventions of government; all this made it impossible to distribute the cost of the war equitably between crown and parliament. Instead the queen chose to squeeze the existing system dry, and in her last years she adopted financial devices as arbitrary as any em-

ployed by the Stuarts, and which provided them, in fact,
with several excellent precedents. She clapped impositions
on currants, she imposed a rudimentary form of ship money
on the maritime towns, she issued patents of monopoly on
a lavish scale, and she levied forced loans on the gentry
in 1599, 1600 and 1601.

Meanwhile, the whole structure was being undermined by
the sale of Crown Lands, resumed on a large scale after the
Armada. As a result it became increasingly difficult for the
queen to alienate further estates to courtiers, however small
the amount, while the loss in regular crown income meant
that the proceeds from the remaining Crown Lands must
be increased, or at all costs maintained, in face of inflation.
So from 1600 to 1640 crown tenants were subjected to
exactions and extortions that mounted as prices rose and
the total area of Crown Lands dwindled. Even then, the
corruption of administrative officials and the resistance of
tenants made it impossible to maintain income from land
at its previous level; ecclesiastical first-fruits and tenths
dropped off, too, and even the income from recusancy fines
declined with the relaxation of persecution.

The effects on the court were disastrous. The slump in
crown income, the dwindling of crown patronage, made it
increasingly difficult for a new generation of gentry to make
their way at court, and even for those already at Whitehall
there was scarcely enough to go round. As the queen
entered upon her old age her personal grip relaxed, and
so did Burleigh's. The court began to split into exclusive
factions of a type fatal to the continuance of the Tudor
system, which had always flourished on the free flow of
new men and new ideas. With the growth of faction came
the attempt to monopolise offices and perquisites as they
fell, leading to clientage and pluralism. The process was
accelerated by the fall in value of individual perquisites,
and by the increased corruption attendant on faction rule.
Elizabeth was slow to move against a situation that had
already threatened her once in the person of the great
Earl of Leicester; she allowed the " Cecilians ", led by
Burleigh's son Robert Cecil, to consolidate their position

against her personal favourite, Essex. Essex's revolt destroyed him, leaving the Cecilians triumphant.[8]

Essex's *putsch* was mainly supported by indigent lower gentry who had turned to war as a profession, by papists, and by Welshmen—an interesting combination. Its near success, and the sympathy it evoked, emphasised the weakness of Tudor rule, and the queen's current unpopularity. The gallant earl was the popular champion against faction rule and petticoat government. It also emphasised the failure of the Tudors to solve the problem of the nobility. The failure of the English nobility to survive as a military caste had left them with no inherited function, while strict application of the rule of primogeniture had prevented their extension through land-owning society. (On the Continent a patent of nobility embraced the whole family, in England only its head and to a certain extent his eldest son.) The natural suspicions of the Tudors made them reluctant to increase their numbers, or use them for any distinctive purpose; the strong, confident Henry VIII probably employed them more than any other member of the dynasty, but Mary was soured by Northumberland's attempt to keep her from the throne, Elizabeth by the Northern Rebellion and the Duke of Norfolk's treason. Great seigneurs like Essex and Leicester were given command of military expeditions abroad, but in peacetime their political influence bore no relation to their great wealth. Most of their energies were channelled into palace intrigue, and Essex's revolt was as much a protest against this general state of frustration as against any specific injuries.

At the turn of the century, in fact, the nobility were in the middle of a transition period that was to last until 1660. Poised uneasily between the status of feudal barons and eighteenth-century " men of influence ", they were only intermittently effective in war or politics. The careers of Essex and the Duke of Buckingham savour strongly of late-mediaeval or " bastard " feudalism; the Earls of Bedford and Pembroke, with their gifts of negotiation and debate, their

[8] See the gloomy picture painted by Sir John Neale in his Ralegh Lecture for 1948, *The Elizabethan Political Scene.*

nucleus of Commons support, look forward to the great
Earl of Shaftesbury, and beyond him to the Duke of Newcastle. But for the moment the influence of the House of
Lords, as distinct from the crown, was negligible, and individual nobles were uncertain in their handling of social
or political influence, and largely ineffective in guiding or
controlling their social inferiors, the gentry.

The Stuarts were more generous than the Tudors in their
creation of peers (they even made it a source of income),
but James I and Charles I did little more than make good the
losses occasioned by failures in the male line over the
last century—nor were their creations always well chosen.*
In other respects their reigns merely accentuated existing
social and economic tendencies. The domination of the Cecilians was confirmed, and set a pattern for the future. The
income of the crown continued to fall, and what fiscal
reform there was tended to concentrate that income in a
narrowing circle. By the 1620s the shortage of patronage
was acute. There were eight contenders for the Provostship
of Eton in 1623, all of them courtiers and crown servants
of the first rank; and the post went to Sir Henry Wotton, the
Venice ambassador, largely because the government could
not pay his arrears of salary.⁴ Moreover, after a brief
recovery in the early 1600s, trade and industry slid off
into a steep economic decline lasting throughout the thirties
and forties. These economic conditions did not ruin the
parliamentary gentry; they were a capable, well-organised
class, and with some inevitable casualties they weathered the
storm. But they were made to realise that they had as yet
no stable position in the state. They were poised uneasily
between the crown above and the ravening, pullulating mass
of the aspiring gentry below. The economic decline of
the crown restricted the careers open to them at court and
made it almost impossible for them to escape from the
neurotic rat-race in which their class was constantly engaged.
It was the social tension thus created that provoked an
explosion in 1640 and 1641 and divided the Long Parliament
into two competing groups: one advocating co-operation

⁴ David Mathew, *The Jacobean Age*, pp. 213-15.

with the crown, the other, domination of the crown; both seeking social stabilisation.

Religion was the other great cause of dissension and disunion in seventeenth-century England. But this does not excuse the extraordinary abuse of the term "Puritanism", which has been used to cover every type of opposition to the Stuarts, for whatever cause.

The greatest single difficulty in discussing Puritanism is the fact that nine-tenths of those who supported it at various times were virtually dumb, and the vocal one-tenth were by no means the most important, and were probably not even representative. The literary output of the Puritan clergy, their hagiographers and pamphleteers, has been subjected to the most ruthless analysis, but it is misleading to infer, as some do, that such analyses give us a clear picture of the "Puritan movement", as a politico-religious phenomenon. The hard truth is that Puritanism would never have advanced an inch without the support of the gentry, particularly in parliament; yet these gentry preached no sermons, they wrote very few books and even their parliamentary speeches are either brief and elusive, or turgid and confused. (The great majority never opened their mouths within the walls of Westminster.) So the motives of these men can rarely be reconstructed from their utterances, only deduced from their actions.

And their actions were erratic; there was no broad sweep of development as amongst the reformist clergy. The opening of Elizabeth's reign found the nation disunited and drifting. The mediaeval concept of society had been based on the two great pillars of Throne and Altar. Henry VIII had knocked one of these essential props away, and only his extrovert dynamism, coupled with a unique capacity for focusing authority, had convinced the nation that no fundamental change had in fact taken place. The reign of Edward VI exposed this conjuring trick, and Elizabeth made no attempt to emulate her father. Those who accepted the Elizabethan church accepted it as part of the system of government, a quasi-spiritual projection of the secular state.

Many did not; and for the first thirty years of her reign the reformist clergy, supported by influential allies in parliament and at court, strove to convert the church into something more expressive of the national genius and farther removed from Rome. The New Dispensation was to be confirmed by the issue of a revised prayer book, nearer to the Calvinist ideal, and would proceed to the reform of the clergy and the abolition or modification of episcopacy.

But in the 1580s, quite suddenly, the majority of the gentry removed their support. They belatedly realised that to support the reformist clergy to the bitter end would be to surrender the church to the control of ministers who were abler and more aggressive than most of its present leaders, and it was never part of the gentry's plan to strengthen the organisation of the church. In fact, the key to an understanding of their attitude, from 1529 to 1641, is their rabid anti-clericalism. Their aim, not achieved until 1660, was a gentry-dominated church subject to parliament; the creation of a strong church independent of crown and parliament alike would merely weaken their own social position, worse still, it would threaten their own direct influence on the clergy through the rights of presentation to benefices they had inherited with the monastic lands.[5] Worse still, the rejection of episcopal discipline could lead to the rejection of all discipline, and the fears thus aroused were to be amply confirmed in the 1640s. The growth of Sectarianism, or Brownism, in the later sixteenth century alarmed the gentry more than the survival of popery. The Calvinistic doctrine that all men were so far beneath God as to be equal in his eyes, that salvation was open to all men, and had in fact been arbitrarily awarded to some men, not others, in an archetypal lottery conducted long before the social status of either Elect or Reprobate was decided; all this had the most destructive social implications, which were driven home by the scurrility and subversiveness of the Puritan Marprelate Tracts published in the 1580s. Hastily the gentry

[5] These rights also conferred economic benefits, which are brought out by Christopher Hill, in *Economic Problems of the Church from Archbishop Whitgift to the Long Parliament.*

closed their ranks, right about turned, formed up behind the bishops, and advanced with fixed bayonets on their former allies, the leftist clergy.

The watchful truce thus established lasted without significant interruption into the 1620s. In 1604 the moderate reformist clergy tried to secure from James I some minor reforms in church ceremonial, and the gentry were willing to back their demand for a learned, preaching ministry. But the bishops suppressed this incipient reform movement at the Hampton Court Conference, and though in each successive parliament there were demands for the abandonment of romish practices and the reform of the clergy, these were advanced more to keep alive parliament's claim to superintend the church rather than in expectation of immediate action.*

The seventeenth-century gentry were intensely religious, most of them, bitten by the personalisation of the Christian life effected by the Reformed Religion, which dramatised the individual and his rôle in the struggle against life's temptations. But, like their fathers and grandfathers before them, they remained resolutely anti-clerical. They willingly supported and encouraged individual left-wing clergymen, loquacious, learned and stimulating, within the framework of the established church, but they were unwilling to embark on any wholesale programme of reform unless it would redound to their own interests, and in view of the announced attitude of the king and bishops on the one hand and the Puritan clergy on the other this seemed unlikely. Since the reforming clergy took their political strength from gentry support it was not easy for them to disturb the *status quo*, nor were the bishops likely to do so unless they could find a new, aggressive leader and secure the firm support of the king.

This support was not forthcoming from James I. Like most English bishops, he accepted the dogma of the Genevan church, but not its system of government. His belief in episcopacy was inspired by its obvious utility as an adjunct to central power, and by his hatred and fear of the unruly presbyters who had blighted his earlier years in Scotland. He hated this God-besotted tribe even more than he did the Jesuits. Moreover, though his outlook on religion was confused and emotional, he was never a persecutor; he even had difficulty in persecuting the papists, whose aimless plotting frightened him half out of his wits. In 1604 he issued a proclamation ordering all ministers to conform to the doctrine and ceremony laid down in the Prayer Book, but he encouraged his new Archbishop of Canterbury, Richard Bancroft, to interpret it liberally, and ultimately less than a hundred, perhaps as few as sixty, ministers were deprived. The High Commission, its jurisdiction in dispute with the common laywers for most of the reign, was too harried to launch any ambitious campaigns of its own, even had Bancroft desired it. As it was, his aim was a decent conformity, and when he died in 1611 James chose as his successor a man of similar spirit, George Abbott. Both archbishops encouraged the universities to produce more preachers, with the result that in 1622 James had to forbid any priest below the rank of dean or bishop to meddle with "the deep points of predestination, election, reprobation, or the universality, resistibility or irresistibility of God's grace", and confine them to genteel improvisation on the Thirty-Nine Articles. The difficulty now was not to discover preaching ministers but to restrain the multitude available.

By 1622, in fact, the church was drifting. James's ecclesiastical appointments had gone in favour of the sophisticated and accommodating—the laodicean rather than the pauline—and, as under Elizabeth, some of the most influential men at court favoured and sympathised with the clerical reformers. Buckingham, perhaps emulating the great Earl of Leicester, was an active patron of earnest and aggressive reformers; of William Laud, but also of John Preston, one of the leading Puritan reformers, who was, a trifle ironically, appointed chaplain to the future Charles I, then Prince of Wales.

But it was perhaps inevitable that this laxity should bring on a reaction, a reform movement from the episcopal side, directed by Laud, supported by Charles I. It was this, the first determined assault on the *status quo* in forty years, that compelled the gentry in the thirties to identify themselves with the Puritan reform movement. Even then, the Long Parliament was to show that they were united only in that negative anti-clericalism which had been theirs from the start.

Religion, then, drove no clear division between the opposing sides; but neither did secular political thought. Neither king nor parliament was much concerned with such abstract concepts as "sovereignty", which imply the existence of a formalised or even written constitution. What concerned them was the actual operation of government—a continuous process, having no known beginning and no foreseeable end, which comprehended the interaction and interrelation of a number of unchanging and unchangeable components: monarchy, parliament, common law, prerogative and so on. Precise definition of their functions was difficult, alteration impossible. Nor did the seventeenth century want to alter them, it sought to operate them correctly. That there was one unique, foolproof mode of operation no one doubted, though few could agree on its nature. Moreover, the seventeenth century was loth to admit the theory of absolute sovereignty; writers like Bodin, in France, were feeling towards it, but when Hobbes first expounded it in all its naked simplicity it was at once rejected. Men clung instead to the mediaeval concept of natural law, a code God-given and beyond the power of mortal man to alter, which regulated the operation of human laws. This romish doctrine was naturalised in England as the law of reason, expressed in certain fundamental legal principles and natural, inalienable privileges confirmed time out of mind. But the patent futility of the Petition of Right in 1628—the first attempt to codify these rights—sent both sides back to older concepts still. The theory of Divine Right notwithstanding, the king's supporters and the parliamentarians took as their starting-point the ancient constitution of the kingdom, which imposed duties on the ruler as well as rights, rights on the subject as well as duties. Each side accused the other, with varying degrees of accuracy and sincerity, of exceeding their customary rights or neglecting their customary duties, and the arguments to which they resorted were naturally historical. We see the constitution as advancing, or developing, over the centuries, but this is merely a concomitant of nineteenth-century ideas of progress. The seventeenth century, like the Middle Ages, regarded man as unprogressive and imperfectible, and his institutions likewise. Since government was static and undeveloping, prescription was of the first importance, and any historical incident could be compared directly with the present.

The reading of history was not only useful but fashionable, offering sound information on the governance of men combined with effective moral uplift. The Bible and theology apart, it was the only literature that equipped a gentleman to grapple with this world without obviously prejudicing his chances in the next. Ralegh's *History of the World* was a best-seller, and Oliver Cromwell's favourite secular reading. Still more significant was the great vogue enjoyed by the English chronicles of Hall or Holinshed, brought up to date in Elizabeth's reign by Grafton and Stow.

The chronicles gave their many readers an episodic and at the same time static view of English history. The greatest stress was laid on military prowess, but the political rôle of the feudal baronage was so stylised that they figured merely as good or bad fairies according to the arbitrarily-decided badness or goodness of the contemporary king, while the unity of the nation was always assumed. Most important, English history was conceived as extending in space rather than time, so that the parliaments of Edward I, for instance, were for all intents and purposes identical with those of James I, and the Tudors—naturally—were just another dynasty. There was no nonsense about a " new monarchy " or a " renaissance despotism " in the chronicles, just as there could be no break between the mediaeval and modern world; there were no Middle Ages, just History, which existed in past, present and future, showing variations only in detail.

This is why so many parliamentary debates in the seventeenth century were concerned, not to prove that this or that element of government was good or bad in itself, but whether or not it had existed at the time of the Black Prince. And the fact that many parliamentary leaders were trained lawyers encouraged this sort of sterile logic-chopping. There is no greater delusion in seventeenth-century history than that the lawyers had any contribution to make to the solution of contemporary problems. The Civil Wars occurred, and Charles I died, simply because the Law solved nothing. Its study gave its practitioners a certain dialectical skill and elasticity in debate, a mastery of rules and procedures that came naturally to them. But of broader conceptions it gave them none. Even the legalistic Clarendon discerned " in the great herd of common lawyers many pragmatical spirits, whose thoughts and observations had been contracted to the narrow limits of the few books of that profession, or within the narrower circle of the bar oratory ". Their belief that every legal precedent, of whatever antiquity, was of equal weight dovetailed neatly with the universalist history culled from the chronicles, but it did not equip them to solve any of the issues of their time. The historico-legal investigations of the early seventeenth century brought them up against two irreconcilable sets of precedents drawn from mediaeval law, one declaring for the unfettered power of monarchy, the other for the sovereignty of parliament. Faced with an unthinkable choice, the lawyers succumbed to what can only be called a neurosis; at the end of the 1620s those who had not already fled to the royal camp washed their hands of constitutional issues. By 1637 men like Finch on the one hand, St John on the other, were not seeking accommodation but defending convictions.

Professional lawyers apart, most sons of gentlemen rounded off their education with a term or two at the " third university ", the Inns of Court. Existing in a state of almost continuous litigation*, they must be able to thread their way through the complexities of the land law (if only so that they could superintend their professional advisers); they must also be able to dispense rough-and-ready justice in their capacity as magistrates. But all this required was a smattering of law, picked up during a twelve-months' resi-

dence amongst the pleasures and distractions of the capital.
That it was only a smattering is indicated by the huge
sales of Lambarde's *Eirenarcha,* an elementary handbook for
justices which was published in 1581 and rarely went out of
print before 1640. It is indicated, too, by the fog of half-
baked legal learning that hangs low over these early Stuart
parliaments, stultifying debate and confusing the minds of
the contemporary audience and later readers alike : the
prosy discourses on the Great Charter, the laboured parallels
between Charles I and Richard II, the legal tags, the mangled
and often irrelevant precedents, the spate of misleading cases
and tendentious exceptions; the whole spiced with snippets
of classical legend and gobbets of chronicle history. In the
Addled Parliament of 1614 this gimcrack constitutionalising
reached the heights of farce, and Lord Chancellor Ellesmere,
declining to confer with a Commons committee, remarked with
withering sarcasm that they " go both high and low, and
look at all things that concern their purpose, and we can
say nothing, having not seen records. They perhaps will
tell us of the Law of Nature and Nations, being able and
learned gentlemen, who have studied this case long. If any
man in this House thinks himself able to dispute with
them, let him do it; for myself I must desire to be excused."[6]

What emerged from this welter of half-learning was a
very simple concept, whose patent unreality only heightened its
persuasive effect. The gentry remembered with nostalgic
reverence the early years of Elizabeth and what they had
been told of the reign of her father, Great Harry, and the
chroniclers amply confirmed the fact that the Tudors were
the greatest dynasty ever to sit on the English throne. So
naturally they sought a balanced constitution modelled on
what the sixteenth-century constitution seemed to have been;
for in that golden century government had apparently reached
perfection. Rejecting ready-made theories, they sought the
solution of a constitutional problem in the day-to-day operation of government, trying to limit the king's prerogative
here, extend the rights of parliament there, straining after
some visionary polity in which a parliament of loyal and

trusty men would give beneficial advice to a powerful, capable, but well-intentioned ruler, using his reserve powers temperately and for his subjects' good, by and with the advice of a paternal and tactful Privy Council. Even Charles I recognised the appeal of this vision in January 1641, when he offered to return "all matters of religion and government" to "what they were in the purest times of Queen Elizabeth's days". It was the ideal of Pym and Coke, as well as Wentworth and Bacon; it was the ideal of Edward Hyde in 1641 and of the Earl of Clarendon in 1661. It was probably the ideal of James II, ostensibly that of Bolingbroke.

But throughout its long history it remained an ideal, not a working basis for government, which is why all attempts to establish it in reality, in 1641 and 1661, failed. The nation moved impatiently on from squirearchy to oligarchy, an oligarchy of nobility recruited from the gentry but no longer of them.

Altogether, most modern commentators have taken the Stuart gentry too seriously. They expect too much of them. The gentry had great social and political impetus, enough to launch the Great Rebellion; but they were too selfish, too individualistic, to accept the discipline that would have enabled them to consolidate their gains and build anew. Their outlook on government was essentially amateur, and provincial; they could not handle central government, they could only impede it. Even during the Great Rebellion their central war effort was entirely dependent on two or three men; as soon as these died off the Long Parliament fell to pieces, and to save themselves its Members had to call upon the suppressed classes below them, who promptly overwhelmed them. In retrospect, they committed class suicide by restoring the monarchy in 1660. Unable to work with the gentry, the later Stuart kings called upon the services of the large landowners, and the rising importance of the nobility, in parliament, in elections, in the counties generally, is the index to the gentry's decline.

Their local administration was always slovenly, shapeless

and selfish. Their education was narrow and blinkered, if deep. The Reformation, the civil wars in Germany, France and the Netherlands, had cut them off from the mainstream of European culture; patriotic resistance to the Counter-Reformation had fostered in them a rabid Protestant nationalism—" God is English!" cried one excited Tudor bishop. Puritanism confirmed the belief that they were the chosen race of Israel, the receptacle of God's direct Grace—for did not " Wycliff beget Huss, who begat Luther, who begat Truth "? Even in the opposite camp, Laud's appeal was to insular nationalism, in his concept of the *ecclesia anglicana* as the true church of Peter, unique and undefiled.

Their possession of a unique form of law confirmed them in their isolation. Of foreign politics they understood little, cared less, and their concept of war was based on the inspired piracy of Elizabeth. Their almost total ignorance of economics ill-equipped them to wrestle with some of the most intractable problems of their age. Sir John Eliot was by no means an unlearned man, but he was capable of making a long speech to the Commons in 1624 in which he betrayed an inability even to distinguish between monopolies and impositions.* Nor, apparently, did any of his audience feel qualified to correct him.[7] The philistinism and ignorance of the gentry are noticeable even in matters of taste. Shakespeare, Jonson and Inigo Jones, Donne and Launcelot Andrewes, Thomas Hobbes; all the great poets, writers, thinkers and artists of the first half of the seventeenth century—even Milton—were supported by the court, the leading citizens of London, or a small circle of dilettante noblemen. Experiments in architecture, too, were left to the crown and its high servants, and the semi-fortified manor houses of the gentry, their exteriors still reflecting the Wars of the Roses, moved with glacial slowness towards the newer fashions of a more peaceable age. (Though it must be admitted that the toughness and defensibility of these houses were to prove useful in the Civil Wars.) Charles I was to assemble one of the greatest collections of paintings

[7] Harold Hulme, *Sir John Eliot*, p. 45.

this country has ever known; it was broken up and sold
by the Rump of a gentry parliament.

In short, the gentry were neither an intelligent nor a
sophisticated class. Their actions exhibited no consistent
political plan, even in the great crisis of 1641. They were
an elemental political force, driven on by complex economic
pressures and incentives they did not even begin to understand; they were destructive, not constructive. And what
was more, though they had no wish to fight their king the
climate of the age was not conducive to civil peace. In
the House of Commons gentlemen showed a greater sense
of decorum than they did, for instance, on Quarter Sessions
or at County Court, but even there, in the crucial debate
on the Grand Remonstrance in 1641, men "took their
swords in their scabbards out of their belts and held them
by their pommels in their hands, setting the lower part
on the ground". "I thought we had all sat in the valley
of death," wrote Sir Philip Warwick, "for we, like Joab's
and Abner's young men, had catched at each other's locks,
and sheathed our swords in each other's bowels." According to the contemporary Dutch historian Van Meteren (and
his opinion is typical of many), the English were "bold,
courageous, ardent, and cruel in war, fiery in attack, and
having little fear of death". "They are not vindictive," he
went on, "but very inconstant, rash, vainglorious, light and
deceiving, and very suspicious, especially of foreigners, whom
they despise."[8] It did not augur well for the foreign dynasty
that succeeded the Tudors in 1603.

---

[8] W. B. Rye, *England as seen by Foreigners in the Reigns of
Elizabeth and James I* (1865), p. 70.

CHAPTER II

JAMES I

1603-1625

Queen Elizabeth died at Richmond on 24 March 1603, her titles passing to her Scots cousin James VI, the great-grandson of Henry VIII's sister Margaret. On Sunday, 3 April, James took a solemn farewell of the Scots people at St Giles's, Edinburgh, and two days later he left for the south, accompanied by a host of retainers, well-wishers and casual greeters that swelled ever larger as he came up to and crossed the Border. Arriving at York, his first act was to write to the English Privy Council for money to proceed; he had entered upon his inheritance, as he was ultimately to leave it, penniless.

Nevertheless, the councillors who hastened to meet him were determined to find no fault in their new monarch, and they found plenty to impress them. James's quick brain, his aptitude for business, his willingness to take decisions, right or wrong, were welcome enough after Elizabeth's tedious procrastination over trifles. They were charmed, too, by his informal bonhomie; they found him "very facile, using no great solemnities in his accesses, but witty to conceive, and very ready of speech". Only the moody Francis Bacon sounded a jarring note. Listening to the king's stammering chatter, he observed that "his Majesty rather asked counsel of the time past than of the time to come".

James was thirty-seven, but looked rather younger, with his straggling adolescent beard, watery-blue eyes and thin, brown hair. He was tall, and the breadth of his shoulders and chest was accentuated by contrast with his thin, spindly legs. (Like his son Charles, he walked badly, rode a horse well.) His tongue was "too large for his mouth, which ever made him speak full in the mouth, and made him drink very uncomely, as if eating his drink, which came out into the cup of each side of his mouth". He dressed with an affectation of simplicity that later degenerated into slovenliness, and "his skin was as soft as taffeta sarsnet, which felt so, because he never washed his hands, only rubbed his fingers' ends slightly with the wet end of a napkin". His sense of humour matched his personal habits; always coarse and anatomical, it rose sometimes to "a fluorescence of obscenity".[1]

There was an element of buffoonery in all he did, and a strong dash of improvisation. Restless in mind and body, he was for ever tramping from room to room, his courtiers and ministers scrambling after, or riding from one palace to the next, the whole court lumbering behind. At dinner his vulgarity, obscenity and uproarious pedantry had full play, as he slobbered in his drink, cracked bawdy jests, and swapped texts and references with the ecclesiastics who stood behind his chair, capping all with a casual blasphemy. He was very rarely drunk; but with his slurred speech, his heavy Scots accent and his restless, rolling eye, he must often have seemed so. Even at the conference of divines at Hampton Court in 1604 his conduct was far from decorous. When the reformer Reynolds, a bachelor, objected to the use of the words "with my body I thee worship" in the marriage service, James remarked with a leer, "Many a man speaks of Robin Hood who never shot in his bow." The bishops "said that undoubtedly his Majesty spoke by the special assistance of God's spirit". "I wist not what they mean," added one cynic, "but the spirit was rather foul-mouthed." With the Scots he was more explicit: "I give not a turd for your preaching," he yelled at one Presbyterian minister.[2]

This unpredictable homeliness was carried over into the king's public utterances, and the French ambassador, accustomed to the more stately pronouncements of St Germain and St Cloud, coldly remarked, "Where he wishes to assume the language of a king his tone is that of a tyrant, and where he condescends he is vulgar". He told the parliament of 1621, in his solemn Speech from the Throne,

[1] D. H. Wilson, *James VI and I*, p. 36.   [2] *ibid.*, p. 71.

that " A spice of envy hath made all my speech heretofore turn like spittle in the wind upon mine own face "; yet when he wished, as in July 1604, he could produce orations every bit as dignified as Elizabeth's, and better, because simpler. In fact, behind James's mask of drivelling tom-foolery lurked a penetrating mind, and he possessed to a high degree that sense of the dignity of kingship for which his son and grandsons were renowned. Naturally, he could not comprehend that his character and physique ill befitted him to translate these ideals into reality.

His nervous and excitable temperament was undermined from the start by the warmth of his reception in England, occasioned by the universal relief at the end of petticoat government and the establishment of the succession after nearly half a century of doubt and worry. The gentry and nobility who came flocking to meet him ploughed the Great North Road into a morass, and his tumultuous reception in London went to his head like wine. Always apt to translate political actions into personal terms, he never suspected that the English were applauding the occasion, not the man; that they would have welcomed with equal rapture any king possessing the usual number of arms and legs and no tail, provided he was a staunch Protestant with a strong claim to the throne and sons to succeed him. He later recalled with unctuous self-satisfaction how " the people of all sorts rode and ran, nay, rather flew, to meet him, their eyes flaming nothing but sparkles of affection, their mouths and tongues uttering nothing but sounds of joy, their hands, feet, and all the rest of their members in their gestures discovering a passionate longing and earnestness to meet and embrace their new sovereign ".

He had always been highly conceited; now he was more so, and his fondness for biblical allusion and his belief in the Divine Right of Kings led him to couple his own name with the Deity's in a manner that provoked his hearers either to mirth or embarrassment. He had succeeded to the throne of Scotland in swaddling clothes, and since the age of fifteen, when the Regent Morton was executed, he had been for better or for worse King of Scots. True, it had often been for worse; but whatever humiliations he had suffered at the hands of his half-tamed nobility he had always been the central pawn in their intrigues, the steady focus of interest; and even when his authority extended only over the house in which he lodged, the room in which he cowered, of that he had been undisputed monarch. He never knew the chastening experience of being a mere prince of the blood; he never had the competition even of brothers or sisters. Raised in poverty, loneliness and pomp, he had learned to think highly of himself, simply because if he did not no one else would. Moreover, by 1603 he had some cause for conceit. Despite his chronic poverty and insecurity, he had learned the difficult art of playing faction off against faction, and by the end of the 1590s he had established control over four-fifths of his unhappy, uncivilised kingdom. He had luck, but he also displayed considerable finesse, and at moments of crisis a courage generally regarded as foreign to his character. By 1597 he had brought the proud Kirk to heel, and in 1599 he even imposed titular bishops on it. He left Scotland with the reputation of a strong, efficient ruler, and it is understandable that he should announce himself as " an old, experienced king, needing no lessons ".

Nobody realised, James least of all, that his best years were behind him, that the enervating South would steadily sap his remaining powers. His views on monarchy were expansive in the extreme, fashioned out of his omnivorous reading in statecraft, and sharpened by his political impotence in youth. He celebrated his eventual triumph over lawlessness and faction by composing *The True Law of Free Monarchies,* published in 1603. In common with all James's literary works, this contained little that was original, but was a particularly decisive and pithy restatement of current theory regarding the Divine Right of Kings—their absolute legal sovereignty, their untrammelled freedom of executive action, their sole responsibility to God. Clearly he believed that the wealth and ancient authority of the English monarchy, the higher standard of life and culture in the South, had enabled his predecessors to translate such ideas into reality.

His task therefore was not suppression but consolidation and exploitation. At the Hampton Court Conference he embarked on " a gratulation to Almighty God . . . for bringing him into the promised land, where he sat amongst grave, learned, and reverend men, not as before, elsewhere, a king without state, without honour, without order, where beardless boys would brave him to his face ".

Elizabeth's Scots poor relation had been dazzled by the irritated glare she always focused on him; by the ubiquity of her intelligence service, the efficiency and subservience of her ministers, by her great wealth, which enabled her to foment revolt in France and the Netherlands, suppress it in Ireland, wage war against Spain, and at the same time pay him a handsome pension. If ever he doubted her absolute authority, he had only to recall her summary execution of his own mother, the anointed queen of France and Scotland. His principal informant in London was Robert Cecil, who naturally failed to stress the restlessness of Elizabeth's last parliaments, the malaise in court and government. The Puritan offensive of the seventies had broken on the crest of the wave and dissolved; all over Europe the ancient estates of the realm were going under to monarchical power, and it seemed that England's parliament would go the way of Scotland's, declining into a docile talking-shop, or at worst an arena for noble intrigue.

Here James's Scots experience misled him further. In Scotland it was the nobles who wielded political power, aggressive and disputatious men, each with a small army at his back and a decisive voice in the counsels of Kirk and State. On his arrival in England his preconceived notions led him to ennoble a group of crown servants—Sackville, Knollys and Cecil himself—who could ill be spared from the House of Commons, and to favour members of the older nobility, like the Howards, whose political power was not extensive enough to compensate for the mischief they did the crown. His conduct in this respect helped to perpetuate, and intensify, the factions at Whitehall which had been such a sinister feature of Elizabeth's declining years. Arguing from his Scots experience, he consistently under-estimated the

English gentry, too. They were associated in his mind with the Scots lairds, a mean, blinkered, embittered class, scraping a precarious living from their stony acres, presbytery-ridden and disunited.

His first encounter with parliament, in 1604, should have taught him a lesson, but did not. Like Elizabeth's later parliaments, the parliament of 1604-11 was in a perpetual rumble of discontent, which only occasionally came to a head on some general issue*. Some Members were concerned with the state of the clergy, many more were feeling the economic pinch; there was sporadic agitation for a " learned, godly ministry " and the abolition of the king's feudal rights of purveyance and wardship. Elizabeth had ridden out such agitation easily enough, taking care to provide the Commons with strong government leadership, and herself moving swiftly to suppress any general issue that seemed likely to provide a rallying-point for opposition—like the question of monopolies in 1601. Unfortunately, James had denuded the House of efficient managers, it could vote no money, for the taxes voted in 1601 had not all been collected, and the end of the war, now in sight, made it impossible for him to appeal to the Commons' patriotic emotions. Finally, he went out of his way to provide them with a specific grievance by disputing with them the Buckinghamshire Election Case. His handling of this case established a dismal pattern, repeated in 1610 and 1621. Ignoring the facts in dispute, he at once took his stand on broad general principles which it was unnecessary and dangerous to raise; of all the alternative arguments at his disposal he chose the weakest; and he advanced so far in its support that he was unable to make a dignified withdrawal. Instead he hung on until the last possible moment, then fell back in disorder. His son was to display the same technique. The privileges claimed by the Commons were enshrined in a singularly impertinent document called *A Form of Apology and Satisfaction*. It was never formally presented to James (may never have passed the House), but he made some thunderous, if oblique, comments on it in his closing speech of the session, in July*. Departing sore and angry, the Members were pursued down to the shires by writs under the Privy Seal for a new forced loan; the government's "softness" towards papists, and the irrationally unpopular peace with Spain in August, completed their disillusion.

However, James was carried through the first seven years of his reign by the ministers he had inherited from Elizabeth; notably Robert Cecil, created Viscount Cranborne in 1603, Earl of Salisbury in 1605. Whatever its disadvantages, the Cecilians' grasp on administration did at least provide an element of stability and continuity that defied the Jacobean disorder, and for a time parried the onset of less responsible ministers. In the sphere of religion, too, Richard Bancroft was adept in smothering reformist agitation. The only notable reform resulting from the Hampton Court Conference in 1604 was the complete retranslation of the Bible—the Authorised Version of 1611. (Typically enough, James supported this because he objected to the annotations in the current Geneva Bible, which, according to him, were " very partial, untrue, seditious, and savouring too much of dangerous and traitorous conceits ".)

But if the reformist clergy were quiescent, the popish issue was still a danger to the king's prestige. Luckily, the uneasy rumours of his correspondence with the Holy See, his exalted schemes of " comprehension ", were swept away by the Gunpowder Plot of 1605, which produced a strong reaction in his favour. In fact, the session of 1605-6, launched by one of James's sillier speeches, passed off in an atmosphere of unexpected cordiality. He told his audience that if he had been blown to pieces with them, " It should never have been spoken or written in ages succeeding that I had died ingloriously in an Ale-house, a Stews, or such vile place, [but] that mine end should have been with the most honourable and best company, and in that most honourable and fittest place for a king to be in, for doing the terms most proper to his office." The Commons, apparently gratified at this compliment (though some may have wondered what would take his Majesty to a beer-shop or a brothel), and certainly relieved at their narrow escape from anarchy, cheerfully voted him three subsidies in direct taxation.

Unfortunately, the success of this session lulled James's advisers into a false sense of security. False, because after 1606 a marked decline in the king's person, court and government soon alienated most of the parliamentary gentry and many of the nobility.

The king's extravagance involved him in a host of difficulties. Transplanted from the grinding poverty of Holyrood to the apparent luxury of Whitehall, he was not easily convinced of the fact that he was still comparatively poor. He spent lavishly and gave generously; he had a wife, Anne of Denmark, who loved little else but extravagant clothes and new jewels, and with two sons and a daughter to maintain in appropriate pomp his legitimate household expenses were much higher than Elizabeth's. The reign opened with a great splurge of expenditure, from which the Treasury never properly recovered. The coronation cost £20,591, Elizabeth's funeral, £17,301, and the arrival of the Spanish plenipotentiaries to sign the peace was the signal for an outburst of regal liberality that shocked many courtiers raised under Elizabeth—like Sir Dudley Carleton, who wrote : " We cannot say that the King hath been behindhand in liberality, for at this one instant he hath given away more plate than Queen Elizabeth did in her whole reign."[3] And even after the close of this exceptional year, 1603-4, the day-to-day expenses of the household continued to rise, absorbing almost unnoticed the money saved by the termination of the war with Spain, the suppression of the Irish revolt and the closing of the Border forts.[4]

James himself was scarcely aware of this increased expenditure, and almost indifferent to the parallel decline in the hereditary crown revenue. He always had difficulty in visualising wealth he could not see and touch—" He was very liberal ", it was said, " of what he had not in his own grip, and would rather part with £100 he never had

[3] F. C. Dietz, *English Public Finance 1558-1641*, p. 101.
[4] *ibid.*, pp. 110-13.

in his keeping than one twenty-shilling piece within his own custody." This put the Crown Lands in a position of peculiar danger; in 1604 Salisbury persuaded James to entail the more valuable estates on the Privy Council, and in 1609 this device was renewed in a stronger form. All the same, the sales of Crown Lands that had been a feature of the second half of Elizabeth's reign continued intermittently under her successors.

Of course, the royal bounty, or patronage, was the natural lubricant of the administrative machine. What was objectionable and dangerous in James's practice was his tendency to concentrate the diminishing number of perquisites or favours at his disposal on a limited circle, a policy continued and intensified by his son. Too often James's generosity was geared to the amount of overt gratitude he could expect in return, and he tended to overlook the parliamentary gentry, who could contribute nothing to the oriental flattery practised by the Whitehall veterans. Nor, despite his many creations, did he appreciably raise the power or prestige of the nobility, and the faction system, which he did nothing to discourage, confirmed in him the tendency to personalise political issues—another trait handed down to Charles I, and James II, too. As one modern historian has remarked, James "did not choose men for his jobs but bestowed jobs on his men".[5]

This was particularly noticed with regard to the Scotsmen who naturally followed their king south and settled more or less permanently at Whitehall. For this generation of Scotsmen, born before the king's accession, could not hold government office or sit in parliament (except through the grant of an English peerage); in other words, they were just so much lumber, consuming patronage without giving effective service in return, and every favour granted a Scotsman deprived the crown of a potential government official or parliamentary supporter.

The most notorious recipient of the king's favour was the handsome but coarse-grained Scots squireling, Robert Carr of Ferniehurst, who was knighted in 1607 and raised to the

[5] H. R. Trevor-Roper, *Historical Essays*, p. 132.

peerage as Viscount Rochester in 1611. From his earliest childhood James's mentors had rigorously excluded him from the company of women, and he fell an easy victim to his fascinating cousin, Esmé Stuart, Duke of Lennox, who came to Scotland in 1579 from the vicious Valois court of France. Lennox's influence was broken in 1582, and in 1589 the young king married the Princess Anne of Denmark. Anne was blonde and shapely, and her husband was never averse to feminine charms, on display, at least. Unfortunately, her stupidity and giddiness, her girlish meddling in Scots politics, her marked deviation towards the Roman communion, only confirmed him in his low opinion of women's character and intelligence. He declined to live in the same place as a woman more than he could help, even with his daughter, and soon after his accession the queen was established at Denmark House, rarely accompanying him on his continual progresses.

James's critics knew perfectly well what to make of his relations with Carr and other male lovelies. As Sir Anthony Weldon remarked, sensibly enough, " The King's kissing them after so lascivious a mode in public, and upon the theatre, as it were, of the world, prompted many to imagine some things done in the [re]tiring-house that exceed my expressions no less than they do my experience." But homosexuality was an imperial vice, after all, and contrary to popular belief sexual indulgence alone has rarely contributed to the downfall of rulers, or even noticeably undermined their prestige. In fact, men reserved their strongest criticism for James's more innocent pursuits, which, until the advent of George Villiers, had a much greater impact on politics and government.

For instance, his love of hunting, evident since youth, had now become an over-mastering obsession, and for the greater part of the year he proceeded from one hunting seat to another across the home counties : from Theobalds to Royston, Huntingdon to Richmond, Windsor to Oatlands and back. He stayed in the saddle all day without a thought of leaving it, and, the kill made, it was his delight to plunge his legs into the stag's bowels. Sir John Harington remarked of one such jaunt : " The manners made me devise the beasts were pursuing the sober creation." At dusk he retired early, petulant or roisterous according to the fortunes of the day. This made him difficult of access to any but the most important ministers or the most intimate courtiers; indeed, after the first few months of the reign, gentry out of court rarely clapped eyes on their sovereign, the common people never. The demonstrativeness of the English people soon palled —" The access of the people made him so impatient that he often dispersed them with frowns, that we may not say with curses", and on being told that they only wanted to look upon his face he cried out in a tantrum, " God's wounds! I will pull down my breeches and they shall also see my arse!"

Moreover, when his liege subjects were vouchsafed a glimpse of their lord and master, at some notable public revelry, the sight was not particularly edifying. He had a strong head for liquor, and in trying to match his consumption the majority of his English courtiers fell by the wayside. Harington has left a classic account of the orgy at Theobalds in 1606, when Salisbury entertained James and his bibulous brother-in-law, Christian IV of Denmark. " A great feast was held, and after dinner the representation of Solomon's Temple and the coming of the Queen of Sheba was made, or (as I may better say) was meant to have been made, before their Majesties. . . . The Lady who did play the Queen [of Sheba]'s part did carry the most precious gifts to both their Majesties, but, forgetting the steps arising to the canopy, overset her caskets into his Danish Majesty's lap, and fell at his feet, though I rather think it was in his face. Much was the hurry and confusion; cloths and napkins were at hand, to make all clean. His [Danish] Majesty then got up and would dance with the Queen of Sheba, but he fell down and humbled himself before her, and was carried to an inner chamber and laid on a bed of state, which was not a little defiled with the presents of the Queen which had been bestowed on his garments, such as wine, cream, jelly, beverage, cakes, spices and other good matters. The entertainment and show went forward, and most of the presenters went backward, or fell down, wine did so

occupy their upper chambers. Now did appear, in rich
dress, Hope, Faith and Charity; Hope did essay to speak,
but wine rendered her endeavours so feeble that she withdrew, and hoped the King would excuse her brevity; Faith
was then all alone, for I am certain she was not joined with
good works, and left the Court in a staggering condition;
Charity came to the King's feet, and seemed to cover the
multitude of sins her sisters had committed; in some sort
she made obeisance and brought gifts, but said she would
return home again, as there was no gift which heaven had
not already given his Majesty. She then returned to Hope
and Faith, who were both sick and spewing in the lower
hall. Next came Victory, in bright armour, and presented a
rich sword to the King, who did not accept it, but put it
by with his hand, and by a strange medley of versification
[she] did endeavour to make suit to the King. But Victory
did not triumph for long, for, after much lamentable utter-
ance, she was led away like a silly captive, and laid to sleep
in the outer steps of the ante chamber. Now did Peace
make entry, and strive to get foremost to the King, but
I grieve to tell how great wrath she did discover unto those
of her attendants; and, much contrary to her semblance, most
rudely made war with her olive branches, and laid on the
pates of those who did oppose her coming." And so on.[6]

The decline in standards of conduct, the inaccessibility
and increasing intemperance of the king, the personalisation
of court service, all this strained the social ties that had
formerly bound monarchy, nobility and gentry together in
one social structure based on court and parliament. And
it strained those social ties just at a time when their financial
justification was being undermined by a Treasury bent on
making the government at least approximately solvent. Salisbury's reform of the Court of Wards increased the government's revenue from that source, but only at the expense

---

[6] It is evident, of course, that Harington thoroughly enjoyed himself here, just as Evelyn did at the court of Charles II. The
perversity of human nature caused James I and Charles II's courts
to be censured for their debauchery, those of Charles I and William
III for their dullness.

of patronage. The same could be said of his stringent administration of the Crown Lands—the redrawing of boundaries, the taking in of encroachments on the Forest, the doubling and trebling of rents, the imposition of increased fines on inheritance—all this, in an era of rising prices, pressed hard on the landowning gentry. The relations between king and parliament might have withstood social or financial friction alone, they could not withstand both at once. The result was seen in the session of 1610, when the last of the great Elizabethan parliaments broke with the last of the great Elizabethan ministers, and was dissolved.

This was particularly deplorable because Salisbury's Great Contract of 1610, by which the king was to surrender his feudal rights in return for a guaranteed annual income, offered the only constructive solution of the crown's financial difficulties, and the one finally adopted in 1661. But the falling-off of patronage had already weakened the loyalty of the courtiers in the Commons, and the encouragement James gave to faction in-fighting and the unscrupulous display of personality prevented Salisbury from offering the leadership of the House to a strong man like Francis Bacon. This was doubly so after the advent of Robert Carr, when it became clear that James was tiring of his " little beagle ", this unlovely, ageing hunchback with his wearisome insistence on sobriety and economy. Instead, Salisbury tried to control the Commons from the Lords, by unsparing use of conferences between the two house. But it was in the nature of this system that once it collapsed it could not easily be replaced by a more rational method. The crown lost control of the Commons in 1610, and never regained it.

The break came on the question of impositions, or extra import duties levied by the crown, which had been legalised by a decision of the Court of Exchequer in 1606. James's attempt to prevent the reopening of this question in 1610 was maladroit in the extreme. Deprived of his natural advisers by his irresponsible decision to spend the session at Newmarket, he again forsook the specific issue, on which he had a strong case, and took his stand on general principles, where the precedents were contradictory and debatable. Outmanœuvred on his chosen ground, he incurred all the odium of forbidding debate without the advantage of preventing it. After three months' adjournment the Commons returned in November in a worse mood than ever, and James acknowledged that his ministers' liaisons with parliament had broken down altogether by sending for certain Members himself, " to ask of them some questions ". In the ensuing debate on privilege his Scots favourites were very freely criticised, and despite Salisbury's protests he prorogued parliament in a huff. In January 1611, again over Salisbury's protests, he dissolved it.

Conscious that the king had withdrawn his favour, weighed down by failure, tormented by physical ills, Salisbury left this parliament a broken man. He died in May 1612, and with him the Tudor era. The death of Archbishop Bancroft in 1611 was another sign of changing times, as was the sudden death of Henry, Prince of Wales, in November 1612. Henry's physical prowess, his bluff manliness and dignified sobriety made him a marked contrast to his father. His virtues were exaggerated, naturally, but he commanded men's respect and won their affection on fair terms, and the prospect of his eventual succession had done much to reconcile them to the inadequate present. The succession now passed to the unknown Charles.

As for Salisbury, he had trained no successor, and the ideals for which he stood—such as they were—lapsed with him. Not until 1629, when Wentworth was appointed to the Council of the North, did the crown secure another great minister combining powers of leadership with administrative skill.

The death of Salisbury was James's chance to show his mettle, to rule as untrammelled monarch. But he was too old, and too indolent, to take advantage of the opportunity. He could plan great things, but he lacked the courage and initiative to carry them out, and his senile meddling merely prevented the emergence of a minister or faction strong enough to implement any positive policy at all, good or bad.

The most able man at court was Francis Bacon, but his

career had been retarded by Salisbury's jealousy, and by lack of money or influence; he did not attain even the attorney-generalship until 1613. Instead, such power as was going went to the Howards, who were interesting and significant not for what they did (which was little enough), but for what they were. They were an old-fashioned political clan, commanding retainers rather than influencing followers, all of them related to or descended from Thomas III, the great Duke of Norfolk executed in 1572 for treasonable conspiracy with Mary Queen of Scots. On his accession James had restored his mother's friends to all their honours, excepting only the dukedom. Their leader was Henry Howard, Earl of Northampton, the last duke's brother and an accomplished intriguer; chief amongst his supporters were the duke's son Thomas, Earl of Suffolk, and his grandson Thomas, Earl of Arundel. The circle also embraced Northampton's son-in-law, Lord Knollys, and the Armada veteran, Charles, Lord Howard of Effingham and Earl of Nottingham, Lord High Admiral of England.

In 1613 their personal influence was strengthened by two events. Frances, the Earl of Suffolk's nymphomaniac daughter, became the mistress of James's reigning favourite, Robert Carr. She obtained an annulment of her marriage to the young Earl of Essex on the grounds of his impotency, after a hearing farcical even by modern standards, and had the effrontery to marry Carr in the white dress and flowing hair of a virgin. James took a prurient interest in the annulment proceedings, and genially presided over the wedding, which was celebrated with unparalleled magnificence and debauchery in September 1613; two months later he created the bridegroom Earl of Somerset. Secondly, there arrived from Madrid a cleverer man than any in English politics, the Spanish envoy Sarmiento, later Count of Gondomar. Gondomar soon won James's affection and entire respect, and with the support of the Howards, Queen Anne and Somerset he kept English policy orientated on Spain for more than a decade.

For by inclination and family tradition the Howards—apart from Lord Nottingham—were active Roman sympa-

thisers. They urged James to marry his son to the daughter
of Philip III of Spain and use her huge dowry to pay off
his debts, with the ultimate aim of reconciling the English
church with Rome. James's devotion to Protestantism, and
perhaps a certain deference to public opinion, had caused him
to marry his daughter Elizabeth to a Protestant prince,
Frederick, Elector Palatine, in 1613. He now felt free
to pursue other plans for his son, and the idea of a Spanish
match tickled his vanity. Essentially he was a parvenu,
a poor relation who had succeeded to a shining inheritance;
both he and his wife, stemming from minor, peripheral
nations of Europe, were profound snobs, and marriage into
the great Hapsburg dynasty was the one thing that would
give them final assurance of their own regality. Moreover,
since his accession James's cloudy mind had been aswim with
dreams of reuniting the shattered Continent, perhaps even
by a great Council of the Church under the joint-presidency
of himself and the Pope. The assassination of Henry IV of
France in 1610 had left him, on paper, the most influential
monarch in Europe. Spain languished under the pietistic
Philip III, France under the child-king Louis XIII, Germany
under the hermit emperor Rudolf II. To James it seemed that
a Spanish match would merely confirm his natural primacy.

But these grandiose schemes of foreign policy were in
direct conflict with his pacific instinct, which forbad any
venture that might conceivably lead to war. It was always
recognised that "he naturally loved not the sight of a
soldier, nor any violent man". As a result he was plagued
by indecisions that left him incapable of directing policy
himself, though he would allow no one else to attempt it.
His gambit of playing one group of advisers off against another only reduced his counsels to an angry muddle, which
was reflected in the parliament of 1614. He infuriated the
Howards by calling another parliament, and at the same time
he took no precautions to see that it worked.

The absence of any firm guidance from above was particularly disastrous in 1614, for the conduct of the Commons
indicated that while they were ready to abandon their predecessors' habit of ultimate obedience to the king and his

ministers, they had yet to find men who could lead them in a campaign of constructive opposition. With the court group leaderless, too, there was no one to rein in the House when it was stampeded by one of those waves of anti-popish hysteria that swept in measured intervals across the seventeenth-century scene. In 1614 the causes of the alarm were more nebulous even than usual, but horrendous rumours of the Spanish match unluckily coincided with rumours of papist agents who had "undertaken" to smother opposition at elections. The council's feeble efforts to interfere in some elections lent colour to this yarn, and they were encouraged by inspired "leaks" from Lord Northampton. After a confused two months spent in unprofitable argument and counter-argument James dissolved the Addled Parliament, observing darkly, "I am surprised that my ancestors should have permitted such an institution to come into existence."

The failure of the Addled Parliament should have consolidated the Howards' position, and ensured the adoption of their policy. But with a debt of half a million, a mounting annual deficit and no prospect of parliamentary aid, James could not afford the commitments of a Spanish alliance; nor was Philip III anything but lukewarm. Both sides were free with high-sounding statements of aspiration and intention, but nothing positive was done, nor even attempted. Northampton died suddenly in 1614, leaving his followers adrift, and two years later Somerset was swept away in the backwash of the Overbury murder.

Somerset's friend Sir Thomas Overbury had bitterly opposed his marriage to the tarnished Countess of Essex, and in 1613 Somerset persuaded the king to place him in "protective custody" in the Tower. But Overbury knew enough to blast Frances Howard's reputation, even in the lax Jacobean court, and as soon as he was released he would talk. Frances was madly in love, and dabbling in black magic had undermined what little mental balance she possessed. She had Overbury poisoned in the Tower not long before her triumphant second marriage. In 1616 the scandal broke, and James ordered a special investigation. He insisted on impartial justice, and got it, but he had identified himself too closely with the annulment, the remarriage and Overbury's imprisonment to wash away all the mud that now bedaubed him. Many believed, incorrectly, that he and Somerset had connived at the murder; it was obvious enough, anyway, that those whom the king delighted to honour had dabbled in adultery, witchcraft and perjury. Lady Somerset pleaded guilty; her husband denied all the charges, but he was convicted by his peers; both were sentenced to death. James reprieved them and they were released in 1622, but only on condition that they lived in strict retirement.

James's parting with Somerset at Royston, when he left to stand trial, was typical of the man, his sentimentality and his shallowness. "The king," we are told, "hung about his neck, slabbering his cheeks, saying, 'For God's sake, when shall I see thee again? On my soul I shall neither eat nor sleep until you are come again.' The earl told him, 'On Monday.' 'For God's sake let me [see you then],' said the king, 'Shall I? shall I?' Then lolled about his neck, [saying], 'Then for God's sake give thy lady this kiss for me.' In the same manner at the stair's head, at the middle of the stairs, and at the stair's foot." But no sooner had Somerset climbed into the coach than James turned away, remarking flatly, "I shall never see his face more." His concupiscent eyes were already lolling on a new catamite, his handsome young Cupbearer, George Villiers.

Love came late to James I. When he met Villiers at Apethorpe in 1614 he was only forty-seven, but already verging on senility. The dithering vacillation that characterised his policy was now evident in his manner. "He was of middle stature, more corpulent through his clothes than his body, yet fat enough, his clothes ever being made large and easy, the doublets quilted for stiletto proof, his breeches in pleats, and full stuffed. . . . His eye [was] large, ever rolling after any stranger [that] came into his presence, in so much as many for shame have left the room, as being out of countenance. . . . His legs were very weak . . . , [and] that weakness made him ever leaning on other men's shoulders; his walk was ever circular, his fingers ever in that walk fiddling about his codpiece."

The new Dulcinea was in painful contrast to this elderly Don Quixote. At the age of twenty-two George Villiers had that rather over-ripe masculine attraction that trembles on the verge of femininity : tall and beautifully-proportioned, he had a heart-shaped face framed in dark chestnut hair and short beard, an exquisitely-curved mouth, and the dark blue eyes of the highly-sexed. He was the son of a Leicestershire knight by his second marriage, and his elder half-brothers stood between him and the modest family estates; he had precious little money and no prospects. But he was taken in hand by his widowed mother, Mary Beaumont, a woman of relentless ambition. She provided the money to send him to France, where he perfected his skill in dancing, duelling, horsemanship and music; in 1614 she bought him a wardrobe and sent him to court, where he was soon appointed Cup-bearer. The following year, with Somerset grown spoilt and petulant, and the first rumours of Overbury's murder flying about, he was made a Gentleman of the Bedchamber. As Somerset fell, Villiers soared past him like a rocket. He was appointed Master of the Horse, dubbed a Knight of the Garter and created Viscount Villiers all in the same year, 1616. In 1617 he was made Earl of Buckingham, in 1619 Marquess.

James was head over heels in love with his " sweet Steenie gossip ",[7] his " sweetheart ", his " sweet child and wife ", and a few days' absence was enough to set him throbbing with desire. " My only sweet and dear child," he drooled, " I pray thee haste thee home to thy dear dad by sunsetting at the furthest . . . , and so Lord send me comfortable and happy with thee this night." Buckingham met this cloying affection, and returned it in kind; he cosseted and teased his " dear dad and gossip ", pandered to his senile whims, and flattered him to the top of his bent. But at the same time Buckingham was always in command. His intelligence,

[7] Buckingham's pet-name was derived from his supposed resemblance to St Stephen.

while it existed at a low level, undoubtedly existed; this cannot be said with the same certainty of Somerset. Moreover, Somerset had had to deal with a much more able, assertive and virile monarch. Buckingham's boyish flirtatiousness enabled him to cross James with impunity, emerging rather with enhanced influence; his letters bubble with nonsensical charm and lovers' baby-talk, but there is a pertness even in his unvarying valediction, from " Your Majesty's most humble Slave and Dogge, Steenie ". Like a giggling dowager James revelled in it all, and when he gave this mettlesome but rather vulgar adolescent an earldom in 1617 he explained himself to the Lords of the Council in his own inimitable fashion : " I, James, am neither God nor an angel, but a man like any other. Therefore I act like a man, and confess to loving those dear to me more than other men. You may be sure that I love the Earl of Buckingham more than anyone else, and more than you who are here assembled. I wish to speak in my own behalf, and not to have it thought to be a defect, for Jesus Christ did the same, and therefore I cannot be blamed. Christ had his John, and I have my George."

With such overwhelming influence at work, the remaining Howards could not expect a long lease on office. They had survived the fall of Somerset only because no one could summon up enough energy to remove them. But the administration of the Treasury by the Earl of Suffolk was almost farcically venal—even his wife took bribes—and the difficulty involved in financing the simplest excursions was beginning to bring the situation home even to James. His visit to Scotland in 1617 was postponed again and again because the Treasury could not find the comparatively modest sum needed to finance it, and only his angry stubbornness set the affair in motion at all. Returning, he crossed the Border penniless, only to find that the expected remittance had not reached Carlisle; there was nothing for it but to push on into England. Thirty miles beyond Carlisle the Treasury wagon hove in sight, guarded by a posse of troops. The courtiers surrounded the wagon, the covers were thrown back, and the royal eyes peered suspiciously into the cavernous interior; on the floor reposed a tiny canvas bag, containing £400. James sent off a furious protest; from the Treasury came the enigmatic answer: " If your wants are so great now, what will they be after your return?"

But in 1618 James discovered a new finance minister, and Buckingham an ideal ally. Sir Lionel Cranfield's keen economic brain had raised him from the dirt to be one of the wealthiest merchant financiers of his day*. His ostentatious vulgarity and bristling bad temper made him a poor courtier, but he was a superb financial technician and a man of overwhelming vigour, and in the years 1618-21 he succeeded where even Salisbury had failed, in drastically reducing James's domestic expenditure. On Suffolk's dismissal in 1618 he was appointed a Commissioner of the Treasury, Master of the Wardrobe and Master of the Court of Wards. His investigations led to Suffolk's conviction on charges of corruption, and in 1619, supported by Buckingham, he switched his attention to the Admiralty. Lord Nottingham was dismissed for incompetence, and Buckingham succeeded him as Lord High Admiral while Cranfield overhauled the naval administration.

But this vigorous reform at home only emphasised the drift in foreign policy. The Spanish policy of the Howards lived after them, partly because of Gondomar's influence, partly because the continued paralysis of France left no obvious alternative, but mainly because no minister had the ability to frame a new policy and the character to impose it on the king. The Privy Council was a bear garden of contending factions. Buckingham might have used his influence to impose order, but it was not in his interest to do so, nor in his nature; he was a mere opportunist, who took his chances as they came.

It was in this atmosphere that the tragedy of Sir Walter Ralegh was played out. Once Ralegh had clashed with the Spaniards on the Orinoco James had little choice but to comply with Gondomar's demand for his head; the criminal folly lay in allowing him to sail on this visionary quest for El Dorado at all. And it was a coward's way out to have him executed under the sentence of death passed on him for treason fifteen years before. It says much for the peculiar genius of the Stuarts that James contrived to transform Ralegh from one of the best-hated men in England, as he was in 1603, into one of the most highly respected and deeply mourned.

The war between Spain and the Protestant Dutch added fresh fuel to popular passions already inflamed by Ralegh's death, and in 1619 the crisis in central Europe began to impinge on England when James's son-in-law Frederick accepted the Bohemian crown in defiance of the new Hapsburg emperor. English opinion was vaguely, emotionally, in favour of some intervention on James's part, far distant as the conflict was. The Counter-Reformation was gathering momentum, and Elizabeth of Bohemia was one of the few Stuarts who enjoyed almost universal popularity; in the court circle she was always (even as a stout old dowager) " The Queen of Hearts ", the living embodiment of regal virtue and beauty in distress, while to the common people she seemed a reincarnation of the great Elizabeth from whom she took her name, the Judith of European Protestantism. But James had no money, and his diplomacy was palsied; unable to seek expert advice from Bacon or Buckingham, he tried to handle his own foreign policy and fell down on the job. Complaisant in the belief that nothing could be done, or the hope that nothing need be done, he was caught out by the Spanish invasion of the Palatinate in 1620 and the emperor's march on Prague. The reign of the Summer King and his Summer Queen was nearly over, the next move lay with the British Solomon.[8]

It was obvious that James could not offer his son-in-law worthwhile aid unless he summoned a new parliament, but it would have been difficult to imagine a less auspicious time for it. The war in Germany and the Low Countries had finally prostrated the English cloth trade, already weakened

---

[8] James's controversial writings had earned him this title, but it was usually employed sarcastically. For instance, Henry IV is said to have remarked " that he hoped that he was not David the fiddler's son "—a reference to Mary Stuart's music-loving secretary, David Rizzio.

by injudicious attempts on the part of a group of London merchants to break the monopoly of the Merchant Adventurers. The collapse of this basic industry had economic repercussions that were to last until the mid-century; in 1620 and 1621 it brought many rural areas to the verge of destitution, paralysed the towns and caused a shortage of money which forced down the price of land. The parliamentary gentry were hardly in a mood to loosen their purse strings, especially as they blamed the crisis on the Council's meddling, and James's lack of money on his own extravagance. They also attributed the shortage of bullion to the monopolies in gold and silver thread held by Buckingham's brothers.

Such devices as monopolies, designed to offset the decline in royal patronage, emphasised the gulf opening between the courtiers and the rest of the landowning classes, between central and local administration. All monopolies could be portrayed as economic evils : some were social evils, too. The monopoly of inns and ale-houses, for instance, wounded not only the pocket but also the *amour propre* of the local justices. Yet this growing division between court and country was officially ratified by James in 1617, when he ordered all gentlemen who did not own a town house to leave the capital forthwith and repair to the country, there to manage their estates and administer local government.

So the great majority of that class that would compose the next House of Commons had been firmly excluded from any contact with the king, any insight into his policy. Cranfield's reforms, however beneficial to the Treasury, also reduced still further the amount of gentlemanly pickings to be had at Whitehall, and made faction necessary as well as desirable. Buckingham, like his master, welcomed the growth of faction and clientage and the personalisation of political relationships. Men who were for the marquess were "made", the rest, nowhere; as one country gentleman remarked, Buckingham was "of a kind, liberal and free nature and disposition—to those that applied themselves to him, applauded his actions, and were wholly his creatures". In fact, he created a system of clientage that embraced every aspect of government, its upper échelons manned by his own relations, as *arrivistes* as the Buonapartes. And James, in his lovesick folly, complacently approved. At a banquet in 1618 he toasted the assembled Villiers family and said, " I desire to advance it above all others; of myself I have no doubt, for I live to that end."

Buckingham's clamorous mother was a caricature of the precarious *nouveau riche*; avaricious, gossiping and intrigante, she moved up each step of the aristocratic ladder in step with her illustrious son—Countess of Buckingham in 1618, marchioness in 1619, duchess in 1623. The flourishing marriage market she set up at Whitehall was not the least unpopular feature of the Villiers empire, and she crowned a career of tactlessness by turning papist in 1622.

Buckingham's half-brother Edward Villiers rose with him, too, and so did his brother-in-law, Sir William Fielding. Both had glimmerings of real ability, but the same cannot be said for his blood brothers, Christopher and John. Kit was so stupid and unattractive that even the omnipotent Buckingham had difficulty finding a niche for him, and he humbly admitted that " his want of preferment stemmed from his own unworthiness rather than from the duke's unwillingness ". John Villiers had the reputation of a mental defective, but in 1619 he was created Viscount Purbeck and married off to the attractive and intelligent daughter of Sir Edward Coke. After a year she went off with another of the ubiquitous Howards, this time Sir Robert, the Earl of Suffolk's younger son; defying the thunders of the High Commission Court, she lived with him in Shropshire for more than ten years and bore him several children.

The enmity of Sir Edward Coke was to have serious repercussions. After a long and fierce campaign against the courts of Chancery and High Commission this turbulent lawyer was dismissed the post of Chief Justice of King's Bench for rank insubordination, in 1616. His daughter's marriage was a last desperate bid to re-establish his position against his life-long rival Francis Bacon, now Lord Chancellor; failing, he entered the parliament of 1621 intent on making trouble. Always a fierce and narrow defender of the common

law, he now came forward as the champion of parliamentary
privilege. It was "Captain Coke" (as James contemptuously
called him) who succeeded in rallying the Commons of 1621,
maddened though it was by anti-popery, economic distress
and hatred of the court, and it was his commanding influence,
exerted alike over battle-scarred veterans like Sir Edwin
Sandys and green newcomers like John Pym, that prevented
a repetition of the Addled Parliament.

Meanwhile the reaction against Buckingham and Cranfield
had produced a strong opposition group in the House of
Lords for the first time since 1485. Its leader was the great
Earl of Southampton, Shakespeare's patron, who "liked
not to come to the council board, because there were so
many boys and base fellows there".[9] Buckingham, the
laughing opportunist, had made no serious preparations for
parliament, and he was astonished to find he could command a
majority in neither house. The Commons sturdily blamed
the king's own extravagance for his financial difficulties, and
attributed the economic crisis to his fiscal gerrymandering.
They declined to vote more than two subsidies, even for
a war they approved, and instead launched a full-scale attack
on the monopolists. Coke's revival of the mediaeval device of
impeachment, or trial before the Lords on the Commons'
indictment, demonstrated the ominous understanding between
the two houses. Impeachment destroyed Mompesson, the most
notorious monopolist, and then Bacon. Bacon's fall, followed
in September by Cranfield's retirement to the Lords, removed
the government's last pretence of controlling parliament.
In November, after a grand debate on foreign policy, the
Commons decided to petition for the abandonment of the
Spanish match. When their deputation waited on James at
Newmarket he showed a wry appreciation of the situation—
"Bring stools for the ambassadors!" he cried—but he had
in fact learned nothing from a similar experience in 1610.
When he once more forbad the Commons to debate policy
and war on the general grounds that their privileges depended
on him, their answer was to write into their journals the

famous Protestation of 18 December 1621, asserting that
their privileges were " the ancient and undoubted birthright
and inheritance of the subjects of England ". James acknowledged their moral victory by at once adjourning them, dissolving them in January 1622, and then going down to Westminster to tear the offending page out of the journals with
his own hands.

The king apart, Buckingham was the man most to blame
for this fiasco, but his power was undiminished as a result
of it, perhaps even strengthened. Queen Anne had died in
1619; James was physically ill, and sinking into a dotage
from which he henceforth emerged only rarely. Foreign
envoys swapped scabrous anecdotes of his unnatural lusts
and extreme cowardice. " The king alone seems free from
anxiety," wrote the French ambassador in January 1622,
" and has made a journey to Newmarket, as a certain other
sovereign once did to Capri. He takes his beloved Buckingham with him, wishes rather to be his friend than king, and
to associate his name to the heroes of friendship in antiquity.
Under such specious titles he endeavours to conceal scandal-
ous doings, and because his strength deserts him for these,
he feeds his eyes where he can no longer content his other
senses. The end of all is ever the bottle."

His body too feeble to indulge in hunting, his brain
no longer equal to literary pursuits, James had little with
which to occupy the long weary hours of every day. So
he came to take an increasing interest in Buckingham's immediate family—in his wife, Lady Catherine Manners, whom
he married in 1620, in his children, and his small nephews
and nieces. He liked to have the children near him, he
watched their illnesses with anxiety, bought them presents,
even played with them. Lady Buckingham was in high favour,
as were her sisters-in-law, Lady Fielding and Lady Purbeck.
Observers were flabbergasted at the king, " who formerly
would not endure his queen and children in his lodgings;
now you would have judged that none but women frequented
them."

Moreover, Buckingham had taken steps to perpetuate his
influence by winning over the heir to the throne. " Baby

Charles ", as James always called him, had lived a lonely and unhappy childhood, overshadowed in his father's eyes by his brother Henry, by Lord Somerset, and lately by Buckingham. For years he was madly jealous of Buckingham, but once the favourite, encouraged by James, turned the full force of his charm on to this shrinking, tentative young man, he melted in a rush. Starved of affection and, like his father, strictly monogamous, the young prince gave all his devotion to this glittering creature who excelled where he was deficient— in swordsmanship, dancing, conversation, drinking and love. Charles was nothing if not heterosexual, but he was a rigid virgin, mentally as well as physically; by loving his dear Steenie he surrendered to a passion that could never mar that virginity, while he took into his life a tumult, a glitter, a romance it sadly lacked.

It was a romantic impulse that drove Charles and Buckingham to embark on their first and most insane escapade together. Parliament would not finance a war, so the only hope of recovering the Palatinate was by a Spanish marriage. Philip IV, however, proved as cryptic as his father, and in 1623 Buckingham persuaded the prince to go with him to Madrid incognito, and there press his suit in person. They arrived in March.

It had taken twenty-four hours' alternate bullying and cozening to secure James's permission, but his failing mind was soon taken up with the tinsel glamour of their mission— " My sweet boys and venturous knights," he called them, " worthy to be put in a new romanzo." But this drivel was soon cut short by the Lords of the Council, who took the opportunity provided by Buckingham's absence to air their opinions freely. Their gloomy prognostications reduced James to flabby panic—" Alas," he babbled, " I now repent me sore that I ever suffered you to go away. I care for match nor nothing, so I may once have you in my arms again; God grant it, God grant it! Amen, amen, amen!" Buckingham replied amiably enough that " none ever longed more to be in the arms of his mistress " than he did to throw himself at James's feet. But he was growing sick of all this senile adulation. One of his letters from Spain ended:

" So craving your blessing, I kiss your dirty hands and end,
your Majesty's most humble slave and dog, Steenie."

The fact is that, having captured baby Charles, he had
no further need of his dear dad and gossip. And he had
some excuse for thinking that his lucky star would carry
him over any disaster. He had departed for Madrid straight
from the fiasco of the last parliament, yet in his absence
the king had made him a duke—the only dukedom granted
outside the blood royal between 1485 and 1660. The
Madrid expedition was another fiasco. Philip IV might just
conceivably marry his sister to a heretic; he certainly would
not compel his Austrian cousin to re-establish another heretic
in the Palatinate. Charles's refusal to see this prolonged the
negotiations through the summer of 1623; and when he did at
last see it there was a moment when it seemed that, sick with
self-created romantic passion as he was, he might consent to the
marriage without conditions. But the moment passed, and he
and Buckingham returned that October with their tails between
their legs, dogged by the news that the Emperor had granted
Frederick's lands and honours to Maximilian of Bavaria.

Yet even this could not unseat Buckingham. On the
contrary, he found any criticism of his actions overwhelmed
by a wave of national rejoicing at the prince's safe return
from the clutching talons of the Inquisition. Fattening on
failure, he was strong enough to ride down the remnants of
opposition at court and pervert the foreign policy of a nation
to the satisfaction of a personal vendetta. For he and Charles
both considered that they had been tricked at Madrid
(whereas they had practised the only deception, on themselves), and they now had but one thought : war against
Spain. Without more ado they bullied James and the Privy
Council into reversing every assumption upon which English
foreign policy had been based for the past decade, and negotiations were at once opened for an alliance with Louis XIII
of France and the hand of his sister, Henrietta Maria. Another parliament was summoned in February 1624, Buckingham won over most of the opposition leaders to his new
" patriotic ", anti-Spanish policy, and the old king, a pathetic
figure, was bullied into requesting the Commons' advice as

to whether he should break off relations with Spain—thus surrendering the very issue on which he had quarrelled with the parliament of 1621.

This was one precedent that Charles I would find it difficult to ignore, and the session was not very old before it provided another. To cement his unholy alliance with the Opposition Buckingham decided to sacrifice his last serious rival, Cranfield, now Lord Treasurer and Earl of Middlesex. Impeached for embezzlement and peculation, this autocratic and unpopular minister was swept away in a matter of weeks, his fall as swift as his rise. James could only commute his sentence, and deliver himself of some prophetic remarks to Buckingham. "You are a fool," he told him, "you are making a rod with which you will be scourged yourself." Turning to his son, he added, "You will live to have your bellyful of impeachments."

Continuing discord between king and prince prevented the government from presenting its case to parliament honestly or even competently. Left to themselves, the Commons naturally fell back on the unrealistic "country" view of foreign policy, a hangover from the high piratic days of Drake. They demanded a maritime war on Spain coupled with an all-out persecution of papists at home. How either measure was to assist in the recovery of the Palatinate was not clear, but the Palatinate had receded into the distance now, and no government spokesman recalled it. Sir John Eliot gave voice to the common sentiment with his usual hysteria: "Are we poor?" he cried. "Spain is rich! There are our Indies! Break with them, [and] we shall break our necessities together!"*

It would have been difficult to explain to the Commons that Spain was far from rich, and that war was never self-supporting, anyway; that the French marriage must involve increased toleration for Roman Catholics; and that Buckingham planned to raise an army for the German campaign under the unsavoury condottiere Mansfeld. The trouble was, no one so much as hinted at all this. James tried to, but his words were cynically explained away by his son in the Lords. The result was that when the Commons finally produced a money bill for the inadequate sum of £300,000, they fastened to it a preamble directing that it should be used only for the defence of the realm, the navy, Ireland or aid to the Dutch. When he came down at the end of the session James tried to emulate Henry VIII. He raged and stormed, vetoed several minor bills with a flourish, and announced his intention of altering the preamble to the money bill. But he was no Tudor; routed by an indignant hum from the Commons behind the Bar, he signed the bill as it stood.

Charles and Buckingham made no protest; gambling on success, they simply ignored the preamble to the money bill, and the views on war policy enshrined in it. In September 1624 they concluded the French treaty, and Mansfeld's army began to assemble in southern England. Terrible were the disagreements between James and Buckingham, particularly over the declaration of war, and half-a-dozen times it seemed that the final break must come. But the old man was feeble now, and Steenie was a drug he could no longer do without; with the approach of Christmas he capitulated. He had usually known the right thing to do, always he had lacked the strength to do it. " I cannot content myself," he wrote, " without sending you this billet, praying God that I may have a joyful and comfortable meeting with you, and that we may make at this Christenmass a new marriage, ever to be kept hereafter; for, God so love me, as I desired only to live in this world for your sake, and that I had rather live banished in any part of the world with you, than live a sorrowful widow-life without you. And so God bless you, my sweet child and wife, and grant that ye may ever be a comfort to your dear dad and husband."

It is to be hoped that Buckingham was kind, for the old man was sinking fast. Early in the new year, 1625, he began a last restless peregrination, which early in March brought him limping into his favourite hunting lodge at Theobalds, in Essex. There he died, on Sunday the 27th. His son was with him, and so was Buckingham (who was inevitably accused of poisoning him). Through the usual smokescreen thrown up by his legion of physicians, it seems that he was brought low by advanced senility, and a general physical breakdown was accelerated by a stroke. His funeral was stately and prolonged, but John Chamberlain's remark on it might stand against the reign as a whole—" All was performed with great magnificence, but the order was very confused and disorderly."

CHAPTER III

CHARLES I

1625-1649

Charles's marriage soon after his accession might have been expected to wean him from his dependence on Buckingham. But his heart had always been set on the Spanish match and in his mind's eye was still the Hapsburg woman, languorous and inbred, "of a fading flaxen hair, big lipped, and somewhat heavy eyed". Henrietta Maria of France was no substitute for this sensual vision. Time would bring her something of her great father's compelling charm, but at the age of sixteen she was still a gawky adolescent, with enormous eyes, bony wrists, projecting teeth and a minimal figure. At the sight of her new husband she burst into tears. Charles, as always, displayed great dignity and exquisite good manners, but he could not drop his guard with this child, nor could she pierce his elegant façade. Personal incompatibility was emphasised by religious differences, an aggressive Catholic, she declined to be crowned with Protestant rites, or even witness Charles's coronation from a place of concealment in the Abbey. Only Charles's chivalry and sense of duty saved his marriage at all, but even after two years he and his wife still led lives apart, coming together at intervals only to keep up appearances, utterly without mutual sympathy, love or understanding. Unable to blame herself, or in justice her husband, Henrietta vented her jealousy on the ubiquitous Lord Admiral.

Buckingham was scarcely devious enough deliberately to sow discord between king and queen, but certainly he profited by it, and under Charles he achieved a freedom of action that James, even at his most doting, had been careful to deny him. Unfortunately, he appealed exclusively to the weaker side of Charles's character, the false romantic, which visualised war, for instance, in terms of glamour and martial glory, not

blood and financial privation, which regarded politics as a
regal diversion and made a personal plaything of some of the
most serious issues of the 1620s. He fostered in him the
Stuart trait of regarding politics in the light of personal
emotion, while at the same time his extrovert temperament
crushed and distorted his master's budding personality. Left
to his own introspective musing, left to make friends and
enemies naturally, Charles might possibly have come to terms
with politics, and men in politics; it was the duke who
forced him to assume a romantic bravura and "dash" that
were really foreign to his nature. This explains so much
that is palpably artificial in the mature Charles I. All his
adult life he was acting a part; he was the nervous man afraid
of seeming nervous, the shy man afraid of seeming shy. He
always over-acted slightly; he was always advancing to occupy
untenable positions, then defending them with pathetic hero-
ism against impossible odds. The end-product is the martyr-
king of Van Dyck's portraits, with the heavy lidded eyes,
the compressed mouth, the long, handsome, wistful face
and effeminate hair, a composition in suffering and Christ-
like resignation. These Van Dyck portraits, painted during the
happiest period of his life, slotted perfectly into the post-
humous martyrologies, when the realistic, human features of
Bower's portrait in 1649 had been forgotten.[1] But every
face that Charles presented to the world was in some
sense a pose, a defence against a world he did not care to
understand.

Buckingham must take the blame for initiating Charles in
a policy of violent and continuous action which the monarchy
was not strong enough to sustain, but Charles must share the
responsibility for its almost total failure. Neither of them
saw the least reason why they should explain the abandonment
of the war policy to which they had by implication pledged
themselves in 1624. Constitutionally, of course, there was
no reason why they should, but prudence and commonsense

---

[1] When the sculptor Bernini saw Van Dyck's "Charles I in
Three Positions" in 1637 he was deeply moved. "Never," he
said, "have I beheld a countenance more unfortunate."

might have suggested some compromise. Their refusal to explain or justify Mansfeld's expedition soon alienated the new parliament of 1625, which would have gone halfway to meet a young monarch who was in most outward aspects a distinct improvement on his late father. Disgusted by his stubborn refusal to explain himself, they only voted him two subsidies, declined to grant him the tunnage and poundage duties for life (as with James I and the Tudors), and accused Buckingham of rank incompetence, if not worse. At the whisper of impeachment they were promptly dissolved, in August 1625.

Subsequently only overwhelming success in war or diplomacy could have justified Buckingham in parliament's eyes; as it was, he merely stumbled from one failure to the next, weighed down by shortage of money, a corrupt, traditionless administration, and his own military inefficiency. Mansfeld's unruly army fell apart at Ostend in a chaos of disease and desertion, and the conduct of the expedition against Cadiz in October 1625 was distinguished by every possible martial vice, even drunkenness. Meanwhile, another part of the fleet, refitted at public expense, was besieging the French Protestants in La Rochelle under the orders of a cardinal of the Roman church. But Charles was not even consistent in perversity, and in 1626 a series of petty quarrels, aggravated by Buckingham's bad diplomacy, culminated in a war against France that postponed indefinitely any attempt to recover the Palatinate.

If it had been difficult to justify Buckingham's war policy in 1625 it was now impossible, and his attempt to muzzle Charles's second parliament, in 1626, by excluding Sir Edward Coke, Sir Thomas Wentworth and most of the other Opposition leaders, only surrendered the initiative to that unbalanced demagogue Sir John Eliot. Under Eliot's leadership the Commons refused further taxes, and instead launched forth on Buckingham's impeachment. Charles's inelasticity of mind, and his belief that the Opposition were inspired by personal motives, always ruined his parliamentary tactics; he could never think himself into the minds of his opponents. But in 1626 his whole strategy was faulty, too. His assumption

C

of complete responsibility for Buckingham's actions, his panic dissolution in June, frustrated a trial which would almost certainly have ended in the duke's acquittal, if only for lack of evidence. As it was, the charges against him were left hanging in air, and Charles's refusal to let him meet them offered strong presumptive evidence of their truth.

This faulty strategy must be attributed not so much to Charles's quarrel with the Commons as to his failure to win back the Lords, who had maintained an attitude of unusual reserve towards the Crown, and marked hostility towards Buckingham, since 1621. Charles's attempt to prevent the attendance of the hostile Earl of Arundel sparked off an explosion in 1626, but Arundel was followed by a still more terrifying *revenant,* in the person of John Digby, Earl of Bristol.

Strafford apart, Bristol was the greatest crown servant of his generation; as a close confidant of James I, and periodically his ambassador to Madrid, he had been in charge of the negotiations with Spain ever since 1611. Yet it was this man whom baby Charles selected as the scapegoat for his own folly in 1623. King James scarcely took his son seriously, but when the great ambassador returned in 1624 he was ordered to keep to his country seat, and Charles and Buckingham were free with their accusations of treason. However, as soon as Charles realised that he needed no scapegoat for the Madrid fiasco he cooled down, and on his accession he sent Bristol a gracious letter intimating that if he acknowledged his errors he would be restored to favour. But Bristol was the last man to admit a non-existent fault, and after a further exchange of letters in 1625 and 1626 Charles, in a fit of puerile fury, accused him of trying to convert him to popery at Madrid. Bristol at once demanded a trial, and the Lords forced Charles to issue a writ of summons. In defiance of the king's orders the terrible earl made his appearance in April 1626 and told the Lords that Buckingham was so frightened of him he dare not let him sit. Thus provoked, Buckingham laid charges of treason against him; he riposted with similar charges against Buckingham;

and the Lords decided that the two trials should run concurrently. They were still in progress at the dissolution.

The Bristol case, more than any other incident, opened the eyes of influential men to the true character of their sovereign lord. It was one of Charles I's least endearing traits that in the execution of his public duties he did not consider himself bound by the rules of honour that governed his conduct as a private gentleman. The continued application of this double standard, especially when dealing with opponents, made it impossible to trust him except where self-interest ensured his fidelity. It was an attitude that could only be justified by the possession of overwhelming strength; yet within two years of the dissolution of 1626 his weakness forced him to summon yet another parliament.

Denied a parliamentary grant in 1626, Charles passed on the cost of the war against France as best he could. The gentry were invited to contribute to a forced loan, the maritime towns were ordered to fit out a fleet, troops were billeted on the civilian population, and as a coercive measure several counties were placed under martial law. Finally, Charles ordered that those gentry and nobility who declined to pay the forced loan be thrown into prison, and the judges declined to free them on a writ of *habeas corpus*. All this notwithstanding, Buckingham's expedition for the relief of La Rochelle in 1627 was a humiliating failure, and he advised Charles to call a new parliament for the following March.

The result was not so explosive as might have been feared. Wentworth, Coke and Pym returned and forced Eliot to drop the charges against Buckingham in favour of a campaign to restrict the king's powers of arbitrary imprisonment, which placed the property of all his subjects at his mercy. The method chosen to enforce what Wentworth called our " ancient, sober and vital liberties " was the Petition of Right, to which Charles was requested to assent as he would to a statute;[2] it declared that imprisonment without cause shown,

[2] Shortage of space compels me to over-simplify the legal subtleties involved. For a detailed discussion see Miss Helen Relf's authoritative monograph, *The Petition of Right*.

taxation without parliamentary consent, forced billeting and the subjection of civilians to martial law, were illegal. The Commons' tactics revealed the damage already done to Charles's reputation as a man of honour. His attempt to bypass the Petition by giving his "royal word" to abide by its provisions was parried with oriental suavity by Wentworth and Noy: "We are ambitious his Majesty's goodness may remain to posterity," declared the one, and, "Were the king immortal," chorused the other, "I would be content with his Majesty's word." The truth was, Charles's royal word was not worth a farthing, and everyone knew it. This assumption was handsomely confirmed by his unworthy evasions and backtracking, which culminated in an attempt to shuffle the Petition through without giving his assent in legal form. Another defeat off La Rochelle broke his obstinacy, but he did not give his assent until 7 June.

The passing of the Petition of Right was a famous victory, but within a month the Commons had thrown the ball back to Charles. Their numbers were depleted now, Coke and Wentworth had relaxed their grip, and the way was left clear for earnest zealots like Eliot, who resented the concessions demanded by Wentworth's policy of co-operation with the Lords, and Buckingham's escape. Other Members were agitated by the fact that Charles had been levying tunnage and poundage illegally since 1626; many more were alarmed at the aggressive church reform movement initiated by Charles's religious adviser and confidant, William Laud, Bishop of Bath and Wells, and in particular at the manner in which some "Laudian" divines were openly justifying royal absolutism. Richard Montague had been censured by the previous parliament; now it was the turn of Roger Manwaring, who had published a sermon in 1627 declaring the refusal of forced loans to be an offence against the laws of God. In June 1628, lashed on by Eliot's unscrupulous mob oratory, the Commons impeached Manwaring and submitted a remonstrance to the king complaining of the conduct of the Laudians and the government's laxness in persecuting the papists. Eliot's new hate campaign against Buckingham so inflamed the London mob that it tore the duke's physician to pieces in the street, and in the last days of the session the Commons took the revolutionary step of appealing to the nation on their own initiative—for their remonstrance declaring tunnage and poundage illegal was clearly addressed to the merchants. Not surprisingly, Charles at once prorogued them to the end of the year.

In retrospect the most important single result of Eliot's conduct was to drive Wentworth back to court. Like Danby later, Wentworth found himself balanced between an unsatisfactory monarch and an unsatisfactory parliament, and, like Danby, he chose the path of order, discipline and strong government towards which his authoritarian nature inclined him. He joined the trickle of parliament men back to Whitehall, and with the assassination of Buckingham at Portsmouth on 23 August his position was assured. In December he was raised to the peerage and appointed Lord President of the Council of the North.

Buckingham's removal was the signal for the return of other men of ability—notably Bristol and Arundel—who endowed Charles's policy with unaccustomed skill and commonsense. It also acquired a new edge. He was at morning prayers when they brought him the news of Buckingham's murder. The service shuddered to a standstill, but the king, stony faced, ordered the chaplain to proceed; not until he reached his bedchamber did he break down. He blamed the House of Commons—Eliot in particular—for reviving popular hostility to the duke and even guiding the assassin's hand, and he was shocked beyond measure at the public rejoicing that greeted the event. (This is forgotten by many who criticise his treatment of Eliot later.) He had little further taste for war, and after a furious attempt to carry out his friend's ambitious plans, he ordered peace negotiations to be opened. This relaxation of policy allowed him to crush Eliot at his leisure, and he moved to his revenge with a hard, cold determination that had nothing in it of his former boyish petulance.

His answer to the Commons' remonstrance on tunnage and poundage was a council order for the imprisonment of re-

calcitrant merchants and the impounding of their goods.
A fortunate death or two in the church made his answer
to their remonstrance on religion even more decisive. In
the second half of 1628 he transferred Laud to London,
appointed Richard Montague to Chichester, promoted two
of Laud's staunchest allies on the episcopal bench, and
presented the impeached Manwaring to a handsome crown
living. This was followed in December by a royal declaration
that the reform of the church was no concern of parliament's. Having thrown down the gage, Charles then ordered
the Commons to reassemble on 20 January 1629.

Eliot fell headlong into the pit dug for him. Baffled by
Charles's serene refusal to shift the blame for the merchants'
imprisonment onto the Council, he turned instead to the
arraignment of the leading Laudian divines, and pushed
through a series of left-wing resolutions on religion which
left the majority of the gentry far behind. The desertion
of the moderate Opposition leaders, like Coke, Pym and
Digges, and the refusal of the Lords to countenance any
of his actions, or even notice them, merely lashed him to
a frenzy of intemperance, fanaticism and irresponsibility.
Threshing and stamping like some wounded dragon, he spat
out his venom indifferently right and left, and under his
half-demented leadership the session reached its climax in
the final disgraceful scene on 2 March, when the Commons,
in hysteria, forcibly postponed their own dissolution by
locking Black Rod out and holding the Speaker down in
his chair. In this unconstitutional atmosphere they passed the
notorious "three resolutions", declaring that anyone paying
tunnage and poundage, advising its collection, or bringing
in innovations in religion, was "a capital enemy to this
kingdom and commonwealth". After that they dispersed.

So, contrary to all expectation, the first part of Charles I's
reign ended in the suicide of the House of Commons, and
it was not to be resuscitated for eleven years. Raised as we
are in the text-book doctrine that Eliot was an apostle of
liberty, and 2 March 1629 a grand climacteric in parliamentary history, it is difficult for us to appreciate the impact

of these events on a generation that reserved its deepest reverence for forms of law. One bigoted parliamentarian, Sir Simonds d'Ewes, noted in his diary: "The most gloomy, sad and dismal day for England that has happened in five hundred years", but he added: "The cause of the break and dissolution was immaterial and frivolous, in the carriage whereof divers fiery spirits in the House of Commons were very faulty and cannot be excused." In fact, the Commons' revolutionary fury forced a majority of the nation to Charles's own conclusion, that "this House proceeds not upon the abuses of power only, but upon power itself". And now, as in 1642, the gentry could not face the situation created by the removal of sovereign power from the king: as Wentworth said, "The authority of a king is the keystone which closeth up the arch of order and government, which containeth each part in due relation to the whole."

The lawyers took this lesson closest to heart, naturally, and their defection set the seal on Eliot's betrayal of the Petition of Right. Of Coke's supporters, Noy followed Wentworth to court and was made Attorney-General, Digges was appointed to the High Commission in 1633, the Mastership of the Rolls in 1636, Lyttleton accepted the recordership of London and ultimately the Great Seal, and John Selden turned his pen to the justification of the ship-money fleet. More important still, the judges declined to accept the rôle envisaged for them by Coke, of independent arbiters between king and parliament; ignoring the Petition of Right, they retreated on a judicial practice that had long preceded Coke, and would long outlive him. In a series of judgments beginning in 1630 with Eliot's *habeas corpus* and culminating in 1637 with *Rex v. Hampden*, they consistently found in favour of the king in all doubtful issues at common law.

Unfortunately, Charles could never take advantage of any swing of public opinion in his favour. His high concept of the nature of kingship set him apart even from his closest advisers; after Buckingham's death he had no friends, only servants. The Scots accent he never lost, his falsetto voice and nervous stammer, kept acquaintance at a distance; his eyes did not dwell on those around him, but looked through them and beyond, finding no point of rest. He was intellectual without being intelligent, and he lacked entirely the common touch so obvious in his father and his eldest son, Charles II. His was never a masculine character, and his feminine delicacy of feature, his *tristesse*, that Pre-Raphaelite droop so attractive to the old ladies of Anglo-Catholicism, had a limited appeal to contemporaries. His perfect good manners, his gentle sweetness of disposition, suffused with calvaric melancholy, imposed on those who came in daily contact with him, but they were not attractions communicable to the nation at large. To those outside a small inner circle he remained something of a mystery, and even those who knew him best could never respect him; William Laud's crushing verdict was: " a mild and gracious prince who knew not how to be, or be made, great ". For not only was he ill-equipped for kingship, he never enjoyed the act of ruling as his father and his sons so clearly did. The duties imposed on him by God he fulfilled with a kind of petulant distaste that struck a chill into those around him. He expected nothing from political life but a crown of thorns; he anticipated betrayal and neglected to reward loyalty, taking it as his due.

So Charles was not so much hostile to the classes outside his little court circle as quite indifferent to them, which meant that the intermission of parliament was a period not of reconciliation but of truce, or, in its later stages, armed truce. For one thing, the depression of the thirties, accentuated by the German war and Dutch competition, caused a distinct worsening in the financial position of the crown. The Lord Treasurer, Portland, returned to the stringent administration of the Crown Lands, the enforcement of the king's rights as feudal overlord, which had been so unpopular a feature of Salisbury's régime. The mediaeval Law of the Forest was strictly enforced by special commissions issued for Waltham, Rockingham, the New Forest and the Forest of Dean, and even the boundaries of ecclesiastical lands were redrawn in an attempt to make first-fruits and tenths more profitable. In 1637 the circumference of the Forest of

Rockingham was extended from six to sixty miles, and fines totalling £51,000 were imposed on the neighbouring gentry and nobility. Another obsolete mediaeval device that seemed perversely designed for the irritation of the landowning classes was suddenly revived in 1630, when it was decided to fine all those owning freehold land to the value of £40 a year or over who had not applied for the honour of knighthood at Charles's coronation. Merchants and manufacturers were goaded in their turn by the new monopolies, or " projects ", many of which were placed on necessities, like soap and salt, and organised as regular industries. They were freely blamed for the depression, as were impositions, which continued to be levied, most notably on colonial tobacco reshipped to Europe.

On the other hand, it should be remembered that monopolies were one of the few financial perquisites remaining to the average courtier, whose economic plight was more desperate by far than his " country " cousin's. Even the Caroline notable Endymion Porter was at various times in the thirties a collector of fines to the Star Chamber, surveyor of the Petty Customs in the port of London, a participant in the soap monopoly, in a Lincolnshire fen drainage scheme, and in Sir William Courten's association of East India traders. It is scarcely surprising that service at court had become almost a profession, handed down in a restricted circle of families increasingly isolated from the rest of the nation. Sir Julius Caesar, for instance, held the Mastership of the Rolls from 1614 to 1636. In 1639 the office fell vacant again, was put up for auction, and went to his son, Sir Charles Caesar, for £15,000.

Meanwhile, in the absence of parliaments, fewer gentry came up to London, and on 20 June 1632 Charles gave this process official sanction by reissuing his father's proclamation ordering the gentry to stay in the provinces. Offenders were to be smelled out by judges of assize, and at least one was fined £1,000, though he protested that he had sold his estates and was a Londoner by residence. It was always in Charles's nature, and in his concept of monarchy, to regard those who differed from him as criminals or traitors, and in the fussy paternalism of his government there was much that seemed to have no other purpose but to annoy the gentry and depress their standing. The efforts of the Council to put the Elizabethan vagrancy laws and the statutes for the regulation of trade into effective operation; its attempt to restrain enclosures, to improve roads, dig canals, drain swamps and regulate alehouses—all these activities, applauded by posterity, were regarded in the seventeenth century as an aggressive and dangerous extension of monarchical power. Particularly odious to the gentry were the commission on depopulation, appointed in 1635 to detect and fine enclosing landlords, and the commission on clothing, which kept wages in the depressed cloth industry artificially high.

The Tudors had been content with the state of the nation so long as it presented a picture of average prosperity and tolerable civil order, irrespective of what oppressions were being perpetrated in dark corners, what under-privileged classes were being persecuted and oppressed. They viewed society as a whole; their aim being peaceful government, not social justice. Charles I's doctrinaire attempt to make local government work as it was supposed to work earned him the outraged hostility of the most powerful political elements in the nation, while the depressed classes he favoured—the evicted tenants, the vagabonds, the unemployed weavers and the miners—showed him no gratitude. When such men did attain to political power in the New Model Army they were the most determined advocates of Charles's execution and the abolition of monarchy.

Finally, the aggression with which Charles countered passive resistance drove him to acts of chicanery the more odious for being tricked out in the garb of abstract justice —as in 1636, when he quarrelled with the City of London and in retaliation prosecuted the Common Council in Star Chamber for technical infractions of the Londonderry charter (a colonising venture that had cost the members of the Council a great deal and brought them little return). The charter was resumed, with the land, and the Council was fined £70,000. In 1639 the fine was reduced to £12,000, paid, and at once handed over to the queen as a birthday present. Yet Charles was bewildered when the City refused his request for a loan in 1640.*

It is a characteristic of weak governments to govern harshly, and the use of the Star Chamber in the thirties is a fair illustration of that fact. In the hands of Laud it was transformed from an instrument supplementing and strengthening the common law courts into a self-sufficient tool for the subjugation of the localities. Its unpopularity, and the unpopularity of its sister court of High Commission, date almost entirely from this decade, and they had no small share of the responsibility for the final collapse of church and state.

William Laud provided the English church with the decisive, aggressive leadership it lacked, but in so doing he upset the balance of forces that had tended towards religious peace since 1604 or earlier. His theological doctrines are not important,[3] his first concern was always with " decent order " and unity within the church. He regarded Puritanism " as a wolf held by the ears ", and believed that the increase in the number of reformist preachers having no cure of souls—an increase marked since 1620—threatened the stability of the church. The death of Buckingham and the intermission of parliament gave him his opportunity, and in 1629 he persuaded Charles to issue Instructions which forbad preaching without cure of souls, forbad corporations to maintain " lecturers ", and enforced the use of prayer book and surplice. The high death rate amongst bishops in the late twenties and early thirties enabled him to staff the episcopal bench with divines of his own choosing, and the courts of Star Chamber and High Commission were unsparingly used to suppress Puritan propaganda and enforce conformity on clergy and laity alike. In 1630 he

[3] He and his followers were often styled " Arminians " but this is meaningless; Bishop Joseph Hall of Exeter, the author of *Episcopacy by Divine Right*, also formulated one of the clearest, most decisive statements of orthodox, anti-Arminian Calvinism. As applied to James I, Charles I and their divines, the word " Arminian " is merely a term of abuse—like the terms " Trotskyite " or " Titoite " in Communist circles to-day.

was appointed Chancellor at Oxford and at once launched himself on a fierce campaign to extirpate Puritanism in that university. In 1633 he succeeded to the see of Canterbury and at once revived the device of metropolitical visitation for the enforcement of order and conformity in this huge province.

His campaign against exaggerated sabbatarianism, his attempts to reinstate stained glass, and move the altar, or communion table, from the centre of the church to the east end, loom large in the controversies of the time. But, though they laid him open to charges of popery, these were largely peripheral matters; it was the broad, positive dogma of "Laudism", not its detailed application, that roused fear and hostility. For to the nationalist ideal of Puritanism Laud opposed the equally nationalist concept of an English church claiming apostolic succession not from Cranmer but from St Augustine of Canterbury, a church that had kept Christ's true doctrine intact amongst the popish errors of the Middle Ages and therefore enjoyed a revelation superior to any on earth. Nor should we underestimate the glamour of this concept, nor the appeal of a return to the prayer book, nor the attraction of more beautiful churches, more dignified services. Recent research into the composition of the Long Parliament[4] has established the interesting fact that the median age of the royalist Members was ten years less than their opponents'; and one interpretation of this is that by the thirties Puritanism had lost its appeal to a younger generation to whom Queen Elizabeth was but a name, who had been raised in the church of Donne and George Herbert and could no longer regard it as a mere laodicean compromise. This would go far towards explaining the splenetic hatred entertained for Laud by the older generation of gentry who were the leaders of the Long Parliament. It also explains the abject failure of upper-class Puritanism in the forties.

Moreover, the religious attitude of the older gentry was principally dictated by anti-clericalism, and one of the key-

[4] D. Brunton and D. H. Pennington, *Members of the Long Parliament*.

notes of the Laudian church was its exaltation of clergy over laity. Also it stood in a new and disquieting relation to the king. Charles I was the first monarch raised from birth in the English church, and his relationship with it was not only closer than his two predecessors but different in kind. It had a singular appeal to a man of romantic temperament who was equally allergic to over-ostentation and enthusiasm; in his own words, it was " the middle way between the pomp of superstitious tyranny and the meanness of fantastick anarchy ". Thus his religious life had a consistency and regularity never attained by his Calvinist father, nor by the protean Elizabeth, a Protestant by accident of state : " he was punctual and regular in his devotions, so that he was never known to enter upon his recreations or sports, though never so early in the morning, before he had been at public prayers; and he was likewise very strict in observing the hours of his devotions ". And, whereas James and Elizabeth had been governors of the church, above and outside it, over but not of it, Charles was a mere member of it. For though Laud acknowledged that the king was the church's secular arm, and in some sense its high steward, he always insisted that the bishops and clergy were directly responsible to God alone for the trusts imposed on them.

The high prelatical dignity was maintained by the royal prerogative courts of Star Chamber and High Commission, and neither was gentle or tactful in its dealings with the laity. In 1633 Lord Chief Justice Richardson, the head of the legal profession, was insulted by Laud before the Council and forbidden to ride the western circuit again, for showing too much leniency to the Somersetshire Puritans. He left the council chamber in tears with rage; " I have been almost choked," he said, " by a pair of lawn sleeves." Morality amongst the upper classes was strictly enforced; even Buckingham's sister-in-law, Lady Purbeck, was forced to flee abroad after fifteen years' cosy adultery, and her lover was clapped in the Gatehouse.[5] When Bishop Juxon of London was appointed Lord Treasurer in 1635 it seemed that government was returning to the bad old days of Wolsey, or

[5] See p. 55 above.

even modelling itself on the more sinister cross-Channel parallel of Cardinal Richelieu. Nor did this seem an alarmist hypothesis to the friends of Sir Robert Wiseman, who was sentenced by Star Chamber to be degraded from the rank of knight and baronet and have his ears cropped, for uttering a libel against Juxon in 1638. As High Commission could unfrock a priest, so it seemed Star Chamber could degrade a gentleman.

This was an incitement to anti-clericalism, and hand-in-hand with anti-clericalism went anti-popery. Charles and Laud were so firm in their inner devotion to the English church that they were quite careless of outward observances. But to the eye of prejudice the Laudian reforms in liturgy, vestments and ritual could only portend a reconciliation with Rome, and the fact that Bishop Montague openly preached the reunion of all true believers did not prevent his translation from Chichester to Norwich in 1638. As for Goodman of Gloucester, not even Charles and Laud could seriously regard him as a Protestant after 1635. And this was set in the context of a court that took its distinctive colouring, in dress, festivity and fashion, from a Roman Catholic queen.

Buckingham's sudden death released Charles's emotional reserves just at the time when Henrietta Maria had completed the transition from adolescence to womanhood, nubile and mature. Self-confident in her skilfully-controlled charm, she could go out halfway to meet her diffident but handsome husband, now half-crazed with grief. She comforted him, and in so doing fell in love; and found her love gratefully returned with all the passion of a man who has made his first conquest. She was pregnant in no time; in 1629 she miscarried, but next year she gave birth to a Prince of Wales, the future Charles II. The Princess Mary followed in 1631, James, Duke of York, in 1633, and others in 1635, 1636, 1639 and '40. These were years of mutual love and faith, an inseparable uxorious bliss that startled Europe in a son of James I and a daughter of Henry IV.

Until 1641 the queen's advice on policy counted for little,

and was rarely, if ever, proffered, but Charles's love for her obliged him to accept conditions in his own household that were not of his choosing. Henrietta was not a violent romaniser, but she was the undoubted mistress of taste at Whitehall, and popery was one of the fashions she set. Papal agents like Con and Panzani were in almost continuous residence, priests celebrated mass daily without the least pretence of concealment, while the Jesuits, the bogeymen of all honest Protestants, were particularly active; they made several notorious conversions, and more were expected daily. Nor was this merely the euphoria of the proselytiser; a cosmopolitan minority religion had a natural appeal for a cosmopolitan minority class. Laud warned Charles of the danger from " the queen's party ", but short of repudiating his wife there was little he could do.

It was not the least of Charles's tragedies that the source of his greatest personal happiness should be incomprehensible to the majority of his subjects. Though she spoke fluent English, though she made scores of English friends, Henrietta remained a foreigner to the end; as her biographer points out, her " salient characteristics were best described by words that have no English equivalents ", for she was *chic, petite, difficile and dévote*.[6] Similarly, the greatest glory of the Caroline court, Charles's magnificent collection of paintings, and his patronage of Rubens, Van Dyck and Jordaens, merely emphasised the gulf that lay between him and his philistine subjects. When he purchased the art treasures of the Duke of Mantua for £25,000 they complained that he was " squandering away millions of pounds upon old rotten pictures and broken-nosed marbles ". And Van Dyck's portraits in their turn exactly recapture the " withdrawn grandeur, frigid magnificence, and brittle elegance "[7] of this epoch, so miserably truncated and left marooned in time. The king and his intimates were not so much misunderstood as completely outside the main stream of English experience and national life.

This is demonstrated most significantly in Charles's foreign

[6] Carola Oman, *Henrietta Maria* (1939 ed.), p. 114.
[7] Whinney and Millar, *English Art 1625-1714*, p. 60.

policy. The struggle between Spain and the Dutch in the thirties, the civil war in Germany, were watched with anxiety by a public that believed the future of European Protestantism was in peril; and Charles's studied neutrality was far from popular. In particular it was noticed that when his sister, the ever-popular Elizabeth of Bohemia, was left a widow in 1632, she politely but firmly declined his proposal that she make her home in England, the implication being that she was dissatisfied at his failure to support her eldest son's claim to the Palatinate and Bohemia. Like his father, Charles hoped to reinstate his nephew by a *rapprochement* with Spain, but this could not fail to be misunderstood in England, especially when it led him to intervene against the Dutch. Spain's great problem was to pay her armies in Flanders in face of the Franco-Dutch blockade of the Channel, so every year from 1630 onwards her transports landed their bullion at Plymouth, whence it travelled overland to London. There Charles took his cut and re-shipped it through Dover into the Spanish Netherlands, by the shortest possible sea route. There it was used to pay the papist armies whose ultimate object was the extirpation of Dutch Protestantism.[8] It is in this context that Charles's most famous fiscal device, ship money, must be viewed.

There was strong political or military justification for such a tax; the English fleet was in disrepair, the Barbary corsairs were a constant threat to the western coasts, and Dutch, French and Spanish warships were continually flouting the King of England's titular sovereignty of the Narrow Seas, and even invading English territorial waters with impunity. The judges, consulted beforehand, had no doubt that the king, as chief executive, could levy such a tax for the defence of the realm, and it was duly imposed on the maritime counties in 1634, and extended inland the following year. It was equitably levied, all proceeds were devoted to the navy, there is no evidence of concerted opposition (or of much opposition at all), and the percentage yield

8 See Miss C. V. Wedgwood, "The Causes of the Civil War, a New Analysis," in *History Today*, Oct. 1955 (v. 170).

was astonishingly high for a seventeenth-century tax—98%, 97% and 96% in the first three years.[9] Opposition was not mobilised until the uses to which the "ship money fleet" might be put became more apparent. In 1635 it raised the French and Dutch siege of Dunkirk in the Spanish Netherlands; and while it was engaged in this un-English activity Dutch and Spanish warships were fighting two pitched battles in English territorial waters, one in Scarborough Bay, the other off Blythe in Kent, where the victorious Dutch landed and pursued their opponents two miles inland.

If any one issue caused the Great Rebellion it was the question of Charles's reliability as commander of the armed forces and director of foreign policy. And his trafficking with Spain in the thirties and his misuse of the fleet revived serious doubts that had been allayed by Buckingham's death. In 1636 resistance to ship money became vocal, the yield dropped sharply, and John Hampden took the issue to court. The judges gave against him in 1637, but by then the final crisis was under way, provoked by Laud's insistence that an Anglican prayer book be imposed on the Scots. The resultant reaction produced the Scottish National Covenant in 1638; a nation united under a militant clergy and a godly nobility, with formidable Bible-banging army generalled by veterans of the German campaigns and supported by the prayers and pence of the faithful.

Charles was helpless in face of this terrible phenomenon. The English gentry, reluctant to recruit a decent army for him, conscripted the riff-raff of town and countryside; the effort of transporting, feeding, clothing and arming them emptied the exchequer and swamped the commissariat. The officers, whether gentry or courtiers, had no stomach for the fight, and the tenants-in-chief, summoned to the host at York, were mutinous and obstructive. One brief skirmish ended the so-called First Bishops' War. But the Peace of Berwick in June 1639 could be no more than a truce, for unless Charles could suppress the Covenant he would lose

[9] Miss M. D. Gordon published the full figures in *Trans. of the Royal Historical Society* for 1910.

England as well as Scotland. He at once sent to Dublin for his strong man. Thomas, Viscount Wentworth, landed in England on 22 September 1639, and assumed control of the state.

Wentworth raised in semi-civilised, feud-torn Yorkshire, was essentially a man of the frontier, and it is not surprising that as Lord Deputy in Ireland he had achieved his greatest success. For Ireland stood in much the same relation to seventeenth-century London as did Kansas or Colorado to nineteenth-century New York. Outside the area within striking distance of Dublin Castle (the "Pale", or fence) lay the Wild West: a subject population ruthlessly exploited by settlers entrenched in fortified manor houses dominating huge estates, themselves torn by savage disputes between the different waves of "pacifiers" and colonisers which had landed from England at various periods since the reign of Henry II. It was a land given over to rustlers and cowboys (or kerns and gallow-glasses), a boiling morass of disorder across which his Majesty's judges padded swiftly and infrequently, under the escort of a small army, while the sullen waters of bribery, intimidation and graft closed without a ripple behind. It was Wentworth's almost total ignorance of any but the seamiest side of government that made him one of the Stuarts' most unusual servants; he came in 1639 like some great barbarian consul from the Dacian Marches, summoned to the defence of the empire's capital, and surveying with brutal wonder the fluorescence of a rotting civilisation—the eunuchs and the Mysteries, the Emperor worship and the dancing girls; the *ecclesia anglicana* of William Laud, a French queen with her French fashions, the plaintive, fainéant world of Mr Secretary Windebank and Sir Antony Van Dyck.

A lawless frontier under barbarian pressure can be governed only by authoritarianism backed by military force, perverting the forms of law or simply ignoring them; Wentworth imposed such a government on Ireland with gusto, and the effect was to exaggerate his latent brutality, his impatience of restraint*. He did not forget his old allegiances, but contemptuously rejected them. Of Coke he wrote: "I shall not rest till I see my master's power and greatness set out of wardship and above the exposition of old Sir Edward Coke and his year books." His rage at John Hampden was terrible, and he seriously urged that he be whipped—a felon's punishment that no other seventeenth-century minister could have recommended for a gentleman and landowner. The lengths to which he himself was prepared to go were indicated by the "framed" court-martial of Lord Mount-norris in 1636, described by Clarendon as "the most extravagant piece of sovereignty that in time of peace had been ever executed by any subject". In England he was an advocate of strong, ruthless government such as he had imposed on Ireland, and he exhorted Charles thoroughly to subdue the three kingdoms before experimenting with ecclesiastical luxuries—"The foundation well and truly laid," he wrote, "what, under the greatness of Almighty God, could be able to shake this monarchy, or stay the wheel of your Majesty's triumph?"

Wentworth's enemies, preceding him into England, had spread the news of his doings far and wide. Black Tom the tyrant was a figure of horror; his mellifluous voice issuing incongruously from a ravaged, parchment face periodically suffused with angry blood, his hooded eyes intermittently blazing as of some searing inner light, or glazed; his heavy body twisted by gout over its supporting stick. In his awful presence questions of taxation, privilege, vestments, even doctrine, faded into pallid obscurity, because he envisaged a polity in which such things had no place. He was a revolutionary, much more so than his opponents, and his implied attack on the fundamental assumptions of parliamentary government drove the Commons leaders right off the sterile ground of legal quibble onto the treacherous questions of sovereignty and executive power.

Charles neither understood Wentworth nor liked him; a theoretical absolutist like Manwaring was within his comprehension, a practical despot not. Henrietta Maria disliked him for the smell of mud and blood about him, and so did her mincing adherents, Windebank and Vane. Not that

that mattered for the moment, for Wentworth simply blotted out any interference not transmitted on his particular wavelength; the king became a cardboard puppet, and Laud, for the first time in ten years, exclusively an ecclesiastic. What defeated him was not the court, nor even principally the gentry, but the very machinery of state. Like Buckingham, he found that the corrupt and inefficient administration of Caroline England simply could not be made to fight a war.

He did his best. As soon as he landed he insisted that Charles appeal to parliament before the next campaigning season, and the writs issued in December 1639. In January commissions were issued for a new army of 23,000, and the high military command was drastically remodelled. He himself was created Earl of Strafford. But the "Short Parliament" that assembled on 17 April 1640 would vote no money, and the attitude of both houses was ominous to a degree. Its sole achievement, in fact, was to establish the leadership of John Pym, a colourless but supremely able tactician, who was the sole survival of the front-bench opposition leaders of the twenties. (Eliot had died in the Tower in 1632, of much greater service to parliament as a dead martyr than a living leader.) When it became clear that Pym was in touch with the Scots, or at least acting in concert with them, Strafford abandoned any prospect of a "constitutional" or legal solution, and at a famous Council meeting on 5 May he urged Charles to dissolve parliament and prosecute a strong forward policy. He told him that, "being reduced to extreme necessity," he was "loosed and absolved from all rules of government", and could do "all that power might admit". Immediately upon the dissolution he translated these words into action. Three Members were imprisoned and their houses searched, in disregard of parliamentary privilege, and mob rioting by the City apprentices was punished by *vigilante* justice; two youths were summarily hanged, one of them being tortured before death. When the City aldermen declined Charles's request for a loan, Strafford committed four of them to prison, and told the king, "Unless you hang up some of them, you will do no good with them." But even Strafford's demonic energy could not bring victory in battle, nor even assemble a tolerably efficient army. On 29 August the advancing Scots routed the English vanguard at Newburn, and on the advice of a Great Council of the peerage hastily summoned to York Charles offered terms to the Scots and summoned another parliament. By the treaty of Ripon the Scots occupied Durham and Northumberland and received a subsidy of £25,000 a month pending the satisfaction of their claims to compensation. This subsidy shackled Charles to his last parliament, which met for business on 3 November 1640 (and finally dissolved itself on 16 March 1660).

The few trusty courtiers elected to the Long Parliament were swept away in the pogrom of November and December against monopolists, projectors, ship-money judges and crypto-papists. But the Opposition was imperilled by its very supremacy. Lack of opponents sapped its discipline; all had grievances against the king's government, fiscal or religious, but no sizeable group could agree on any one thing in need of immediate legislation, and had they been allowed to dwell on such questions as church reform they must speedily have disintegrated. But luckily almost all of them were united on the simple issue of Strafford. The knowledge that he was negotiating abroad for mercenary troops, the fear that he might forestall any reform at all by appealing beyond parliament to the arbitration of force, compelled them to unite under Pym's leadership for his destruction. Without that unifying motive the history of the Long Parliament might have been very different. Strafford went to the Tower as soon as parliament met, and proceedings for his impeachment began. Laud followed him into imprisonment, but he was to remain there, almost forgotten, until 1645; for the moment the question of the church's future was gratefully shelved.

Nothing left so deep a scar on Charles's character, and his subsequent reputation, as the death of Strafford. Almost his last words on the scaffold were, " An unjust sentence that I suffered for to take effect is punished now by an unjust sentence upon me." But it was not Charles's signature on any death-warrant that killed Strafford so much as the whole course of his policy in the first six months of this parliament, and it is not easy to see what alternative course he could have taken. True, a policy of complete reconciliation and co-operation with the Commons might have saved Strafford, but the earl himself rejected such a surrender, as did the queen. So Charles could only play for time, hold himself aloof from the Commons, and in his public pronouncements offer revision rather than reform—" A skilful watchmaker," he told parliament in February, " to clean his watch, will take it asunder, and when it is put together it will go the better, so that he leave not out one pin of it."

Of course, it was a policy that appealed to Charles's passivity, the negativeness of his character. Throughout the forties he declined to offer any solution himself, preferring instead to pick and choose amongst the schemes put forward by others. Meanwhile Strafford's mantle fell on Henrietta Maria, with her greater decisiveness, her surer touch with men and servants. She carried on the great earl's policy as best she could, negotiating with Spain and Holland for aid and intriguing with the discontented officers of the English army. These intrigues erupted in the ineffectual First Army Plot of April 1641, and the engagement of the Princess Mary to William, eldest son of the Stadtholder Frederick Henry, Prince of Orange. Meanwhile Charles himself obstinately refused all requests from the Commons that he disband the Irish Army. It was this policy of active reaction, Strafford's own, that created the hysterical public demand for his death.

Charles relied on the Lords, unwilling to condemn one of their number for executing the king's orders, and alienated by the mounting mob violence and religious anarchy in London. His hopes were answered when the Lords adjourned the trial in April, but isolated in Whitehall he could not keep a grip on them, and when the Commons passed a bill of attainder the upper house let it through, assuming he would veto it. On Sunday, 9 May, after wrestling with his conscience all day, Charles signed a commission for his assent to Strafford's attainder and the " Self-Perpetuating Act "—

a revolutionary measure prohibiting the dissolution of parliament without its own consent. As he scribbled his signature he said, in tears, "My lord of Strafford's condition is happier than mine." Perhaps it was. The earl was beheaded on Tower Hill on 12 May.

Strafford's death could have been the great blood sacrifice that averted the omens of civil war. For with him died the threat of revolutionary violence, and the rule of law returned. On his side Pym spent June and July pushing through a series of reform acts which were never repealed and which formed the basis of the Restoration Settlement—the acts abolishing Star Chamber, making tunnage and poundage dependent on parliamentary grant, declaring ship money illegal, and so on. It was Charles who declined to regard these reforms as establishing a working compromise, and he was justified to some extent by the Triennial Act, passed in March, and the Self-Perpetuating Act, both of which infringed the fundamental law by restricting his undoubted prerogative of summoning and dismissing parliaments. He could also point to the mob law that reigned in the capital. In addition he drew the wrong moral from Strafford's death; as time went by he came to attribute it not to his own obstinacy in refusing concessions but to his pliancy in making any at all, while at the same time it confirmed him in the belief that all opposition was conceived in malignancy and treason. He made no effort to find a party amongst the warring Commons groups, and instead increased the general suspicion regarding his motives by departing early in August for Edinburgh, where he hoped to find supporters amongst the Scots nobility.

He came like a lamb into a veritable lions' den of intrigue, and left it shorn of his last few tufts of reputation. His pathetic attempt to play one section of the Scots nobility off against the other only implicated him in a mysterious brawl known as "The Incident", generally regarded as an abortive *coup d'état*. This confirmed the English parliamentary leaders in their belief that the king could not be trusted to act like a man of honour. The religious differences between Lords and Commons, and between different sections of the Commons, which erupted in vicious squabbling during July and August, also convinced Pym that it was high time the dispute was transferred to simpler, safer ground.

So as soon as parliament reassembled in October 1641, after a short recess, Pym brought forward the question of Charles's fitness to be trusted with executive power by releasing details of " The Incident " and ostentatiously throwing an armed guard round Westminster. Charles, still in Edinburgh, took up the challenge; he began to negotiate with the London aldermen, and he notified the Lords that he would take his stand on the defence of the established church. Pym countered by releasing another instalment of Henrietta's clandestine intrigues with the Army, but these petty revelations were thrown into the shade when news arrived on 1 November of the Irish revolt. " The Queen's Rebellion ", as it was generally called, raised in the sharpest possible form the question of the king's fitness to command troops. Charles hobnobbing with a few discontented grandees and half-pay officers was one thing; Charles at the head of a well-found army, marching through loyalist Wales to the ports of embarkation, was another thing altogether. In the Additional Instruction of 8 November the Commons declared that unless Charles removed his present advisers they would proceed to the suppression of the rebellion themselves, and Pym produced the Grand Remonstrance, a lengthy indictment of the king's policy and actions, for submission to the nation. Quarrels over the religious clauses of the Remonstrance cut his majority down to eleven, but the vital need for union in face of danger gave him command of the depleted Commons for the rest of the year.*

So from the moment Charles returned from Edinburgh on 25 November the issue became essentially a struggle for power, and particularly for control of Westminster and London. Charles courted the City aldermen, consolidated his grip on the Tower, and began assembling armed volunteers for Ireland. Pym still held the Commons, and the London mobs. The balance of power was broken on 21 December, when Pym's allies secured a majority in the elections to the

Common Council. On the 30th the Lords suddenly swung round, and permitted the Commons to impeach the bench of bishops *en bloc*. Faced with the loss of his majority in the Lords and his control of the London government, Charles was forced to hasten his preparations for a *coup d'état*; Pym's threat to impeach the queen brought them forward with a disastrous rush. He impeached Pym and four of his lieutenants, but when he invaded the House of Commons to seize them they had fled. Charles's career is full of tactical failures in projects whose only possible justification was complete success. The attempt on the Five Members is only the most notable.

Charles's guards were designed for a sudden onset against divided enemies, they could not overpower a capital united against him, and on 10 January 1642 he and his wife took the road out of London. He rode in again to his trial in 1648; she saw it again as an old woman, in 1660.

Charles's departure did not affect the issues between him and parliament; but their true nature was now recognised. The religious issue, for instance, was now dead; in February the king even gave his assent to a bill to exclude bishops from the Lords. Controversy centred on the Militia Ordinance; both sides were taking measures to secure fortresses and arsenals, and Charles opened negotiations with Holland and Denmark. Parliament declined to allow him the command of troops, while he declined to surrender it to anyone else— "By God," he told Lord Pembroke, "not for an hour!"

Charles's departure for York in March was an act suspicious in itself. He could not decide between the various policies pressed upon him by his divided counsellors, and as a result he reaped all the disadvantages of being thought a warmonger without any of the advantages that a truly bellicose policy would have brought him. (His obvious designs on Hull, and his dithering irresolution before the city, are typical.) Meanwhile the physical separation of king and parliament set up two contrary vortexes, which began to suck in supporters on either side. Groping for some legal justification, parliament issued in June the Nineteen Propositions, which would virtually have taken all executive power out of the king's hands; they followed it up with a declaration which was to be the only legal basis of their authority until 1648, that, " What they do herein hath the stamp of royal authority, though his Majesty, seduced by evil counsel, do in his own person oppose or interrupt the same; for the king's supreme and royal pleasure is exercised and declared in this high court of law and counsel after a more eminent and obligatory manner than it can be by personal act or resolution of his own." Charles, failing to secure foreign aid, was reluctantly thrown back on a " constitutionalist" position, and at his request the peers who had joined him at York declared that the king did not desire civil war, " but that all his endeavours tend to the firm and constant settlement of the true Protestant religion, the just privileges of parliament, the liberty of the subject, [and] the law, peace and prosperity of this kingdom ".

This stand upon the established church brought in more supporters, and on 15 July first blood was shed at Manchester. Parliament began to raise troops and appoint generals, and on 22 August the king raised his standard at Nottingham. Even then, it is doubtful whether he could have made a fight of it if parliament had not come to his aid, by declaring on 6 September that all those who did not support its cause were " delinquents ", and their property forfeit. This brought in enough supporters to form a sizeable army, and in the reaction against parliament's folly Charles might have seized London and ended the war before it was fairly begun. As it was, his advance on the capital was checked at Edgehill and halted at Turnham Green; he retreated westward and took up his winter quarters at Oxford.

The Civil War was lost, in retrospect, by this failure to break into London. Henceforward it was difficult for Charles to control the satraps who had risen for him in north and west, and his failure to seize the central state organisation, such as it was, made it impossible for him to levy regular taxation. In 1643 parliament imposed the excise and the assessment (the forerunner of the eighteenth-century land tax) on the counties under its control, which were administered by efficient, if quarrelsome, county committees. Charles's one advantage, his possession of superior generals and better cavalry, was inevitably whittled down as the war progressed. He was unable to consolidate the victories of Adwalton Moor and Roundway Down, which gave him control of the north and west in 1643, and John Pym's last act of statesmanship was to call upon the assistance of the Scots. In 1644 the Scots and the army of the Eastern Association pinned the Earl of Newcastle in York. The king's German nephew, Rupert, marched to its relief, but the joint royalist army was routed at Marston Moor, in great part by the cavalry of the Eastern Association, trained and led by Oliver Cromwell. Rupert's high military reputation suffered a blow from which it never recovered.

But parliament, too, had its problems of leadership. Pym and Hampden died in 1643, leaving no obvious successors, and the initiative devolved on the army commanders, accentuating the division between the "presbyterian" Earls of Essex and Manchester, who favoured an agreed peace, and Cromwell, a sectarian in religion and a self-made soldier, who was the spokesman of those parochial gentry, yeomen and artisans who were now coming to the front in the parliamentary armies. Essex and Manchester were now discredited by their abject failure to take advantage of the victory at Marston Moor, and the following winter, 1644-5, Cromwell pushed through parliament the Self-Denying Ordinance, which made a clean sweep of the existing commanders. Another ordinance created a new professional army, centrally recruited and paid from assigned heads of taxation, with Sir Thomas Fairfax in command and Cromwell his Lieutenant-General of Horse. This New Model Army finally and conclusively defeated Charles at Naseby in 1645, dispersed the royalist armies in the west, and took Bristol. In May 1646 Charles gave himself up to the Scots at Newark and in June Oxford surrendered.

The kingship had never been abolished : conversely, Charles had never dared to dissolve the Long Parliament, for this would infringe the Self-Perpetuating Act and by implication

reject the reform legislation of 1641 upon which a large
measure of his moderate support depended. In 1646, as in
1642, parliament maintained that it was the expression of
royal authority, the leader of its opponents a mere *doppel-
gänger*. But this ingenious pretence could not be indefinitely
maintained, and the moment of disillusion, when the adjust-
ment must be made to the king in person, could be infinitely
dangerous. Parliament's heavy taxation, and the depression
of the forties, had driven most of the gentry into their normal
attitude of opposition to constituted authority. Emerging
victor in the struggle, parliament found itself saddled with
the blame for all its attendant privations and exactions, the
losers' depredations being conveniently forgotten. Its legal
status was dubious in the extreme; such mandate as it had
received in 1640 had long ago expired, and it had shed more
than half its original Members anyway. Hanging over it was
a huge army composed mainly of the lower classes, infected
with religious enthusiasm and political radicalism and hostile
to the landed gentry. It was commanded by men like Ireton
and Cromwell, who stood head and shoulders above the
surviving parliamentary leaders. This army must be disbanded,
better sooner than later, yet parliament simply dared not
impose the additional taxes necessary to pay it off. So,
when the Scots surrendered Charles to the representatives
of parliament, at Newcastle in January 1647, he was still
the key to the political situation; in that respect the
Civil War had solved nothing.

Charles made a triumphal journey south to Holdenby House
in Northamptonshire. Thin and slightly haggard, his hair
silver-streaked, *triste* but far from downcast, he looked well
in adversity, and his unexpected personal charm, his dignity,
grace and sweetness of manner, disarmed everyone who
came in close contact with him over the next two years. As
soon as he reached Holdenby parliamentary commissioners
arrived to negotiate a settlement which would put his influence
behind them, and their urgency was underlined by the failure
of their ill-advised attempt to disband the army without back
pay, in March. This only drove the army leaders to approach

Charles too. Such flattering competition for his services
caused Charles to overestimate his strength; it would have
misled a much cleverer man. Secluded as he was from the
world of reality, the politics of 1647 became an intellectual
game to him, almost a pastime, as he played army off against
parliament, parliament off against army, and both ends against
the middle. He was in his favourite position, the passive
arbiter between other people's suggestions. He seemed unaware that though he was the key to the situation, that
situation was not all-embracing; and if the key could not
be made to turn, some men would be prepared to burst the
lock. Yet he had his warning, and apparently took the point.
When Cornet Joyce arrived at Holdenby in June to remove
him to the care of the army at Newmarket Charles asked
him by what commission he acted. Young Joyce turned in his
saddle and indicated the troop of horse drawn up behind him.
The king smiled and said, " It is as fair a commission and
as well written as I have seen a commission written in my
life."

Laud had been executed in a casual gaol-clearing in 1645,
and episcopacy abolished, yet Charles still thought that by
declining all terms offered him he might force one side
or the other to propose the re-establishment of the English
church. In reality his only choice lay between religious
liberty, or " Independency ", and some modified form of
presbyterianism—as Culpeper bluntly told him : " Presbytery
or something worse will be forced upon you, whether you
will or no. Come, the question is, whether you will be
king of Presbytery or No King, yet perfect Presbytery
or perfect Independency to be." Charles presumed too much
on the conservatism of the army's chief negotiator, Henry
Ireton, who wanted a quick constitutional settlement so that
he could eliminate Leveller radicalism at his leisure. But the
mounting royalism of the nation, rallying to a man pathetically
incapable of harm, rebounded off the iron men of the New
Model. Many officers, Cromwell amongst them, had serious
doubts of the necessity of kingship, and in the army alone
survived the feeling that Charles was personally responsible

for the war—a feeling that had been strengthened by the publication of his correspondence with foreign and Irish papists, captured at Naseby field. They hated him as only soldiers can hate an irresponsible statesman.

Needless to say, Charles was indifferent to personal danger; physical cowardice was not one of his many faults. He could visualise events much more disastrous than his own death. With the Prince of Wales in France the succession was secure (he had ordered him to leave Jersey), and such was his reverence for monarchy that he clearly expected his own execution to be the signal for a national uprising in Charles II's favour. Certainly he could not preserve the monarchy (as against his own life) by allying with a usurping army or a junto parliament, neither of them being a valid constitutional organ. On the other hand, if he gambled everything on complete victory and failed, the resultant chaos must in the long run bring the country back to monarchy (as in fact it did). He was quite alone. His wife had gone back to France for good in 1644; she was hopelessly distant from him now in time and thought. (When she taxed him in one of her letters with flirting with presbytery, he tactlessly replied, " I assure thee, I put little or no difference between setting up the presbyterian government or submitting to the church of Rome.") The happy world of the thirties could never be renewed, and he could visualise no future that held any certain place for him. His one fear was for his successor, and when he surrendered to the Scots in 1646 he left strict instructions to his Privy Council, which they were to transmit to the queen. " I conjure you," he had written, " by your unspotted faithfulness, by all that you love, by all that is good, that no threatenings, no apprehensions of danger to my person, make you stir one jot from any foundation in relation to that authority which the Prince of Wales is born to. I have already cast up what I am like to suffer, which I shall meet (with the grace of God) with that constancy that befits me. Only I desire that consolation, that assurance from you, as I may justly hope that my cause may not end with my misfortunes, by assuring you that misplaced pity to me do not prejudice my son's right." In 1647 these orders still stood, and they in some sense define his policy.

In August the army advanced on London and "liberated" parliament and the City government in the usual way (that is, by purging them to a state of anaemic acquiescence). The almost deliriously unconstitutional actions of the army leaders, and the manifest ineffectiveness of parliament, convinced Charles that he must throw himself on the mercies of the Scots nobility, who posed as the leaders of a united nation. In November he fled from Hampton Court to Carisbrooke, Isle of Wight, and on Boxing Day he signed an "engagement" with the Scots. In the first three months of 1648 the massing of the Scots army, the restlessness of Kent and Essex, proclaimed the advent of the second Civil War.

When Charles appealed to the arbitration of the sword the army leaders who had been most vulnerable to his wiles were the first to reject him. Under their pressure parliament broke off all negotiations with the king by the Vote of No Addresses, and on 22 April the whole army held an extraordinary prayer meeting at Windsor, where, wrote a participant, "We were led and helped to a clear agreement amongst ourselves, that it was the duty of our day, with the forces we had, to go out and fight against those potent enemies which that year in all places appeared against us, with an humble confidence in the name of the Lord only, that we should destroy them." And their ominous conclusion was, "that it was our duty, if ever the Lord brought us back again in peace, to call Charles Stuart, that man of blood, to an account for the blood that he had shed, and mischief he had done to his utmost, against the Lord's cause and people in these poor nations".

The suppression of the English royalists, and the defeat of the invading Scots at Preston in August, gave the Army a clear mandate from the Lord of Battles. Parliament flinched, but the victorious army re-entered London in December, purged the Commons to a mere "Rump", and instructed it to set up a High Court of Justice to try the king. Even the republican Algernon Sydney objected to the revolutionary implications of such proceedings, but the messianic Cromwell replied, "I tell you, we will cut off his head with the crown upon it."

For Charles I this was the moment of truth, and he rose magnificently to the occasion. All his life he had been an unwilling actor, but had he prepared half his former parts as well as he did this last he would never have gone to the block. He created the myth of his own martyrdom as surely as Napoleon created Bonapartism on St. Helena.

All evasions, all equivocations were now past; it was his sole function to die well, and in so doing hand down a legend that would sustain his son and his son's cause. He told his daughter Elizabeth that "he should die a martyr, and that he doubted not but the Lord would settle the throne upon his son, and that we should all be happier than we could have expected to have been if he had lived."

His courage and dignity, his evident sincerity before God, impressed all but the most fanatic of his gaolers, and were the basis of a martyrology unprecedented in English history. His face was gaunt, his beard untrimmed, but he looked more virile, more manly, than in his years of prosperity. His dress was deep black, but he still carried a gold-headed cane, as he had always done, and even this produced its own moment of poignancy. When it fell from his hand in Westminster Hall he waited perceptibly; all his life there had been someone to retrieve such baubles and hand them up again on bended knee. Not now. Recollecting this, he stooped and picked it up; the High Court unfroze.

From first to last he declined to admit the legality of his trial and execution. Bradshaw told him, "You are before a court of justice," to which he riposted, "I find I am before a power"; and even at the block he firmly declined to utter the usual words of forgiveness to the executioner, because only God could forgive the slaying of His anointed. He told his audience in Westminster Hall: "It is not my case alone, it is the freedom and liberty of the people of England; and do you pretend what you will, I stand more for their liberties. For, if power without law may make laws, may alter the fundamental laws of the kingdom, I do not know what subject he is in England that can be sure of his life, or anything that he calls his own." (His impediment of speech had disappeared under the stress of this hour.) In his last messages and letters, his last words to Bishop Juxon and his attendant, Herbert, lovingly collected in the *Reliquae Sacrae Carolinae*, he stressed that he was dying for his people and his faith—or, as he put it to his little daughter, "for the laws and liberties of this land and for maintaining the true Protestant religion".

The inevitable sentence pronounced, he prepared himself composedly for death, with Juxon as the spokesman of that church he had always loved. Laud he did not apparently regret, and he may have been in his mind's eye, with Buckingham, when he told his son: "Never repose so much upon any man's single counsel, fidelity and discretion, in managing affairs of the first magnitude (that is, matters of religion and justice), as to create in yourself or others a diffidence of your own judgment." Strafford he did remember, and the wound still rankled, but he was soon to make the only possible atonement. The day before he died he said goodbye to Princess Elizabeth and Henry, Duke of Gloucester, his only children available: to them, and to Juxon and Herbert, he confided his few personal possessions; and to his last gaoler, Colonel Matthew Thomlinson, who had become his friend, he gave a keepsake, too, his gold toothpick. The action is significant; even a year ago he would have regarded Thomlinson's devotion as no more than his due, but he had learned at last that devotion must be won, loyalty earned, and that both deserved gratitude. He told the princess to tell her mother "that his thoughts had never strayed from her, and that his love should be the same to the last". To the Prince of Wales he sent a long letter of sensible advice, and confided to his care "your mother, my wife", who had been "content with incomparable magnanimity and patience to suffer both for and with me and you". But it was five years since he had set eyes on Henrietta Maria, and she was slipping away down the slope of

S.   D

memory. His main concern now, as he told Charles, was for " my own soul, the church and my people, and you also as the next and undoubted heir of my kingdoms ".

And so to the day itself, the 30th of January 1649, its details etched deep into the consciences of generations to come. They were so etched because the king, by his great command over himself, his sense of balance, his inner faith and peace, never put a foot wrong. It was not just a courageous end—many have made that—it was a great baroque drama, magnificently staged by the Army, superbly sustained by their chief actor. The communion at Juxon's hands, with the awesomely apposite lessons—the Passion according to Matthew, and Jehovah's vengeance on Pharoah for his disobedience to his anointed, Moses. Then the double shirt, lest he tremble and be thought afraid—" I would have no such imputation," he remarked, " Death is not terrible to me; I bless my God I am prepared." Then the long walk across the Park, past the Spring Garden, which held so many happy memories of the thirties, and still he did not falter, even as he passed through the Banqueting Hall, under the great Rubens ceiling he had commissioned and cherished—through and onto the scaffold.[10]

All his life Charles had been separated from the people, even from the ruling classes, by barriers of mutual suspicion and misunderstanding. This was to his advantage now, for his words and actions on the scaffold gave this generation their only clear view of him, at a time when he was transfigured and ennobled by the imminence of death —when he was going, in his own words, " from a corruptible to an incorruptible crown, where no disturbance can be ". And a few moments before he lay down, and the axe fell, he reached out across the ranks of the soldiers, beyond the coopers, malsters, tailors and yeomen who were their officers, beyond the London proles, to the gentry whom Pym had led, the men who had defeated their king and were now themselves defeated. To a communion of misfortune he added a unity of purpose: the restoration of the right order of

[10] This Rubens ceiling survives, as one of the great lesser-known sights of London.

society, in rank and degree. "As for the people," he told Juxon, "truly I desire their liberty and freedom as much as anybody whatsoever; but I must tell you that their liberty and freedom consists in having government, those laws by which their lives and goods may be most their own. It is not their having a share in the government, that is nothing appertaining to them. A subject and a sovereign are clean different things; and therefore until you do that—I mean, that you put the people in that liberty—they will never enjoy themselves." Such were the principles, suitably modified, on which the gentry brought back his son in 1660.

The axe flashed, the crowd flinched; but it was not an end.

CHAPTER IV

CHARLES II

1649-1685

In February 1649 the Rump prudently abolished the monarchy as being "unnecessary, burdensome, and dangerous to the liberty, safety and public interests of the people". For the next eleven years Charles II was a wanderer in western Europe.

He was at the Hague when they brought him the news of his father's death; the following year he sailed for Scotland, to conclude that cynical alliance with the Kirk that ended in his total defeat at Worcester in 1651. Returning, he took refuge with his mother, who as a Daughter of France was permitted to reside in Paris on a small state pension. The Netherlands were now closed to him by the death of his brother-in-law, William II of Orange, in 1650, leaving as his heir the posthumously-born William III. In face of the republican States General, Mary of Orange, a pretty, scatter-brained eighteen-year-old, could do little to aid the brother she idolised. In 1654 the dawning reconciliation between France and England forced Charles to move on to Cologne. In 1656 he signed a secret treaty with Spain and transferred his court to Brussels, where it remained.

From the moment when he left his father at Oxford in the spring of 1645 and went out to assume nominal command of the royal armies in the west, the young prince had dragged with him a gaggle of meddlesome, quarrelsome and presumptuous advisers. Their personnel might change between Truro and Scilly, Scilly and Jersey, Jersey and Paris, Paris and Amsterdam, Amsterdam and Edinburgh, but their incestuous bickering and wrangling—"brangling", to use Lord Balcarres's expressive term—was always the same. On Charles I's death this aimless unpleasantness was polarised into a struggle between the "Louvrians", the queen mother's clique, who favoured a restoration by French arms, and the Anglican constitutionalists, led by Edward Hyde, chancellor of exchequer, and the Marquess of Ormonde, titular lord lieutenant in Ireland, who looked to a national uprising in the new king's favour. There was no love lost between Henrietta Maria and her husband's last advisers, who blamed her, she knew, for his defeat. In 1659 she lost her temper and told Ormonde that "if she had been trusted the king had now been in England"; to which the marquess replied that "if she had never been trusted he had never been out of England".[1]

However, it was soon made clear to Henrietta that her reign was over. Her first act when she had recovered from the news of her husband's death was to write to Charles II at the Hague requesting him to return to Paris to discuss the appointment of a new Council. He replied that it was already chosen, and forthwith dismissed her favourite Digby from his Secretaryship of State. Henceforward Charles treated his mother with all the deference that was her due, and an affection he sincerely felt, but he ignored her advice completely except when it chimed in with his own intentions. But this threw him back on his courtiers, and he did not find it so easy to snub men who were twenty, thirty, even forty years his senior, and were used to treating him as a mere boy. His attempt to appoint Francis Wyndham to a Secretaryship of State in 1649, against the Council's advice, showed him what he was up against from the start. The seventy-five-year-old Lord Cottington came to him one morning and begged a place for an old servant of his, a falconer. Charles asked, what place? and Cottington replied, a royal chaplaincy. The king, falling for the trap, objected that the man could have no qualifications for such a place, to which Cottington replied, poker-faced, that he was as well qualified for a chaplaincy as Colonel Wyndham was for a Secretaryship.

Charles I would have dismissed Cottington and appointed Wyndham; Charles II did neither. He had inherited most of his father's failings, but not the weakness that flouts opposition in an attempt to prove its strength; his pride

[1] F. C. Turner, *James II*, p. 29.

was a convenient piece of apparatus, to be stood upon or kicked aside as occasion served. But it is not surprising that he seized the first opportunity to escape from his embarrassing mentors of 1649 by departing for Scotland. By rejecting their considered advice he abandoned the Anglican cause for which his father had died, and betrayed one of his father's noblest servants, the Marquess of Montrose—a piece of Stuartism that wrecked his reputation for honour and probity at the outset of his public career.

He sailed from Holland in 1650 a mere youth of twenty, affable and courteous, but moody and uncertain of himself; he returned in 1651 a man. In the interval he had undergone experiences not commonly part of the education of English kings. For six months of his stay in Scotland he had led a life of sustained hypocrisy; he had talked lies, sworn lies, prayed lies, he had eaten lies and drunk them, he had gone to bed with them at night and risen with them in the morning. To preserve his sanity he had adopted a cynical reserve that remained with him thereafter. He had led men to war, and fought courageously at Worcester; and after that defeat he had lived as a fugitive for six weeks, hiding in trees, barns and priestholes, masquerading as a manservant, hobnobbing with cooks, ostlers and serving wenches. He was at ease now in any society, and would be always. He was still reserved, but only when he chose to be, and he had an easy air of command.

He towered over most of his contemporaries in height, but he had inherited his father's graceful stride, together with a slenderness of face that gave old servants an occasional glimpse of Charles I through the Bourbon-Medici mask. His hair and eyes were very dark brown, almost black, his face swarthy, split by a wide, ugly mouth—" A tall, black man, six foot two inches high ", ran the parliamentary " wanted " notices in 1651. In his teens he had been rather plump, and more conventionally handsome, but war and suffering had already pulled in his cheeks and dug great hanging lines of cynicism down his face; his eyes were glinting, but mocking and slightly *dégagé,* often resting on some private joke that excluded his audience. He was arresting rather than attractive, and his easy charm was dependent on an inner spark that was often lacking; then he appeared surly and bad-tempered.

His occasional fits of anger were frightening in their intense bitterness, but there were few other sanctions he could apply against his titular ministers in their neurotic squabbling, intensified by dim poverty and enforced idleness. Even the few whom he trusted were a trifle wearisome : Hyde, portly, complacent, and always in the right; and Ormonde, his passive, self-conscious perfection a constant irritation to the fallible. Unable to demand lesser, concrete things, they all clamoured ceaselessly for the king's confidence, and intrigued spitefully or railed impetuously against those thought to possess it. Inheriting his father's reserve, his love of quiet, mindless contemplation, Charles avoided these questing, torturing mental fingers either by retreating into gloomy silence or by adopting a pose of ready geniality and agreeing sunnily with everybody. The development of such traits, coming hard upon his betrayal of Montrose, caused Charles I's old servants the greatest anxiety; it seemed all too likely that the son was a rather more supple and intelligent version of the father. Hyde told Edward Nicholas gloomily, " The king loves both you and me, and thinks us very honest and useful servants, but he will sometimes use another, of whom he hath not so good an opinion, as well or better than either of us."

At Cologne and Brussels the obvious decline of the royalist cause, instead of uniting the ministers, merely inflamed their mutual suspicions, and the discovery and execution of the Cromwellian spy Henry Manning in 1655 did nothing to mitigate the rather feral atmosphere in Charles's counsels. The king's increasing frivolity called forth a magisterial rebuke from his young cousin Louis XIV, already something of a prig. " The King of England," remarked Louis, " should rather with tears seek to appease the wrath of Almighty God than follow his amours at Brussels ", and in 1658 even Ormonde admitted : " I fear his immoderate delight in empty, effeminate and vulgar conversation is become an irresistible part of his nature, and will never suffer him to animate his own designs and others' actions with that spirit which is requisite for his quality and much more for his future."

Charles most obviously lacked the veneer of domestic respectability a wife would have given him, yet marriage seemed to be passing him by. There had been talk in 1649 of a match between him and his cousin Sophia, the Electress Palatine's youngest daughter, but she went on instead to marry Ernst Augustus of Hanover and bear him a son, the future George I. The queen mother's attempts to mate him with his French cousin, Mlle de Montpensier, came to a similar end. Of course, Charles did not lack for women; the conditions of exile tended to break down moral conventions dependent on a stable society, and he had already taken several mistresses from amongst the well-born camp followers at his court in the Netherlands; notably Lucy Walter, who bore him a son, James, in 1649, and Elizabeth, Lady Shannon, eight years his senior, who gave birth to a daughter in 1650. In Paris he consoled himself with Eleanor, Lady Byron, a member of his mother's household, before turning in 1652 to Isabelle-Angélique de Montmorenci, the widowed Duchess of Châtillon. Isabelle was so dazzling she even captivated the much married Edward Hyde, who described her as "a lady of great beauty, of a presence very graceful and alluring, and a wit and behaviour that captivated all who were admitted to her presence". Even so, he could not visualise her as queen of England, and Charles for once agreed. But there was a deep and mutual affection between them; cut off from it, he sought sexual satisfaction in quantity and wide variety—or, to quote an inimitable Victorian gloss, "He sought forgetfulness in the coarse and sensual pleasures of the gay city, and plunged himself into a career of shameless vice."[2]

The carping hints of his courtiers are no more specific, while the gloating blast of Cromwellian propaganda credited the English "Tarquin" with the rape of every virtuous matron and the seduction of every helpless virgin within the arrondissements. All that happened, apparently, is that Charles avoided the French court—where he would meet

[2] Eva Scott, *The King in Exile*, p. 482.

his match-making mother, and the Duchess of Châtillon—
and turned instead to the Parisian brothels. Charles's taste
in women was catholic, ranging in later years from the
ice-cold, ice-blue loveliness of " la belle Stuart " to the
black-ringleted voluptuousness of actress Nelly : he was not
a gourmet so much as a gourmand. All the same, when he
left for Germany the following summer, 1654, he spent his
last night in France with the Duchess of Châtillon, at her
château of Merlou.

No sooner had Charles left France than his mother made a
singularly ill-advised and inept attempt on the Protestantism
of her youngest son, Henry, Duke of Gloucester. Her
failure, and the removal of Henry to the Netherlands, was
the prelude to a series of further squabbles that almost broke
up the Stuart family.

The trouble centred on James, Duke of York, who had
escaped from England in 1648 and joined his mother in
Paris. The maternal joy with which he was greeted—he
was a fair-haired, dashing youth of fifteen, friendly and
more open-natured than his brother—soon turned to impre-
cation. He did not approve of Henrietta Maria (even
she soon realised this), and his stubborn devotion was given
to the memory of his father. The queen mother's impulsive
attempt to dictate the composition of his household brought
him out in open mutiny, and Charles returned in 1651 to
find them not on speaking terms. The obvious solution
was to give way to James's demand that he be allowed to
join the French army, where he served with distinction under
the great general Turenne, and soon acquired a regiment of
Irishmen who deserted the Spanish colours *en masse* in order
to serve under him.

James's slow brain, his stubborn, solemn loyalties to this
and that, his utter lack of a sense of humour, always irritated
Charles, and any affection he felt for him is best qualified
by the adjective " rueful ". But he appreciated his brother's
fundamental loyalty to himself as their father's heir, and
recognised that his stupidity was so absolute as to be a source
of strength. For the most part he treated him with wary

condescension, as if he were some dull-witted but extremely
muscular savage. He provoked James in 1656, but he never
made the same mistake again. As soon as he signed the treaty
with Spain in April of that year he ordered his brother to
join him in the Spanish Netherlands, but James mulishly
ignored his repeated orders; he did not resign from the
French army until the end of the campaigning season, and
then he left his Irish regiment behind. Meanwhile Charles's
favourite sister, Mary of Orange, who had also flouted his
commands by spending most of the year junketing in Paris,
arrived at Brussels at the same time, and took James's part.
Goaded beyond endurance, Charles fell into his mother's
error by trying to dismiss James's chosen servants, the
Berkeleys. In January 1657 the duke retired in a huff to
Breda and issued terms of surrender which Charles accepted
unconditionally. His attempts to discipline his sister fared
no better. In February 1658 he abruptly summoned her to
Brussels on hearing of her liaison with Harry Jermyn, the
nephew of Henrietta's Master of Horse. It was bad enough
that the elder Jermyn should be generally regarded as his
stepfather; that the younger should also seduce his sister
was too much. Unfortunately he was scarcely in a position
to play the moralist; his love affairs were the talk of Europe,
and only the previous year Catherine Pegge, the daughter of
a Derbyshire squire, had borne him another son, Charles.
Mary defended herself with great spirit, and he was glad
enough to let her return in triumph to the Hague.

Meanwhile the conduct of the discarded Lucy Walter in
constantly proclaiming that she was Charles's lawful wife
made his prospects of a dynastic marriage no brighter, and
his anxiety to gain control of his eldest son James (later
Duke of Monmouth) made him reluctant to give her the lie
direct. In 1656 she even went to England, where the government naturally snapped up her story and gave it the widest
circulation, and in 1657 she pursued her "husband" to
Brussels, occasioning further "shrewd discourses". As soon
as she died in 1658 he made an offer for the hand of his
young sister-in-law, Henrietta of Orange, with whom he may

just possibly have been in love, but he was frustrated by the joint opposition of his mother and his sister Mary.

Henrietta Maria now hoped to marry her son to the eleven-year-old Hortense Mancini, niece of Cardinal Mazarin, the effective ruler of France. But Charles's political prospects were not such as to attract the great minister. France and Spain, prostrate after nearly thirty years of war, signed an armistice in May 1659, leaving the regicide English government one of the strongest on the Continent, its stability apparently unaffected by the death of Cromwell the previous September and the subsequent re-establishment of the Rump. The failure of Booth's rising in September 1659 seemed the end of royalist hopes, and Charles at once left for Bayonne to throw himself on the mercy of the French and Spanish ministers who were negotiating the peace of the Pyrennees. But they were all noncommittal, and even his request for Hortense Mancini's hand was politely refused. Charles's subsequent conduct suggests that he was settling down to a long exile. At Colombes, on his way back, he was reconciled with his mother, and even created the odious Jermyn Earl of St. Albans. As for James, he was negotiating for the post of High Admiral of Spain.

But since Cromwell's death the Army had thrown up no able and unchallenged leader; it had forfeited its popularity long ago, by the end of 1659 it had lost its authority, too. Ever since 1649 a majority of the parliamentary gentry had wanted the monarchy back; their influence was now exerted on one of the most intelligent and realistic of Cromwell's commanders.

On 2 January 1660 General George Monk struck camp and crossed the Border, London bound with the Army of Scotland at his back. He arrived on 3 February. On the 21st his guards allowed the excluded Members of the Long Parliament to resume their seats. On 16 March parliament dissolved itself, and three days later Monk was in touch with Charles. On 25 April a new parliament assembled, with the House of Lords. On 1 May it took into consideration communications received from Charles. On the 8th it proclaimed him king.

He and his brothers landed at Dover on 23 May, and entered London in triumph on the 29th, his birthday.

So transcendant was the scene of rejoicing on that day that it injected colour and life even into the insipid pages of John Evelyn's diary—" with a triumph of above 20,000 horse and foot, brandishing their swords and shouting with inexpressible joy; the ways strawed with flowers, the bells ringing, the streets hung with tapestry, fountains running with wine; the Mayor, aldermen, all the companies in their liveries, chains of gold, banners; lords and nobles, cloth of silver, gold and velvet everybody clad in, the windows and balconies all set with ladies, trumpets, music and myriads of people flocking the streets, and was as far as Rochester, so as they were seven hours in passing the city, even from two in the afternoon till nine at night. I stood in the Strand, and beheld it, and blessed God."

The English were charmed with their new king, with his quiet dignity, his easy manners, and his effortless selection of the *mot juste*. His tact and studied consideration, however insincere, compared favourably with his father's tongue-tied reserve. Accepting a Bible from a deputation of clergy as he entered London, " he thanked them for it, and told them . . . that the greatest part of that day's solemnity he must ascribe to God's providence, and that he would make that book the rule of his life and government ".

The favour he showed to the older generation of Cavaliers, men like Leicester, Southampton, Newcastle and Northumberland, was particularly well received, in that most of them had received scant thanks from his father. Such thoughtfulness did much to smooth over the inevitable difficulties attendant on the Restoration, and helps explain the ease with which Charles was able to mould together the diverse political elements at his disposal—exiled royalists and stay-at-homes, Cromwellians, Presbyterians and even some so-called republicans. The Act of Indemnity and Oblivion, passed in 1660, wiped the slate clean; only those who had signed Charles I's death warrant (the " regicides ") were called to account, and only the lands of crown and church were automatically resumed. The rest was left for private negotiations or litigation. Charles himself showed no animosity towards those about him who had helped to prolong his exile—he " said smilingly to some about him, that he doubted [i.e., suspected] it had been his own fault that he had been absent so long, for he saw nobody that did not protest he had ever wished for his return ". But he showed his ruthlessness by insisting on the death of the great republican Sir Henry Vane, as being too dangerous to live.

In the melting pot of the Interregnum the old division between " Court " and " Country " had temporarily collapsed, and the names themselves were not revived until the seventies. For ten years after the assembly of the Cavalier Parliament, with its huge monarchist majority, in 1661, Charles II's potential court embraced almost the whole of political society, nobility and gentry. This catholicity of choice, on his part and his brother's, laid the foundations of a new " Court party ", stronger than any that had emerged in this century. It would have been united still more firmly to the crown but for Charles's decision to rely for the first few years of his reign on the talents of the " old guard ".

Charles would have been singularly ungrateful, of course, if he had not rewarded the courage and loyalty of Edward Hyde by confirming him in the Lord Chancellorship he had held since 1658 and by creating him Earl of Clarendon. Moreover, his daughter's marriage to the Duke of York in 1660 gave him a unique position *vis-à-vis* the royal family. James had seduced Anne Hyde in Holland, where she was a lady-in-waiting to the Princess Mary, and when she found herself pregnant he agreed to marry her. Hyde was furious, Henrietta Maria came rushing over from France, but it was James's boon companions who shook him, by loyally asserting that, they had all enjoyed his mistress's favours too. However, Killigrew overdid it when he declared " that he had found the critical minute in a certain closet built over the water, for a purpose very different from that of giving ease to the pains of love, [and] that three or four swans had been witnesses to his happiness ". Even James thought this " greatly out of bounds ", and the lie was exposed. Relief sharpened his determination, and his mother's opposition was the deciding factor. Charles made no objection; unlike Henrietta Maria he could learn from experience.

But if the retention of Clarendon is in every way explicable, the appointment of the inexperienced Earl of Southampton to the Treasury is not. If it were meant as a sop to the older Cavaliers it went too far. A more skilful minister might have secured a better financial settlement for Charles; as it was, the refusal of the gentry to continue Pym's "assessment" meant that crown income was based on the excise, whose yield could never be accurately forecast. The result was that Charles's income in the sixties was usually £300,000 a year short of the £1,200,000 considered necessary by parliament itself, and £400,000-500,000 short of his actual expenditure. The failure to overhaul an out-dated Treasury administration made serious retrenchment impossible, and chronic shortage of money reduced Charles and Clarendon to such unpopular shifts as the Portuguese marriage and the sale of Dunkirk to France.

The Dutch war of 1665-7 exposed not only Southampton's inept financial organisation but also Clarendon's faulty administration. His political development intermitted by war and exile, Clarendon had remained frozen in the attitude of 1641, when he was a "Country" back-bencher. He was thus the only "gentry" chief minister of the century, and his pathetic attempt to focus the day-to-day administration of a semi-modern state on a moribund Privy Council, and his refusal to form a permanent "Court interest" in the Commons on the grounds that this would be contrary to "the constitution", reflect the views of the "Country" opposition in 1679 and again in 1701 and 1710. He deliberately reduced Charles II to the same position *vis-à-vis* parliament as his father in the twenties, with the result that he was helpless from the start to prevent the introduction of a church settlement contrary to the king's wishes and probably his own. The Uniformity Act of 1662 finally abandoned the ideal of a comprehensive English church and substituted for it a persecuting Church of England. The expulsion of about one-fifth of the parish clergy in one year, and their replacement, on the nomination of local

patrons, by men made intolerant by persecution, instituted
the famous alliance between squire and parson, and the Corporation Act of 1661 gave the gentry decisive influence in
a majority of boroughs. The very formulation of this settlement by parliament, and its refusal to sanction the canons
of 1641, settled a dispute just a century old. Convocation
even abandoned its right to tax the clergy, and parliament's
refusal to revive the Court of High Commission ensured
that the king would never regain control of a gentry church.

Clarendon realised the drift of this ecclesiastical legislation too late, and it was left to the king to implement that
" liberty of tender consciences " promised in the Declaration
of Breda, and to redeem his private promises to the Roman
Catholics. But his attempt to suspend the penal laws in 1662
was opposed by Clarendon himself as an infraction of the
constitution and had to be withdrawn the following year*.

That the king was disappointed with the settlement goes
without saying; the church of the Ascendancy was much
nearer Pym's ideal than Charles I's. But his anger was largely
impersonal, his motives political; he was an advocate of
comprehension and toleration largely because of the weakening
effect of persecution upon the state. Charles I's last prayer
was that his son should be vouchsafed " a pious and discern-
ing spirit ", but it had been answered, if at all, in an unexpected way. Such religious convictions as he possessed were
largely negative in character, and closely geared to politics.
His father's example and his own experiences in Scotland had
given him a lifelong aversion to Presbyterianism, and he did
not rest until Argyll was destroyed and episcopacy imposed on
the Kirk. Nor was it likely that he felt much sympathy with
the Anglicanism of the exile—what Halifax called " the
little Remnant of the Church of England in the Faubourg
St Germain ". He admired the Roman church, his debt to the
papists who had saved his life after Worcester was one of
the few personal obligations he scrupulously and consistently
honoured, and the example of his Bourbon relatives undoubtedly convinced him that Catholicism was the only decent
religion for princes to die in. But he postponed his conversion until his deathbed, and from 1651 onwards he was a

regular communicant in the Anglican church. His reaction to
the attempt to convert his brother Henry in 1654 outlines
his attitude admirably. His warning letter to the boy contained no mention of salvation, hell fire or the immortal soul,
and the nearest it came to any spiritual concept was in its
appeal to " the last words of your dead father, which were
to be constant in your religion ". What it stressed were the
deleterious effects of Henry's conversion on his own fortunes and that of his family—" You must never think to see
England or me again, and whatsoever mischief shall fall
to me or my affairs upon this thing I must lay upon you
as being the only cause of it." He was undoubtedly ill-
pleased at James's conversion in 1668. He insisted that his
daughters, Mary and Anne, be raised as Protestants and
married to Protestants, he forced him to baptise the children
of his second, Catholic marriage in the Church of England,
and he forbade him ever to announce his conversion in express
terms.

There were persistent rumours of Charles's own conversion,
and even a man as percipient as Halifax more than half
believed them. But James's conduct at his brother's deathbed
shows that he at least did not regard him as a co-religionist;
nor did the Spaniards in 1656, nor Louis XIV in 1670.
Moreover, in 1668 the Pope declined to allow James to join
the Roman church while continuing to take the Anglican
sacrament, and what he refused James he could scarcely
grant to his brother.

However, despite his bungling of the church settlement,
Clarendon was not dismissed. Instead the king chose to
weaken the Chancellor by giving his patronage to his most
insistent critics : to Thomas Clifford and Sir William Coventry; to the Chancellor of Exchequer, Anthony Ashley
Cooper, Lord Ashley; to Sir Henry Bennet, Secretary of
State; and to the 2nd Duke of Buckingham, who had
inherited all his father's charm and all his dashing folly.
These men were Charles's friends; their attitude to Clarendon
was dictated partly by ambition but partly by devotion to the
king's service, and it was they who accepted the task Claren-

don rejected, of building up a government "interest" in parliament.

This division between the "old guard" and the "new men" was reflected in Charles's social life, which revolved round a set of young, hard-drinking gad-abouts like Buckingham, Charles Sedley, Sir George Etherege, Charles Sackville, Lord Buckhurst (later Earl of Dorset), and John Wilmot, Earl of Rochester, whose verses, witty, unpolished, haunting and disgusted, express the angry futility and emptiness of an age poised between Faith and Reason. They were patrons of, many of them contributors to, a dramatic literature noted for its bawdry and false glamour, but possessing a vitality and drive equalled only by the Elizabethans. Amongst these "angry young men" Charles polished his wit, and acquired a bawdiness of conversation that became habitual with him, even in the presence of women, and ran counter to his usual good breeding.

Such habits of life had worried Clarendon in exile, and worried him more now. "The worst is," he told Ormonde in 1662, "the king is as discomposed as ever, and looks as little after his business, which breaks my heart, and makes me and other of your friends weary of our lives." There was a marked indifference in Charles's attitude towards politics and government which was heightened by his tendency to pass off serious things with a casual jest. It was not that he was lazy, for though he certainly played hard he also worked hard. He had immense stamina and physical reserves, and however late the rout or debauch the night before he was to be found next morning early at the head of the appropriate council or committee.[8] He kept himself fit with a whole battery of manly exercises : riding, dancing, hunting, swimming and tennis, and his easy, "sauntering" stride could wear down the most pertinacious suitor. As late as 1684 he rode his own horse to victory at Newmarket. Clarendon's concept of kingship called for constant superintendence of every branch of government, and Charles was glad to give it;

[8] See E. R. Turner, "Charles II's part in governing England", *American Historical Review*, xxxiv (1929).

little escaped him, good or bad, and if he was slow to act
on such information at least he was not guilty of his father and
grandfather's impulsive and disastrous essays in intervention.
His great defect was that he could not formulate general
lines of policy, or enunciate key ideas that would have drawn
together the random details of administration. It was a defect
visible in other spheres: his deep interest in experimental
science, for instance, which led to the foundation of the
Royal Society, was not accompanied by any grasp of scientific
theory; and though he took a lifelong interest in naval
architecture and the expertise of seamanship and navigation
he knew next to nothing of naval strategy and the function
of the fleet in war. In politics, similarly, he was an experi-
menter, a tactician; any given short-term situation he could
handle with skill, but he was apparently incapable of visualising long-term policies, or even the eventual result of any
particular coup. It was this that led to the confusion and
futility of his early foreign policy, and brought England,
hopelessly unprepared and friendless, to the brink of the
Second Dutch war in 1664.

Charles's women were perhaps symptoms of weakness,
certainly not the cause, as some historico-moralists would have
us believe. They were sexual toys, their influence on politics
negligible. Few of them even engaged his elusive affections.
" It may be said ", wrote Halifax, " that his inclinations to
love were the effects of health and a good constitution, with
as little mixture of the seraphic part as ever man had;
and though from that foundation men often raise their
passions, I am apt to think his stayed as much as any man's
ever did in the lower region." He met Barbara Palmer, a
well-used nineteen-year-old, just before the Restoration, and
in 1661 her complaisant husband was created Earl of Castlemaine; she retained her precarious position as *maîtresse en
titre* for another six years, despite her appalling bad temper
and the passive competition of Frances, " la belle Stuart ".
With her haunted, wistful face and springy slimness, she is
one of the most appealing of Restoration beauties. She is
also the only one of Charles's mistresses, apart perhaps from
Mazarin, who could be described as sexually unbalanced—

or, in Burnet's cutting phrase, "enormously vicious and ravenous". Though Charles acknowledged the paternity of her first child, born in 1661, it was disputed between him, her husband and the Earl of Chesterfield, but he liked easy conquests, and he ignored her manifold infidelities so long as she did not make a fool of him with his own entourage. She bore him four other children, one a year from 1662 through 1665, whose paternity is not seriously in doubt.[4]

In this context his marriage to Catherine of Braganza was a disaster. It would have required a woman of outstanding physical beauty and strength of character to oust Castlemaine; the convent-trained Portuguese princess had neither. Physically she was no more than adequate, she lacked intelligence and wit, and she could scarcely speak a word of English. She forfeited any faint hope of managing her husband when she fell in love with him, a solecism none of his mistresses was so careless as to commit. He was a man easily irked by demanding affection, and his brutal response was to force Castlemaine on her as lady-in-waiting. Her squeaking protests, and Clarendon's chivalrous intervention, only inflamed his rather feminine cruelty, usually hidden from the world. Partly out of shame, he thereafter treated the queen with all the courtesy for which he was justly famous; he even slept with her at regular intervals the rest of his life. But her failure to bear children finally relegated her to the background of society and politics.

Clarendon watched these events with dismay, but his censorious attitude was only a contributory factor in his fall; the prime factor was the need of a scapegoat for the unpopular religious settlement, for the barren popish marriage, for the sale of Dunkirk, for the thousand minor inequities and disappointments attendant on the Restoration, and above all for the Dutch war.

The conduct of this war was marked by a chronic ineptitude in administration that was everywhere taken for corruption. The navy, Cromwell's pride, was poorly equipped, inadequately manned and unimaginatively handled by the royal

[4] A full list of Charles's acknowledged bastards, fourteen in all, is printed in *The Complete Peerage* (revised edition), vi, App. F.

admirals James and Rupert, and after a succession of botched battles and missed opportunities the ministers fell into violent disagreements they took no pains to conceal from the public. Buckingham turned his parliamentary interest against the government and was sent to the Tower to cool off, Ashley and Bennet (now Lord Arlington) were at each other's throats, and all of them took it out on Clarendon, the universal whipping-boy. In these circumstances parliament was understandably reluctant to throw good money after bad, and the war effort, under-financed, languished still further. England's humiliation was driven home in a rhythmic series of catastrophes : in 1665 the Great Plague, in 1666 the Great Fire, and in 1667 the Dutch attack on the Thames and Medway. A peace was hastily patched up in July 1667.

In August Charles abruptly ordered Clarendon to give up the Great Seal and face his accusers as a private individual. Exile stopped his mouth, and his defence in the Lords was left to the loyalty of his son-in-law, James. His exile was made permanent by statute, and for several years he was even denied the company of his children. He died at Rouen in 1674.

Such conduct came as no surprise to those who had known Charles I, or had witnessed Charles II's betrayal of Montrose, but it came as a revelation to a younger generation of ministers. Both Charles II and his father treated their servants with a bland indifference that sprang from the same lack of human sympathy ; one was conscious of it, the other not. (James II's studied, acutely self-conscious loyalty to men and institutions was a reaction—perhaps deliberate—against a trait infinitely damaging to his predecessors.) No one could plumb Charles II's character. It baffled Burnet, who wrote : " He has a strange command of himself ; he can pass from business to pleasure and from pleasure to business in so easy a manner that all things seem alike to him ; he has the greatest art of concealing himself of any man alive, so that those about him cannot tell when he is ill or well pleased." He treated men he liked, men he disliked, with

equal composure and affability, but once in a decade his ruthless animosity against selected victims—Russell and Sydney,
Vane or Argyll—made men wonder what volcano simmered
beneath the stone crust of speculative indifference. Clarendon's
successors were an uneasy race. They turned their backs on
their royal master unwillingly, and as they faced a raging
parliamentary opposition, or furtively negotiated with Louis
XIV or William of Orange, they were conscious always of a
pair of black, slaty eyes, in heavy pouches, probing their
shoulders and their kidneys, seeking the easiest place for
the dismissive dagger. Sweat broke out on their foreheads,
and their knees trembled. If they were untrustworthy, venal
and self-seeking, their eyes always on the main chance,
they were moulded in their master's presumed image. As
one of the more respectable of them wrote : " He lived
with his ministers as he did with his mistresses; he used
them, but he was not in love with them. . . . He tied himself
no more to them, than they did to him, which implied a
sufficient liberty on either side."

No doubt Charles preferred it so. " He has a very ill
opinion of men and women ", wrote Burnet, " and so is
infinitely distrustful; he thinks the world is governed wholly
by interest." His father had accepted loyalty and devotion
as no more than his due; Charles II expected loyalty from no
man, and therefore rarely received it.

Clarendon was succeeded by a group of ministers each
directly responsible to the king. The fact that their initials
form the nickname " C-a-b-a-l " has served to disguise their
mutual antagonisms and jealousies, which enabled Charles
to control them as he could never quite control Clarendon
or Danby. Clifford and Ashley concentrated on financial
affairs; Buckingham sometimes helped, sometimes hindered
Arlington in the administration of foreign policy; and
Lauderdale ruled Scotland, as he had done since the Restoration. Between now and the end of the reign Charles experi-
mented with various ministerial combinations : the exigencies
of the later seventies called for a paramount minister, and

the Exclusion crisis produced a "Country" ministry, followed by two "triumvirates". But after 1681 he returned to a loose assemblage of jarring incompatibles that left him undisputed master. James II tried to copy him, as did William III; but William soon realised, what James never appreciated, that such a ministry by its very nature prevented the adoption of any controversial or even positive policy. Thus the treaty of Dover between England and France in 1670 inevitably disrupted the Cabal.

The open clauses of the treaty of Dover embraced a policy that was politically sound, if morally indefensible. In return for a subsidy Charles was to destroy the Dutch navy, while the French invaded Holland overland. Failure was not anticipated, and at the conclusion of a lightning campaign Charles was to receive certain Dutch ports and his nephew William III was to be established as the ruler of a truncated Netherlands, which would no longer be a serious trading rival. So far so good; but the treaty also contained a secret clause, known only to James, Arlington and Clifford, by which Charles undertook to declare himself a Roman Catholic on the outbreak of war and return England to the Roman communion, using French troops if necessary*.

Even Louis XIV regarded this as impracticable and unwise, and Charles's insistence on it is little less than insane, knowing as he did the weakness of English romanism and the violent prejudice against it. It is out of context with everything else in his life, political or religious, and can only be ascribed to the influence of his sister, "Minette". Mary of Orange had died at Whitehall in 1660, but her place as Charles's favourite relative (he only had room for one at once) had already been usurped by the young Henriette-Anne. Born at Exeter in 1644, she had been raised a Catholic, and her marriage to Louis XIV's brother Philip, Duke of Orleans, in 1661 made her the second woman in France. Her captivating wit, verve and physical charm are not communicated in her portraits, which depict a sly-looking, rather bony young woman with her brother's large nose; all the same, she effortlessly captured the slavish adherence of every man with whom she came in contact. Married to a pervert, she sublimated her own natural instincts by playing on those of others, and her brief career was a medley of magnificent frivolity and deep political intrigue. Those relentless egoists Charles and Louis both gave her all the affection at their command, and neither was quite the same again after her premature death. It was she who overcame the objections of both sides to the treaty, and she came in person to Dover in 1670 to sign it. She was supported by the papist Clifford, by Arlington, whose religious attitude mimicked his master's —like Charles, he sent for a priest on his deathbed—and by the Duke of York, a recent and most important convert to Rome.

James's punctiliousness in the performance of any duty laid upon him had given him in the past the appearance of a greater devotion to Protestantism—or any religion—than in fact he possessed. In early life he had no more interest in such matters than his brother, and his antipathy to his mother and his devotion to the Huguenot Turenne would have retarded any deviation towards Rome. But he grew closer to his mother as he grew older, after the Restoration he was much in the company of Irish papists like Richard Talbot, and even his wife, Clarendon's daughter, had marked leanings towards Rome, which she gratified after her father's exile.

There is much that is still mysterious in the precise circumstances of his conversion, but once he had come to a decision he could not compromise, as his brother felt able to do, and in 1668 he privately renounced Protestantism. He found at Rome a piety Canterbury had not given him, and a mind empty of intellectual conceits was at once filled to the brim with religious zeal. Though he was as great a womaniser as Charles, and the terror of jealous husbands, he even made an effort to restrain his sexual appetite, and there may be some truth in his brother's flippant remark that James's mistresses were so ugly they were clearly imposed on him as a penance. The strain of continence could only have contributed to the souring of a character that had never been precisely sweet, and his lack of any routine employment after 1673 was particularly irksome to one of his temperament. In the working relationship he and his brother had struck up since 1658 the concessions had all been on one side, and Charles now found James's carping criticism, his intolerant advice, an increasing strain on his temper.

For one thing, James's conversion was damaging to the monarchy, as well as his own prospects; so much so that Charles made him take the Anglican sacrament until 1672 and attend Anglican services for several years after. Even then, rumours flew about in 1669 and 1670, producing a proposal from Buckingham and Ashley that Charles divorce his barren wife and marry some fertile Protestant in order to disbar James. The Duke's antipathy to " Minette " weakened his influence still further, and though he was present at the signing of the treaty of Dover, and of course supported it, it is unlikely that he took much part in its inception. Henriette-Anne returned to Paris from Dover and almost immediately died of peritonitis, at the age of twenty-six. It is significant that after that Charles talked no more of his own conversion, let alone England's.

But the damage had been done. Few believed that the Duchess of Orleans had come to Dover for a social visit, and Charles's conversion was widely credited. The attitude of the Commons in 1670 and 1671 made it clear that only if Charles's new foreign policy were crowned with over-whelming success in war could he hope to avoid a serious parliamentary crisis; perhaps not even then. For in January 1672 he had to default on the current government debt in order to find the ready cash to refit the navy, and in March, two days before the declaration of war, he yielded to pressure, perhaps blackmail, from James and Clifford, and issued a Declaration of Indulgence suspending the penal laws against all dissenters, Protestant and Catholic. Even then, his own nephew denied him the victory that was so necessary to him. As the French armies advanced into the Netherlands the Orangist mobs rose against the republic, murdered the Pensionary de Witt, and sent for William III, that silent, brooding, orphaned young man of twenty-two, who had spent most of his life in "protective custody". Elected Stadtholder, Admiral-General and Captain-General of the Provinces, he at once displayed a courage and power of leadership worthy of a man twice his age. Calmly he ordered the dykes to be cut; and as the farmlands of Holland disappeared under water the finest army in Europe, commanded by the century's greatest generals, splashed to a halt within sight of Rotterdam. His navy suffered grievous losses, but it contained the English and French fleets.

Charles postponed the next session of parliament to February 1673, and tried to strengthen his ministers by appointing Clifford Lord Treasurer and Ashley Lord Chancellor, with the title Earl of Shaftesbury. But the Commons also had leaders now. The fall of Clarendon had split the court for the first time in the reign and sent Sir William Coventry over into opposition, where he took over the so-called "Country" party, a loose alliance of gentry driven by the same prejudices as Pym and Eliot : anti-popery, anti-clericalism and xenophobia. In 1673 they attacked not the "patriotic" war but the alliance with popish France and the Declaration of Indulgence. James called for a firm stand, but Charles was supple enough to take the sort of decisions his father and his brother both found impossible. On 8 March he simply cancelled the Declaration, and parliament passed the taxation necessary to maintain the war effort. But they also passed a Test Act, imposing an oath no Roman Catholic could take on all holders of office under the crown.

The Test Act smoked out James, who resigned all his offices that summer. He then gave further offence to public opinion by marrying the most bigoted and francophil Catholic available, Mary Beatrice d'Este of Modena. Clifford resigned, too, and before he died that autumn he told Shaftesbury of the secret clause in the treaty of Dover. Shaftesbury at once went over into opposition, and in October he was dismissed. A revitalised and strengthened Opposition, aided by the Dutch, pulled Charles out of the war in February 1674. A few months later Buckingham joined Shaftesbury, while Arlington retreated to the post of Lord Chamberlain, his nerve broken. Of the famous Cabal, only Lauderdale remained.

Anne Hyde died in 1671. She had ruled her ducal husband with a rod of iron, and it is not surprising that *en secondes noces* he plumped for a fifteen-year-old girl raised in traditions of wifely docility, not nurtured amongst the assertive, cock-sure English gentry. There is some indication that Charles would have preferred a Protestant sister-in-law, for obvious reasons, but he had not practised what he preached, and he knew better than to restrict James's choice. Nor could he or anyone else at court find much fault in Mary of Modena. She was decidedly nubile, and beautiful in the Italian fashion, with an abundance of dark hair setting off a fair, creamy skin; she was intelligent, if inexperienced, and very amiable, and she soon struck up a close friendship with her elder stepdaughter Mary, only two years her junior. She was always on the best of terms with her brother-in-law the king.

Meanwhile Charles had found a woman who, if she never monopolised his affections, secured a greater share of them than any other. Louise de Kéroualle was the daughter of a Breton noble family and maid of honour to the Duchess of Orleans. In the chaos following the duchess's death in June 1670 she was grabbed by Buckingham, who brought her over to England as a new tit-bit for Charles. The duke knew his friend and master well; Charles was taken at once with the girl's dark good looks and baby face, and above all with her quintessential Frenchness. By 1667 he had grown weary of Castlemaine, and he was no longer disposed to ignore her flagrant infidelities, which were widely celebrated in prose and verse: in "The Poor Whores' Petition to the most splendid, illustrious, serene and eminent Lady of Pleasure, the Countess of Castlemaine", for instance, and in that famous mock-pindaric,

> Let Ancients boast no more
> Their lewd Imperial Whore . . .(etc)

Her last folly had been to insult the queen publicly, and this he would not permit. He pensioned her off, and in 1670 created her Duchess of Cleveland.[5] She found consolation in the muscular arms of Jacob Hall the rope-dancer, while he engaged a couple of actresses: Mary (" Moll ") Davis, of the Duke's Theatre, and Eleanor (" Nell ") Gwynn of the Old Drury, who both bore him children in the early seventies.

But Gwynn and Davis were both from a different mould than the Frenchwoman, whose demure virginity, preserved for over a year, only lashed Charles into an even greater state of excitement. She surrendered at last in October 1671, at a house party at Euston, Arlington's Suffolk mansion, and on the 14th Charles celebrated by riding his horse Woodcock to victory in the Newmarket Plate.[6] Louise bore him a son nine months later—Charles Fitzroy, Duke of Richmond —and in 1673 she was made Duchess of Portsmouth. Henceforward she was always regarded as his principal mistress.

He was unfaithful to her, of course, but only with other members of his salaried seraglio, and in any case, the first ardour past, her attraction seems to have been more than sexual. Her tastefully-furnished apartments, the influence of her soothing intelligence, provided Charles with a calm, informal, easy domestic life of a kind he had never known, at least not since the age of ten. She was a good listener, he could confide in her, and she altogether lacked Cleveland's grasping, aggressive, egoistical sexuality. She behaved like a great lady, expected to be treated like one, and was.

Cleveland acknowledged defeat; she went to Paris in 1677 and stayed there. But Charles never discarded, he only added to his hand. So Nell, the frisky comedienne, played on, a licensed court jester and a very good one, presiding over Charles's rakish stag parties, openly vaunting her sexual

[5] According to Dugdale, " by reason of her noble descent from divers worthy ancestors, and her father's death in his Majesty's army, as also in respect of her personal virtues ". Charles acknowledged her daughter Barbara, born in 1672, but the sire was almost certainly John Churchill, later Duke of Marlborough.

[6] Charles won the Plate again in 1674, and contemporaries seem to have assumed that no favour was shown him. See Sabretache, *Monarchy and the Chase,* p. 88.

prowess to the French ambassador, and lifting her petti-
coats to show him her enchanting legs—much better than
Portsmouth's, she said. She satisfied another part of Charles's
nature; she was Portsmouth's complement, not her rival.
Portsmouth's only serious challenge came from another Frenchwoman, Hortense Mancini, Duchess of Mazarin, who arrived
in 1675 with an experience of amorous intrigue in half
the capitals of Europe. She was one of the great beauties of
the age, and Charles was the last man to resist her " experienced and well travelled Lust ";[7] it was a neat revenge,
too, on the dead cardinal, who had rejected his offer for
her hand in 1659. But it was an affair of the flesh only;
Mazarin was shallow in the extreme, and the king's infatuation
died in three months. Arguably it would have died even
sooner but for Portsmouth's open jealousy. She showed better
sense when she effected a public reconciliation with her rival,
who was taken onto the strength and settled at Chelsea.[8]

Arlington and Ralph Montagu had sponsored Mazarin in
the hope of influencing high policy; theirs was a delusion
shared by most contemporaries, but a delusion all the same,
even with regard to Portsmouth. Portsmouth's influence on
appointments, even at the " cabinet " level, was almost limit-
less, but in the seventies certainly, and in the eighties probably, her direct influence on policy decisions was negligible.
Her case was that of James. Because she was always with
the king, knew all his secrets, it was assumed that he followed her advice; and there were always instances when
his actions seemed to reflect her conjectured opinions, or
his brother's. This is mere coincidence; at the sticking-
point he ignored them both. (If he had listened to her in
1680, for instance, he would have allowed the exclusion
bill to pass.) Moreover, she was never of the " French party "
in the seventies, though the French ambassador liked to think
she was. She did not owe her position to Louis XIV,
she owed it to her ability to manage Charles II, and that

---

[7] From the great philippic against her in " Rochester's Farewell ":
Poems by Rochester, ed. V. de Sola Pinto, no. lxxxi.

[8] Her pension was continued by James II and William III, and
she died in Chelsea in 1699.

consisted in hearing his arguments and agreeing. If those arguments sometimes led him towards France they as often led him away, and Portsmouth could only follow.

But from 1674 to 1678 Charles sank into one of his intervals of comparative lethargy, surrendering the greater part of policy-direction and patronage to Sir Thomas Osborne, a tough Yorkshireman who succeeded Clifford as Lord Treasurer in 1673 and was created Earl of Danby in 1675. Danby was one of the few ministers of Charles II who had taken the measure of parliament and was not afraid of it. By judicious use of patronage, in the provinces and at Westminster, by the imposition of strong discipline and the choice of able if unexciting subordinates, he rallied the demoralised " Court party ", re-formed it, and marched it back towards the fighting. He offered the gentry a monarchy based on the Anglican church at home and a " patriotic " anti-French policy abroad, and it is the measure of his success that despite the fluctuations in Charles's actual policy, and its inherent contradictions, he maintained his power for five difficult years and staved off the demand of the Opposition lords, led by Shaftesbury and Halifax, for the immediate dissolution of this Cavalier Long Parliament.

Danby knew that Charles's liaisons with Louis XIV satisfied his desire for a genuine policy of his own and expressed his real admiration for his cousin. Moreover, Charles's known deviations were useful for coercing the Dutch, who were competing with France for England's assistance as the only means of breaking the deadlock in a war that now embraced all Europe. Louis's principal aim must be to force the dissolution or permanent prorogation of this anti-French parliament, and it was better that he do this through Charles rather than through the Opposition leaders. Moreover, in his negotiations with Charles Louis was inevitably on the losing end; from 1675 to 1685 Charles succeeded in blackmailing him by exaggerating the danger from parliament, despite the fact that however francophobe English parliaments might be they were even more opposed (with Charles I in mind) to the raising of an English army.

Most of the New Model had been disbanded in 1661.

But there remained the nucleus of the modern regular
army—Monk's own regiment of foot, known even then
as the Coldstream Guards; the First (later the Grenadier)
Guards; the First and Second Regiments of Life Guards;
and Lord Oxford's Regiment of Horse, "The Blues". The
officers of the three English regiments in the Dutch army,
descendants of sixteenth-century volunteers, returned to England in 1665 and raised the third regiment of the Line, "The
Buffs"; and the famous Scots Brigade of Gustavus Adolphus,
which had taken service under Louis XIV, was recalled in
1670.[9] To the Commons gentry it seemed that there were
more than enough troops loafing around London, without
adding to their number.

In fact, France's main danger came not from the gentry
but from Danby himself, whose power reached its height
in 1677. He had secured Portsmouth's aid long ago; he
now captured James, who was all for an aggressive, show-
down policy in Flanders. An injudicious attempt to force
a dissolution divided Lords from Commons and catapulted
Shaftesbury and three of his associates into the Tower, and
in October Danby and Sir William Temple engineered a
match between William of Orange and James's elder daughter,
Mary. Like her stepmother, Mary burst into tears at the
sight of her intended husband; she was a vivacious young
girl, who had inherited little of Henrietta Maria or Henriette-
Anne's compelling charm, but possessed a greater regularity
of feature and a more conventional dark loveliness. (She
strongly resembled her aunt and mother-in-law, Mary of
Orange.) The young Stadtholder, on the other hand, was
dour and fey, prematurely aged by a lonely childhood and
the precocious assumption of crushing responsibilities. Mary
had enough intelligence, however, to come to value her
husband's qualities, and in a few years, with the resilience
of royalty, she fell in love with him. She soon endeared

[9] In addition there were two regiments, of horse and foot, at
Tangier, which was part of Queen Catherine's dowry. They were
the First, or Royal Dragoons, and the Second, or Queen's Regiment
under Colonel Kirke—known as "Kirke's Lambs" from the Paschal
Lamb of the House of Braganza in their crest. They returned in
1684.

herself to the Dutch people and contributed not a little to William's popularity and prestige in the Netherlands.

But by forcing Charles II to define his foreign policy more closely, this marriage only brought about its collapse. It produced a defensive treaty between England and Holland in December 1677, implemented by the despatch of an expeditionary force to Flanders and consolidated in a general alliance the following March. The effect was to imperil the delicate balance Charles had maintained since 1674, and in May 1678 he hastily doubled back on his tracks and with Danby's reluctant consent signed a treaty of neutrality with France. But by now both Louis and the Dutch regents were anxious to end a war that only enhanced William's power in the Netherlands and gave his shifty uncle a deciding vote in European affairs. In May 1678 the States General by-passed the Stadtholder and accepted Louis's proffered terms of peace.

The peace of Nimeguen in July was an unmitigated disaster for Charles and Danby. Excluded from the European peace settlement, they were left with two contradictory treaties, neither of them ratified, and a useless army that could only be paid off with the assistance of a turbulent parliament grown crazed with age. Their debts were mountainous, their credit blasted. So the Popish Plot, exploded under a reeling government, knocked it prostrate.

The romance invented by Titus Oates and Israel Tonge in August 1678, of a Jesuit conspiracy to kill Charles and enthrone his brother by armed rebellion, focused on one centre all the random germs of anti-popery that had been circulating in the English political system for generations: the fag-end of Elizabethan propaganda, re-ignited by the Gunpowder Plot, fanned to a blaze by the Irish Rebellion, industriously refuelled by the Dutch in the early seventies and redirected against France and the Duke of York. Such heady stuff sent the lower classes reeling, and even their superiors were rocked by the still-unexplained death of Sir Edmund Berry Godfrey, the Protestant magistrate, and the discovery that Edward Coleman, the Duchess of York's secretary, had been engaged in treasonable correspondence with the Jesuit La Chaise, Louis XIV's reputed *éminence grise*.

Charles's failure to handle the matter decisively and realistically from the start meant the surrender of that godly and patriotic task to parliament, which assembled for its eighteenth sitting in October. But even greater damage was done by the revelations of Ralph Montagu, who had been recalled from the Paris embassy in July and disgraced; in revenge he betrayed to a horrified Commons evidence of Danby's secret negotiations with France.[10] To save Danby, and preserve the more dangerous secrets of the seventies, Charles had to prorogue parliament at the end of the year, dissolve it in January 1679, and summon another for March. In the elections the gentry registered their bitter disillusionment with Danby for trafficking with popery behind a smokescreen of Anglicanism, and the courtiers were decimated at the polls. The result was a House of Commons reminiscent of 1640, with a 90% majority against the government, and supported by a London mob inflamed by religious fanaticism and economic hardship to an equal degree. James retired to Brussels just before parliament met, and Danby was impeached, dismissed and sent to the Tower, where he remained until 1684.

Charles's isolation in the crisis that followed, and his ultimate success, have caused him to be credited with almost supernatural sagacity and skill. In fact, his policy and attitude were almost identical with his father's in 1641: passive temporisation, accompanied by a vain search for aid from France or Holland. There is only one significant difference; Charles II changed his ministers as easily and almost as often as he changed his linen, and much of his immunity must be attributed to this sanitary precaution.

On the other hand, the Opposition was never so effective

[10] Montagu had been living with Cleveland in Paris. When she complained to the king that he had also seduced their daughter, Lady Sussex, Charles seized the excuse to rid himself of an obstreperous and unreliable servant. In view of its repercussions this is the most important intervention by one of Charles's mistresses in politics, and the least noticed.

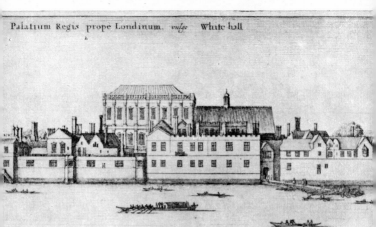

Palatium Regis prope Londinum, vulgo White hall

THE WHITEHALL OF CHARLES I, FROM THE RIVER

from engravings by Wenceslaus Hollar

JAMES I
Peace with Spain, 1604

WILLIAM AND MARY
by George Bower

ANNE
by John Croker

JAMES I
from a portrait attributed to Jan de Critz

CHARLES I

*detail from a
portrait by Van Dyck*

HENRIETTA MARIA

*detail from a
portrait by Van Dyck*

CHARLES I AT HIS TRIAL, 1649

*reproduced from the portrait by Edward Bower by Gracious
Permission of H.M. Queen Elizabeth The Queen Mother*

CHARLES II AS
PRINCE OF WALES

*painted at Oxford, c.164[
by William Dobson*

CHARLES II
IN EXILE

*probably painted in
Paris, 1659;
attributed to
Philippe de Champaigne*

CHARLES II

*from a pastel drawing
by Edward Lutterel*

QUEEN CATHERINE
OF BRAGANZA

*reproduced from a
miniature by Samuel
Cooper by Gracious
Permission of H.M.
The Queen*

JAMES II, 1685
from a portrait by Sir Godfrey Kneller

opposite, SOME OF CHARLES II'S MISTRESSES

CASTLEMAINE; *reproduced from an unfinished sketch by Samuel Cooper by Gracious Permission of H.M. The Queen*
MARY DAVIS, *by an unknown artist*
NELL GWYNN, *after Sir Peter Lely*
LUCY WALTER, *from a miniature by (?) Nicholas Dixon*
PORTSMOUTH, *from a miniature by Paolo Carandini*

MARY II AS
PRINCESS OF ORANGE
c.1677

*reproduced from a
miniature in the
Dutch Royal Collection
by Gracious Permission
of H.M. Queen Juliana
of the Netherlands*

QUEEN ANNE, c.1703

*from a miniature
by Charles Boit*

WILLIAM III

from the portrait by Gottfried Schalcken

PRINCESS ANNE, 1687
from the portrait by John Riley

as its great following in the country would suggest. The majority of the new House of Commons were inexperienced backwoodsmen, their policy essentially destructive and strictly limited in scope; they would be satisfied with the enactment of some draconian anti-popery laws and the exclusion of the Duke of York from the succession. But their self-styled leaders (who in fact had scarcely any control over them) looked to the restriction of the royal prerogative and their own re-establishment as advisers and controllers of a limited monarchy, perhaps even an oligarchy. Such views their followers scarcely understood and distrusted when they did. This was seen in April, when Charles broke the old Privy Council, dismissed Danby's followers, and took aboard the Opposition leaders, Russell, Essex, Henry Powle, Halifax and old Lord Holles (a veteran of 1629 and 1642), with Shaftesbury as Lord President. He then neatly divided his new ministry by proposing a scheme of statutory Limitations on the power of a popish monarch—an idea of Halifax's. Charles almost certainly had no intention of carrying out such a scheme, but its respectability was attested by its likeness to Pym's Nineteen Propositions, and also by the howl of protest it evoked from James; if the Opposition refused it, the onus would be on them.

They had to refuse it. Shaftesbury and Russell had the choice of running on downhill, or being trampled underfoot by their gadarene followers. The result was the introduction of the first exclusion bill to bar James from the throne, which led to the prorogation of parliament in May and its dissolution in July.

The moderate opposition peers, Halifax and Essex, stayed on at court, partly for the significant reason that the issue of exclusion had brought to the fore the question of the next heir. Theoretically, after James came his elder daughter Mary, which meant in effect William, who had a strong personal claim as a grandson of Charles I. William did his best to preserve his contacts in England, but these were not with the exclusionist leaders, who were allied rather with the Dutch republicans, and in any case favoured the claims of the Duke of Monmouth, Charles's eldest bastard. William consistently refused to come to England without the king's permission, in the autumn of 1679, and in the spring and autumn of 1680. Yet Charles and James always suspected him of encouraging Monmouth's pretensions so as to involve him and James in mutual ruin (just as he is still suspected by some of countenancing Monmouth's rebellion in 1685).

In fact, young Monmouth was a liability to anyone who espoused his cause. He had inherited his father's sexual prowess and his mother's brains. Charles had always doted on him, he was a general favourite at court, and his bravery in war, his skill at games, his beauty and personal charm made him popular with the masses, too. His head was turned by his cheap success in suppressing the Covenanters' Rebellion in Scotland in June 1679, and on his return he fell completely under Shaftesbury's control. Monmouth's great attraction for Shaftesbury was that he would make a weak king, amenable to junto control. But—and it was a very important "but"—the very weakness of his title made it impossible to foist him off on the country gentry, because of their loyalty to the theory of Hereditary Succession and Divine Right, and perhaps because the accession of a bastard to the throne might ultimately influence the law of succession to landed estates. This is why such frenzied efforts were made to find the famous Black Box, containing Lucy Walter's marriage lines, why Charles twice put himself to the public humiliation, in 1679 and 1680, of registering Monmouth's illegitimacy in the Privy Council records, and why Shaftesbury was still discussing Charles's divorce as late as October 1679. The truth was, the exclusionist leaders were saddled with a candidate for the throne whose cause they could espouse only through indirect public demonstrations and anonymous pamphlets.

Meanwhile the new elections, in August and September 1679, repeated with emphasis the verdict of February, but the second exclusion parliament was not destined to meet for another year. For in August Charles fell seriously ill, probably of pneumonia on top of influenza, and his brother was sent for in haste. The advent of James was decisive. Charles was convalescent, but still weak; he was arguably never the same again after this illness, and certainly not for nine months or so, and he accepted his brother's simple, authoritarian advice without demur. Shaftesbury was dismissed, Monmouth exiled, and parliament prorogued until December, when Charles announced that he would not meet it until November 1680. The first result was to smoke out Essex and Halifax, the men of compromise, advocates of an agreed solution, with whom James had no sympathy. Next to go were Shaftesbury's followers, who resigned from the Council in January 1680, leaving the way clear for the Duke's men: the Earl of Sunderland, Sidney Godolphin and Lawrence Hyde, the younger son of Lord Chancellor Clarendon. James retired for a few months to Scotland, but returned in February.

The long prorogation soon began to wear down the rank-and-file of the "Country" party, who drifted out to the provinces again, spurred on by a tentative government purge of the local benches. At the same time James's brutal demand that men declare themselves one way or the other produced unexpected results. Shaftesbury's answer was to organise a campaign of petitions for the assembly of parliament which as much as anything demonstrated the strength of reviving royalist sentiment. Counterblasts "abhorring" the unconstitutional practice of mass petitioning gave the two sides the names of "petitioners" and "abhorrers", later shortened to "whigs" and "tories", and the fact that there were now two sides at all must be attributed to the Duke. Unable to make any impression on James's able and conscience-less young ministers, the whigs rapidly lost their initial momentum; by the spring of 1680 they were almost at a standstill.

Charles's rôle was still largely passive. He was slowly recovering his health when he had another, milder bout of sickness in May 1680, which threw him back. He was depressed by the desertion of a great majority of his courtiers, and he had quarrelled with Portsmouth. For once that lady had been over-zealous in support of the French interest after Charles had decided to abandon it, in December 1679, and her attempts to aid the French ambassador brought her a sharp tap on the knuckles. Their association was not broken, but there was an undeniable reserve. The joyous anticipation with which he looked forward to James's return in February indicates that he was not himself, and in the months that followed the royal brothers were unusually close. But even James was strangely passive, and inclined to leave decisions to Sunderland and Hyde; he was perhaps depressed by the death of his three-year-old daughter Isabella in March. He and Charles spent much of their time at Windsor; the king still came up to London or Hampton Court once a week for council meetings, but for the rest he lived the life of a studious country gentleman—"There was little resort to him", noted Sir John Reresby, "and he passed his day in fishing or walking in the park, which indeed he naturally loved more than to be in a crowd or business."

He was only dragged from the semi-retirement by the sudden recrudescence of the whigs in June, which led to the collapse of English foreign policy and the break-up of the ministry. In the light of subsequent events it is clear that this whig revival was an artificial movement, and almost exclusively metropolitan. It was sparked off in June by Shaftesbury's desperate decision to present James as a popish recusant before the Middlesex grand jury, and the Duchess of Portsmouth as a common prostitute. It continued into July with a humiliating defeat for the government in the City elections. When parliament at length assembled in October, thirteen months after its election, the power of the Opposition to a great extent depended on the effectiveness of the London mob, led by Shaftesbury's notorious "brisk boys" from Wapping.

It was the European situation that brought Charles to this risky encounter. The previous December he had defeated an attempt by Louis XIV to make an alliance with the Dutch, but since then all his efforts to form an anti-French coalition with Holland and the Empire had broken down because of the manifest instability of the English government—only Spain had signed a treaty, in June. His decision to meet this "hard-boiled" parliament was his last desperate bid for an independent foreign policy; he requested money for that, and for nothing else. The alternative was a dissolution which

would only raise the provinces to the same critical tempera-
ture as the capital. Of course, though it was tactically right
to keep the issue bottled-up in London, he thereby risked an
explosion. The mounting tension cracked Sunderland and
Godolphin, who embraced exclusion as the only alternative to
civil war, hoping to preserve Mary's rights and keep Monmouth out. A few days before parliament met Charles finally
gave way to their pressure and agreed to send James back
to Edinburgh.

But James's attitude of unbending reaction, which alarmed
even his brother, was the rock on which this final crisis
broke and receded. He made it perfectly clear that if
parliament removed his rights he would transfer the struggle
to the battlefield. No one doubted his sincerity, and he
had the means to put his threats into operation; Scotland was
behind him, he was sure of assistance from Louis XIV, and
he could count on the support of at least half the English
nation. It was the knowledge that exclusion would mean
immediate civil war that enabled Charles to defy the London
mob, the City government and the Commons, and order
the Lords to throw out the second exclusion bill in November
1680. To the great mass of the nation civil war was not
only bloody but futile; for had not 1660 merely restored the
status quo of 1641? In rejecting the exclusion bill the king
could plead that he was averting civil war; if his opponents
took up the challenge they would be indelibly branded as
incendiaries.

Shaftesbury hesitated. London did not rise. Parliament
spluttered and squabbled on into January 1681, but the king's
relentless refusal to prorogue it prevented the introduction
of another exclusion bill and the initiation of a new cycle,
while the growth of the " Williamite " group of exclusionists
forced Shaftesbury into open patronage of Monmouth, whose
standing with the nation, except in the radical west, was
extremely dubious.

For by this time the whole crisis was running down. Fear
of popery was waning, and even the London mob was tiring
of the judicial murder of Catholics that had continued intermittently since 1678. The country gentry had had time

to forget Danby's treachery, and the steadiness of the established church was exerting a cumulative effect. The gentry woke up to find that they had been stampeded into supporting the candidature of a bastard prince in alliance with Dissent, republicanism and lower-class urban radicalism; and while a great patrician like Shaftesbury could mingle with the masses and not catch their fleas the squires were not so thick-skinned.

Charles showed a just appreciation of the situation when he cut the whigs off from the disordered capital in January 1681 by dissolving parliament and ordering the next to assemble at Oxford, in March. Militant urban radicalism and rural dissent still forced most of the boroughs to vote the whig ticket, but that fact in itself was alarming. After three elections in as many years these " levelling " techniques were becoming distressingly habitual, and there were schemes afoot for making them legally permanent. The exclusionist nobility prejudiced their case still further by coming to Oxford with gangs of servants and retainers armed to the teeth, dragging after them their skilled muckrakers and mob-raisers from London. Charles came later, flanked by Life Guards. Even then his retinue was not safe from insult, and the mob at Carfax, mistaking Nell Gwynn's coach for Portsmouth's, gave it a good jostling. The young comedienne threw them into a transport of delight by sticking her head out of the window and shouting, " Pray, good people, be civil; I am the *Protestant* whore!" But the atmosphere was patently dangerous.

That is why Shaftesbury could muster thirty peers for the exclusion bill in November 1680 and only nineteen for the impeachment of Fitzharris (a similar test issue) in March 1681. As the Lords left Christ Church hall on 26 March, he made a dramatic personal appeal to Charles to legitimise his son, but the king calmly replied that though he was second to none in his affection for Monmouth he could not perform the impossible. But, " I have law and reason and all right-thinking men on my side," he went on, " I have the church " —pointing to the bishops—" and nothing will ever separate us."

Charles's alternative to exclusion was an elaborated scheme of limitations, which would have made William and Mary regents after his death. The whigs could have embarrassed him cruelly by accepting it, and so obliging him to drop it or impose it on James by force; instead they put him in an impregnable position by rejecting it outright, and the following Monday, 28 March, he caught them on the wrong foot by suddenly dissolving parliament. They had ridden armed and full of bravado into royalist Oxford, but their leaders could assess the political realities of 1681, and civil war was not amongst them. " Round them were tennis courts and college gardens on which the Commons might have reunited themselves by an oath more solemn than any which they had yet sworn; but they dispersed : some to London, others to the country, and many to the horse races at Burford."[11]

A few days before the dissolution of the Oxford parliament Charles finally abandoned the attempt to conduct an independent foreign policy, and concluded a secret agreement with the French ambassador by which he promised not to summon another parliament for three years. In return he received a subsidy of two million livres the first year, and one-and-a-half million in each of the two years succeeding.

But to reverse the order of motivation, and imply that it was the French subsidy that enabled Charles to dissolve parliament at all, is to exaggerate both his need and Louis's generosity. Hyde's administration of the Treasury and the increasing yield of the excise had put his finances in as good order as they ever would be, and even if he had needed money, Louis's subsidy would not have made the difference between dissolving parliament and retaining it. A sum of £340,000 spread over three years was a useful tip, but no more, and it is only a strange persistence in thinking of *livres tournois* as directly equivalent to pounds sterling that has led so many historians to brand Charles II as a remittance man of France.[12]

[11] David Ogg, *England in the Reign of Charles II* (1955), ii. 619.
[12] See C. L. Grose, " Louis XIV's financial relations with Charles II ", *Journal of Modern History*, i (1929), 177-204.

In fact, the money paid him by Louis XIV over his whole reign, excluding the proceeds of the sale of Dunkirk, did not amount in aggregate to one year's average income from recognised sources. Throughout the exclusion crisis Charles's use of his prerogative of dissolution or prorogation was governed by considerations of policy, not finance. All he did in 1681 was screw another small pourboire out of Louis for adopting a policy he was compelled to adopt anyway. Again Louis fell for the old bluff, that Charles might be able and willing to come to terms with parliament on the basis of a war against France, than which nothing was less likely.

But it is true that the whigs had shot their bolt. As their legions marched out of Oxford into the spring of 1681, raising high the dust in the country lanes, they grew smaller and smaller in the distance. Their tumult and their shouting died on an Anglican wind that had been rising since early 1680. The irreconcilables of the left pressed on, their faces to the front like those antique Romans they so much admired; their obstinacy extinguished the "Good Old Cause" at the Rye House and Sedgemoor. But the great majority of their deluded followers peeled off the marching columns and crept back to their homes down the by-ways, like stragglers from a defeated army. They burnt their whig uniforms, and hid their whig weapons in the thatch against a better day, in 1688; and when next they appeared on their own front step they were cooing soft as any doves for the Divine Right of Kings and the Church by Law Established.

This Anglican reaction was skilfully exploited by Charles and his law officers. Orders in Council, issued in December 1681, reminded the gentry of their power to "regulate" disaffected boroughs under the Corporation Act of 1661, and the lists of magistrates and lord lieutenants were overhauled. Recalcitrant corporations were crushed by writs of *quo warranto*, while nobility, gentry and clergy co-operated in a brisk pogrom against Dissenters under the auspices of the Clarendon Code. The submission of the more important parliamentary boroughs in the provinces paved the way for an attack on London, which was launched in June 1682 by the appointment of a tory lord mayor and closed with the confiscation of the City charter in November 1683.

In 1681 two of Shaftesbury's lower-class lieutenants were rushed through the legal formalities and executed for treason, and the earl himself narrowly escaped a similar fate. The following year he fled to Holland and died, a broken man, in January 1683. The rest of the whig high command made the mistake of associating themselves, however tenuously, with the lunatic fringe of plebeians who concocted the Rye House Plot for the assassination of Charles and James that summer. Lord Russell and Algernon Sydney were condemned and executed, and the Earl of Essex committed suicide. Monmouth took refuge in Holland, followed by the great whig merchants who had been amongst Shaftesbury's most influential supporters. Dismissed from the City government and their livery companies, they were ruined by the imposition of staggering fines for libels uttered against the Duke of York in the heat of the exclusion crisis.

One of the last to join this variegated mob of exiles was John Locke, expelled from his studentship at Christ Church for his heterodox political opinions. For in 1683 the Convocation of the University of Oxford extended the royalist reaction into the intellectual sphere by denouncing twenty-seven whiggish propositions as " false, seditious and impious, and most of them also heretical and blasphemous, infamous to Christian religion and destructive of all government in Church and State ".

Having established his government more firmly than either of his immediate predecessors, the king had every right to indulge his taste for the frivolous and idle. In the declining years of Charles II's court it was always afternoon. Early spring found him at Newmarket, even when the weather was so dismal as to repel all but the most sycophantic. Portsmouth philosophically played crimp and basset while the fashionable young noblemen sipped their fashionable tea. High summer took them all to Windsor, where Charles could hunt stag in Cranborne Chase; on quieter days he fished the river meditatively, or strolled idly on the terrace. Every Sunday he went up to Council at Hampton Court, and he made occasional excursions farther afield; usually to Sheerness, Woolwich or Chatham, to view the docks and defences and see the launching of new ships, the planning and building of others. August would find him at Winchester, convenient for more naval expeditions, to Portsmouth or the Isle of Wight, and for riding, racing or walking across the Downs. A brief visit to London or Windsor, then he would drink summer to the lees at Newmarket again, with hawking, cock-fighting, racing and all the other excitements of the autumn meeting.

Charles was superficially content, but his very absorption in this round of pleasure betrayed an inner uneasiness, and he was conscious now of approaching death. He usually spoke of such things with flippancy—he told Burnet, " All appetites are free, and God will never damn a man for allowing himself a little pleasure "—but as he watched with impatience the rise of his new palace at Winchester he was heard to remark sombrely that " a year was a great time in his life ". The cruelly-exhausting strain of the exclusion crisis, accentuated by illness, had taken a lot out of him. (The wits said he was sexually impotent, a symbolic slander.) He had lost little of his old energy, and he changed little in appearance after 1660, but by 1683 he was a smaller man in ways other than physical. The vicious animosity that had always been a hidden streak in his character was openly displayed in his campaign against the whigs. Even James, the iron man, would listen to those who pleaded for Russell's life, but Charles even brushed aside the intercession of Louis XIV. He told George Legge, " If I do not take his life, he will soon have mine "—the reduction of politics to a personal vendetta. And when every allowance is made for the deficiencies in the seventeenth-century intelligence services and the lack of a police force, the activities of men like Jeffreys, who was appointed Lord Chief Justice in 1683 solely for the terror he could inspire, are a blot on the history of the reign.

Charles was as withdrawn and fathomless as ever, and he

had lost the capacity to laugh at himself. Rochester had died in 1680, but had he been alive he would never have dared circulate such lampoons as:

> We have a pretty witty king
> Whose word no man relies on:
> He never said a foolish thing,
> And never did a wise one.[18]

Charles was still capable of pointing out one of his courtiers as "the greatest whoremaster in England", but it would have been a bold man who replied, as Shaftesbury once had, "Of a subject, sire." "Old Rowley" needed more careful managing now; he was argumentative and unsympathetic, subject to childish suspicions and childish rages, surrounded by managing men and women. His boon ministers reflected something of the change: Sunderland, obsequious enough, but ill-tempered, intolerant and spiteful; Halifax, freethinking and deeply cynical, regarding politics and politicians with censorious disfavour, a brilliant but never a dangerous talker; and Sidney Godolphin, smooth and accommodating, "never in the way, and never out of the way". His instinct for playing one servant off against another had hardened from idle precaution into iron prejudice; Edward Seymour's conspicuous loyalty in the exclusion crisis did not prove the road to preferment, and for presuming to aspire to Danby's position as paramount minister, Lawrence Hyde, Earl of Rochester,[14] was demoted from the Treasury in 1684, despite the protests of his friend and brother-in-law, the Duke of York.

It is doubtful whether the old intimacy between Charles and James was ever revived after the exclusion crisis. The Duke was left marooned in Scotland after the dissolution of the Oxford parliament, and Charles intimated to him that the price of his return would be outward compliance with Anglicanism. James moaned and thundered humourlessly to

[18] Which had evoked the reply: "That is very true, for my words are my own, my actions are my ministers'."

[14] The poet Rochester left an only son, who died without heirs in 1681 and the title with him. It was revived for Lawrence Hyde in 1682.

anyone who would listen, but at Edinburgh he remained. That summer William came over to see Charles, who, " amongst other expressions of his displeasure at his brother's heat, said that if he were once king he would never be able to hold it out four years to an end ".

But when James did return, in the spring of 1682, it was with an enhanced reputation. He had governed Scotland for two years with grim efficiency and resolution, showing himself vigorous and decisive where his brother was indolent and prevaricating; he was also punctilious in demanding the respect due to his rank and blood, and such things had an attraction for stuffier courtiers, who were never at ease with his careless and unpredictable brother. He took his closest friends from amongst the Anglicans—Rochester, Dartmouth and Preston—but he made no secret of his personal faith and practice. In contrast the attitude of Charles, who was generally regarded as a papist or perhaps an atheist at heart, was felt to be unmanly and disingenuous. The natural result was that James attracted to himself his own court, Anglican in tone, which soon rivalled his brother's in numbers and quality. This trend has undoubtedly been exaggerated, but it did exist, and Charles was past the age when he could shrug off such petty irritations. So he got his own back whenever he could. His doting affection for Monmouth in these years was in part a reaction against his brother, and one of Halifax's principal attractions lay in the mutual animosity between him and James. Even their shared enthusiasm for the sea, their many joint dockyard inspections and naval expeditions, did not bring the brothers closer together. There was no reason why James should not have been restored to the command of the navy in 1682, but he had to wait another two years, and then he only obtained it through Portsmouth.

Portsmouth could do impossible things, take liberties denied all others. Her frenzied support for exclusion in 1680 scarcely affected her personal relations with the king, and she continued to patronise Sunderland, the leading court exclusionist, long after his dismissal in 1681. Her control over patronage was all but absolute, and if she intervened in policy very little it was because she was scarcely capable of doing so. She rocked the political world by bringing Sunderland back to court in 1682 and making him Secretary of State in 1683. He then became her "man of business".

Charles's way with women had always been most casual, except when fired by ravening lust—"He had more properly, at least in the beginning of his time, a good stomach for his mistresses, than any great passion for them. . . . His taking them from others was never learned in a romance, [and] . . . his patience for their frailties showed him no exact lover." But Portsmouth always occupied a special place in his affections, more firmly established as he grew older. Halifax preferred to think of their relationship as "an insensible engagement" bred of long familiarity and mutual tolerance, but others did not hesitate to call it love. "His fondness", wrote Burnet, "broke out in very indecent instances", and he "caressed her in the view of all people, which he had never done on any occasion or to any person formerly".

In 1682 she risked a three-month visit to France, and absence only heightened Charles's affection; the unexpected news of her landing brought him scampering down to meet her like any young lover. She had grown plumper and more amiable with the years, and rejoiced in the pet name of "Fubbs",[15] but it is significant that Charles felt a jealousy for her that he would not have displayed, probably not felt, for any previous mistress. He provoked a first-class scandal in 1683 by ordering her too familiar friend Philip de Vendôme out of the country. Again, nothing ever dragged him from the Newmarket autumn meeting (even the sittings of the exclusion parliaments had been geared to it), nothing except the news that Louise had fallen ill in London in October 1684. He found her apparently *in extremis*, and she

[15] A ship of the royal navy was named after her, and therefrom the Greenwich public house *The Fubbs Yacht*. James remarked in 1682 that Charles was "very well pleased with his new yacht, the 'Fubbs', she outsailing all the old ones". Other yachts were the *Cleveland* (1671) and *Portsmouth* (1674). See C. M. Gavin, *Royal Yachts*.

begged him, as her dying wish, that he should let no one come between his brother and himself. Both he and James were reduced to tears.

To her James owed his influence on policy, which was quite open and recognised by 1684, particularly with regard to Scotland and Ireland. Charles resented his meddling, and is said to have told him, "Brother, you may travel if you will; I am resolved to make myself easy for the rest of my life"; and so on. But he had always found it easier to talk than act—in that he resembled his grandfather—and inaction had paid dividends. So he made no effort now.

Cleveland had returned at last from Paris, and one Sunday night, 25 January 1685, the sanctimonious Evelyn was shocked at the conflux of Charles II's women at Whitehall, in "unexpressible luxury and prophaneness, gaming and all dissolution, and as it were total forgetfulness of God"; "The king sitting and toying with his concubines, Portsmouth, Cleveland and Mazarin, etc.; a French boy singing love songs in that glorious gallery, whilst about twenty of the great courtiers and other dissolute persons were at basset round a large table, a bank of at least £2,000 in gold before them." But, added Evelyn, with unctuous satisfaction, "six days after all was in dust".[16]

For while the king was shaving on the morning of 2 February he was felled by a stroke. A daring and quick-witted doctor bled him at once, but it prolonged his life only a few days, and by noon on the 5th he was given over by his physicians.

Portsmouth, overwhelmed with grief as she was, had too much decorum to approach the bedchamber, but she sent for the French ambassador and told him that the king was a Roman Catholic at heart and must be given the opportunity of dying in that faith. Barillon saw James, who gave a typical answer: "I will hazard all rather than not do my duty on this occasion." By a remarkable coincidence the only English priest available was Father John Hudleston, who had aided Charles in his escape from Worcester in

---

[16] Evelyn so relished this anecdote that he included it twice. See E. S. de Beer's edition of the *Diary*, iv. 403, 413.

1651; by a further irony he was ushered up the back
stairs by the Keeper of the Closet, Will Chiffinch, who was
used to fairer visitors. The bedchamber was cleared, Hudleston came in, confessed the king, absolved him and gave him
extreme unction. Afterwards Charles revived slightly, and
" spoke with more feeling and understanding ". " He often
spoke quite aloud to the Duke of York in terms full of
tenderness and friendship; he twice recommended to him
the Duchess of Portsmouth and [her son] the Duke of
Richmond." He also commended to him all his other children,
except Monmouth, and added the famous injunction, " Let
not poor Nelly starve." In the midst of these rather carnal
preoccupations " he often expressed his confidence in the
mercy of God ". Such of his sons as were available came
to receive his blessing (but not their mothers); his benedic-
tion was then extended to the whole room, all kneeling.
As one candid onlooker remarked, " This was so like a
great, good prince, and the solemnity of it so very surprising, as was extremely moving."

Pain kept him awake, and at midnight the queen came to
take her farewell. When he asked for her again she was
too overwrought to come, but " she sent a message to him
to excuse her absence, and to beg his pardon if she had
offended him in all her life ". He replied, " Alas, poor
woman! She ask my pardon? I beg hers with all my heart;
take her back that answer." At six in the morning he asked
what time it was, and said, " Open the curtains, that I may
once more see day." About ten he lapsed into unconscious-
ness, and he died at noon without a struggle. " He died as
he lived," wrote John Drummond, " the admiration of all
men for his piety, his contempt of this world, and his resolution against death."

CHAPTER V

JAMES II

1685-1688

James II's long apprenticeship to kingship had already exposed his principal deficiencies—narrowness of mind, rigidity of temperament and lack of imagination. Lauderdale delivered a classic summing-up in 1679 or thereabouts:[1] "This good prince," he said, "has all the weakness of his father without his strength. He loves, as he saith, to be served in his own way, and he is as very a papist as the pope himself, which will be his ruin . . . [and] if he had the empire of the whole world he would venture the loss of it, for his ambition is to shine in a red letter after he is dead."

Like his father, James found communication difficult. There is no reason to doubt his distress at the tragic death of his baby son, Cambridge, in 1678, but he acknowledged William of Orange's condolences like this: "I keep Cornwall [the messenger] here on purpose to send you word what the express will bring, which will be peace or war; and now that I have said this I will not defer letting you know that I do easily believe the trouble you had for the loss of my son; I wish you may never have the like cause of trouble, nor know what it is to lose a son. I shall now say no more to you, because the bearer can inform you of all things here." All his letters are brief, clumsy, replete with schoolboy platitudes, stock phrases, even recurrent stock sentences, untouched by any emotion save anger, and innocent of any intellectual concept. Even his wooing partook of the same limitations, for there is a ring of truth in Grammont's account of his approaches to Miss Hamilton—"He entertained her with what he had in his head; telling her miracles of the

[1] To his chaplain, whose notes are printed in *Journal of Modern History*, xx (1948).

cunning of foxes and the mettle of horses; giving her
accounts of broken legs and arms, dislocated shoulders, and
other curious and entertaining adventures; after which his eyes
told her the rest." His repeated statements on religion were
apparently culled from some old-fashioned and not very
literate work of standard devotions.

But James's bigotry was always curiously superficial. He
showed an acute awareness of the sacrifices he was making
for his faith, and expatiated on them at every opportunity
with a kind of masochistic fondness. He admitted more than
once "that if he [had] agreed to live quietly and treat his
religion as a private matter . . . he could have been one of
the most powerful kings ever to reign in England, and no
doubt he would also have cut a fine figure in Europe; but,
having been called by Almighty God to rule these kingdoms,
he would think of nothing but the propagation of the Catholic
religion, and this was the true service of God, for which
he had been and always would be willing to sacrifice everything, regardless of any mere temporal consideration".

And the strange thing is that James, the least successful of
the Stuart kings, was the most English. The effect of his
second marriage has been persistently over-estimated; he
needed no Mary Beatrice to make him a conventional bigot,
and it is hardly likely that this convent-trained mouse decisively
influenced an obstinate, opiniated husband twenty-five years
her senior. In her brief appearances prior to his accession
she figures as a piece of ducal luggage, unceremoniously
carted from place to place in James's wake, unhappy, home-
sick for Italy, and frequently seasick. He treated her like
a nice child, and when she suddenly turned on him in 1686
his first emotion was quite clearly shock. Her holy domestic-
ity was never very congenial to a gad-about husband, who
in his youth had played the guitar "tolerably well"; "She
has no other amusement whatsoever", wrote one admirer,
"save that of playing basset every evening—except on Sun-
days and the eve of days on which she receives communion."
She was beautiful, of course, but James was not the man
to be attracted by beauty alone, and since he did not find
in her the overt sensuality he needed his emotional life

was centred instead on two Protestant mistresses of undistinguished appearance, considerable intelligence and rampant sexuality. We may discount the influence of Arabella Churchill and Catherine Sedley: James's Catholic advisers did not. They reigned successively, and with only the briefest intervals, from 1665 to 1687.

Again, James's obstinate loyalty to friends was one of his most notable characteristics; but it is remarkable how few Catholic friends he had—only confessors. Apart from Richard Talbot, Earl of Tyrconnel, and perhaps Harry Jermyn, Lord Dover, his boon companions and his lords of the bedchamber were chosen from amongst the lay Anglicans, like Rochester, Churchill, Feversham and Dartmouth, or the godless, like Kirke and Herbert.

In fact, it is to his first marriage, not his second, that we must look for the guiding influence in James's life; to the love-match with Anne Hyde that brought him into close association with Clarendon and his sons. Clarendon's reverence for established institutions chimed in with the ideas James had imbibed in ultra-royalist Oxford in the forties, and with his own and his father's high concept of monarchy. Clarendon confirmed his son-in-law in his respect and affection for the church which had so steadfastly supported his father, and Clarendon's son Rochester held him to that path almost to the end. The exclusion crisis confirmed the loyalty of the established church, and it was quite natural that in the last two or three years of his brother's reign James should emerge as the leader of the lay Anglicans, "who", he told his first parliament, "have shown themselves so eminently loyal in the worst of times". His respect for the Anglican church survived even the progressive disillusionment of the years 1685 to 1688, and his ultimate anger against it mirrors the depth of his previous attachment. In the first year of his reign he paid it the greatest compliment at his command, by envisaging an English Catholic church modelled on it and parallel to it.

Moreover, he had a respect for law and the authority of parliament with which he is not usually credited. He suspended certain statutes, but he never pretended to abrogate them, and when he thought of suspending the second Test Act in 1687, and Sunderland told him, rather whiggishly, that it would be unconstitutional to tamper with a statute defining the composition of parliament, he agreed docilely enough. In so far as it is amenable to analysis, his conception of kingship was founded on the misty squirearchal dream of Clarendon and Pym—not the authoritarianism of Strafford and Laud, nor the francophil absolutism of Sunderland and Godolphin. He saw himself as a divinely-appointed patriarch, ruling through a staid and eminent council and a docile and tranquil parliament, representative of a godly and satisfied people. He was no more capable than the country gentry, or the great " Country " minister, Clarendon, of appreciating the complex economic, social and political stresses of his time. In other words, his projects were not flawed by bigotry—though all his actions and utterances were arbitrarily clothed in terms of superstitious fanaticism—but by qualities and prejudices that were quite independent of religious belief.

He had inherited his father's belief in the supernatural authority of kingship, and even improved upon it—to the extent that he expected a bastard usurper to assume, or be vouchsafed, its external attributes. He remarked after his interview with the Duke of Monmouth in 1685 that he " did behave himself not so well as I expected, nor so as one ought to have expected from one who had taken it upon him to be king". So, even more consistently than his father, he believed that all opposition to his policy was inspired by the worst of motives. Men displaying such vicious contrariness were uniformly branded as " rogues ", " knaves ", " cattle ", " enthusiasts ", " atheists " or " republicans " (this last a term of deep opprobrium, perhaps the strongest in his vocabulary), and the contemplation of their well-merited sufferings was one of the few things that moved him to recognisable mirth. He described Lord Chief Justice Jeffreys' " Bloody Assize " of 1685 as his " campaign in the west ", a phrase so satisfying that he repeated it in his next letter. Even polite resistance on the part of chosen advisers was an impertinence, and when he dismissed Halifax in 1685 he complacently remarked that he wanted it to be generally known that the only way to secure his favour was "to follow his wishes blindly, and to own an attachment to his interests that was without any qualification or reserve whatsoever".

As a corollary, he regarded any concession made under pressure as an abject sign of weakness. The obstinacy he inherited from his father was strengthened by his father's example—a curious "double-take"—for he attributed Charles I's destruction not to his refusal to make significant concessions but to his weakness in making any at all. The exclusion crisis had confirmed in him the belief that his enemies could be dispersed by courage and will-power alone, and when his more intelligent ministers advised him to pardon the Seven Bishops in 1688 he refused, "bringing forward the examples of the late king his father and the king his brother, who had weakened their authority—and in his father's case brought on his own death—by too great a display of leniency". "He knew the English people," he added, "and they could not be held to their duty by fair treatment."

His terror of the English people, their violent prejudices, their insensate rages, was one of the most important influences on his life. It produced many of the measures—his expansion of the army, for instance, and his abject surrender to Tyrconnel's Irish policy—that seemed most menacing to contemporaries. He lived in daily expectation of rebellion, and in 1687 a French envoy was flabbergasted to find him busy fortifying the great naval base of Portsmouth on the *landward* side. Even his religious policy was primarily designed to erect a defensive shield between him and his Protestant subjects; as Sunderland remarked, the king "had nothing so much at heart as the establishment of the Catholic religion, [for] . . . without it he would never be secure, and always exposed to the indiscreet zeal of those who excite the people against Catholicism".

Apprehension, then, not aggression, is the key to an understanding of James II's policy, with its contradictory lurches from side to side, its pathetic contortions, its obvious omissions, its hazardous reversals out of one cul-de-sac into the next. In the first week of the reign the French ambassador noted that some people " fear there is a design to ruin the Protestant religion and tolerate Catholicism alone ". " This is a project," he added, " so difficult—not to say impossible—to carry out that sensible men do not fear it." And even in 1688 the " sensible men ", like Nottingham and Halifax, continued to regard the Roman church with studied contempt, and stoutly maintained that if the king had any despotic notions they were doomed to failure.

James naturally expected his brother's death to be the signal for armed rebellion; he was astonished when his accession was greeted with restrained but sincere rejoicing, the taxes he felt obliged to collect in anticipation of parliamentary grant were paid with the minimum of grumbling, and the House of Commons elected in February and March 1685 duly reflected the success of Charles II's campaign against the corporations.

Still off balance, he met parliament in May with a wary and belligerent speech. Commenting on the rumour that they intended to secure more frequent sessions by restricting his permanent income, he told them roundly, " It would be a very improper method to take with me, and the best way to engage me to meet you often is always to use me well ". Undeterred, parliament made him the best-endowed of all the Stuarts by voting him all Charles II's revenues for life, plus £800,000 a year for three years to refit the navy. This hopeful session was interrupted in June by the news that Monmouth had landed in the west and proclaimed himself king, but few doubted that when parliament met again it would repeal the penal laws against Catholics, and possibly the second Test Act, which excluded them from the Lords. The king was already hearing mass publicly at Whitehall, but he told the French ambassador that he intended to advance slowly and carefully, always with the countenance and support of the Anglicans.

The counterpart of an Anglican alliance at home was an understanding with Holland abroad, and both William and James seized the opportunity presented by Charles's death to effect a complete reconciliation, which was cemented by the prince's conduct during Monmouth's rebellion, when he at once sent over the Scots and English regiments in the service of the States General and offered to lead them into battle. James was genuinely touched, the more so since this conduct contrasted sharply with that of his much-admired cousin Louis, who declined to give him financial assistance, even at the height of the revolt. In August James formally renewed all the existing treaties between England and Holland, while Louis fumed impotently.

But this halcyon period of reconciliation lasted only a few months. His old fears and suspicions, lulled by the first session of parliament, were at once re-awakened by Monmouth's revolt. The initial success of this undermanned, undersubsidised venture indicated that a national uprising could not be suppressed without aid from abroad, which might not be forthcoming in time, and might be politically disastrous if it were. The only alternative was an immediate expansion of the standing army and the appointment to the new regiments of Roman Catholic officers who were experienced in Continental warfare and whose loyalty was not in doubt. He dispensed them by letters patent from the oath laid down in the first Test Act, pending the decision of parliament, which he hoped would be in favour of repeal.

But by prematurely demanding the repeal of the Test Act he prevented even the discussion of the archaic and discredited penal laws. The dismissal of Halifax before the session opened was rank bad tactics, in that it consolidated opposition in the Lords, and as soon as the session opened they fell upon the question of dispensations, supported by a House of Commons under the leadership of that true-blue tory Edward Seymour. The violent persecution of the French Protestants by Louis XIV did nothing to increase the popularity of his English cousin, though the French ambassador assured Louis that James was overjoyed " at the marvellous success with which God has blessed your Majesty's efforts to convert your subjects ". Early in December James had to prorogue parliament to evade a resolution publicly condemning his policy, and his persecution complex was now dominant; he told the Pope's envoy, the Count d'Adda, that he was faced by "a vast conspiracy of the ill-intentioned".

The failure of this parliament hamstrung James for more than a year. Pious admirers were filled with "wonder and tenderness at the sight of so great a king animated by such ardour for the aggrandisement of our religion", but this hectic romanising zeal was more evident in words than deeds, and it is remarkable how very little James accomplished, or even tried to accomplish, in 1686. A carefully-tailored bench of judges confirmed his power to dispense individuals from the provisions of the Test Acts, but Catholics capable of filling the places now open to them were simply not available; nor were they likely to be available unless the king made some decisive move against the Anglican church. The commission for ecclesiastical causes was set up in July, and at once suspended the Bishop of London for permitting anti-papist rant in the pulpits of his diocese. But after this sudden pounce it slumbered. The prorogued parliament lingered on, and with it the Anglican Lord Treasurer, Rochester.

The truth is, James simply did not know what to do. Without the expected rush of Catholic converts, he could only continue to lean on his Anglican allies, for the Dissenters were still damned as "enthusiasts" and "republicans" in his eyes. On the other hand, he began to realise the disadvantages of Catholic zealotry in February 1686, when the queen, aided by a gaggle of priests, forced him to put away his Protestant mistress, Catherine Sedley, Countess of Dorchester.

Poor James always found sexual continence a great strain, and he told one Frenchman that what he most admired in Louis XIV was his effortless monogamous rectitude—"He is younger than I," he groaned, "but I have much less self-control." He could not withstand the unanimous opinion of his most trusted ecclesiastics, but he had recourse to the scourge to acclimatise himself to Sedley's absence, and even then he dare not dismiss her face to face for fear of weakening—a remarkable admission from a man who prided himself on his inflexible will. She soon returned, but henceforth James regarded his young wife rather more warily. Her pregnancy in 1687 laid the foundation of an ascendancy that in their exile became absolute dominance.

Meanwhile his policy abroad, as well as in Ireland, reflected his profound uncertainty. He had no defined foreign policy, but existed in the vague hope that an attitude of belligerent neutrality would enhance his nuisance value, and thus his prestige. He quarrelled violently with William when the prince refused to appoint a Catholic to command the British regiments in Holland or deliver up the Scots and English refugees who crowded the Dutch towns. On the other hand, Louis XIV was fully as alarmed as William at the expansion of the English army, the refitting of the navy and the extension of the south coast ports and dockyards. James's bellicose utterances did nothing to lower the tension. In October, for instance, he told the Privy Council " that next year they should see as great a fleet abroad as England ever had, and everything in order to secure him from his enemies and to keep his neighbours from insolencies in all parts of the world ".

William, patiently trying to read into his uncle's actions the intelligence and logic that informed his own, could only conclude that he intended to alter the succession in favour of the Princess Anne or his bastard son Berwick, who had been raised a Catholic. In fact, nothing was farther from James's mind; he was too stern a legitimist, and he had suffered too much from exclusion projects himself, to countenance the proposals of his more extreme advisers. It seemed unlikely that Mary Beatrice would bear him a son —all her children had died young, and she had last conceived in 1681—but though he was now fifty-three he had made no serious attempt to come to terms with parliament, nor with his daughters, who would succeed him. It needed Pope Innocent XI to remind him, as late as December 1686, that all his efforts should be directed to Anne's conversion, in the hope that her childless elder sister would not reign long.

Undoubtedly James was thrown off balance by the failure of his schemes of widespread proselytisation, and the lack of a strong Catholic laity forced him to negotiate always from a position of weakness. There were only two well-known Catholic lawyers, Alibone and Brent, neither of them first-rate; there was no Catholic capable of handling the national finances; and, most surprising of all, only one Catholic—the disreputable Irish adventurer Ignatius White, Marquis d'Albeville—who was capable of sustaining a foreign embassy with moderate competence. Despite Louis's expressed wish for a Catholic, James had to appoint two Protestants in succession to the Paris embassy, and for the Rome embassy in 1686 he could only find the Earl of Castlemaine, whose wife's relations with Charles II made him a laughing-stock, and whose aggressive ignorance offended Louis XIV and enraged Innocent XI. Castlemaine returned early in 1687, but he was not replaced until 1688, when James chose Lord Thomas Howard, a man who had spent his whole life managing the estates of his brother the Duke of Norfolk. Foreigners visiting England in 1686 noticed with amazement that James's romanising policy was managed and directed by the Protestant Lord Sunderland.

Moreover, even the Catholic minority at Whitehall was sharply divided into two groups, held apart by training, tradition and policy. The Jesuit "extremists" were led by Father Edward Petre, James's confidential adviser since 1678; their most noted lay agents were the Celtic adventurers, Castlemaine, Tyrconnel, Melfort and Albeville. Ultramontane and pro-French, they favoured violent romanisation at home and an aggressive, anti-Protestant policy abroad. They were strong enough to keep Cardinal Howard, the "Cardinal of England" and the nominal leader of the native Catholics, out of the country the whole reign; in return Innocent XI, no friend to France or the Society of Jesus, persistently refused to grant Petre a cardinalate or a bishopric.

Opposed to the Jesuits were the secular clergy, loyal to the Pope and therefore anti-French, plus the native Catholic peers like Powis, Belasyse, Norfolk, Dover and Arundel, who consistently opposed any measure likely to imperil their estates or the measure of working toleration they already enjoyed. They opposed James's commissioning of Catholics in 1685 and his break with parliament, they opposed the appointment of Tyrconnel as Lord Deputy in Ireland, and they anxiously sought an accommodation with William in 1686 and 1687. Lord Dover constantly threatened to leave the country, and early in 1688 the Duke of Norfolk actually did so; he went to Paris and stayed there the rest of, the year. They opposed the dissolution of parliament in 1687, the recall of the regiments from Holland in 1688, and the trial of the Seven Bishops. In short, James's natural supporters in England steadfastly opposed him in his every important act of state.

In these circumstances it is not surprising that his policy should be slow to develop. But at the end of 1686 he realised that since he could not go back he must move forward. In a sudden burst of activity he dismissed Rochester and his brother Clarendon, appointed Tyrconnel Lord Deputy, and began to exert pressure on Members of Parliament by personal interview—or "closeting". William, seeing Tyrconnel's appointment as the first overt threat to his wife's inheritance, at once despatched a special emissary to England. Dykveldt declined to pledge William and Mary to support James's policy, and soon after his arrival in February 1687 he transferred his attention to the dissident peers, Catholic and Protestant. Meanwhile Albeville, the Hague ambassador, was ordered to attempt the conversion of Mary, and James's priests made a more definite approach to Anne. Finding Anne as great a bigot as her father, but Protestant, they turned to her Lutheran husband, with equal lack of success. In March 1687 Anne tried to visit her sister in Holland, but she was refused permission to leave the country. The Whitehall of the Stuarts was like the court of some Visconti or della Scala princeling, with the ruler's closest relations his most hated and suspected enemies.

But the failure of James's policy was most heavily underlined by the conduct of two creatures he had made from mud: Piercey Kirke, colonel of the Tangier regiment, and Admiral Arthur Herbert, Master of the Robes, whose dismissal for refusing the king his parliamentary support closed the experiment in "closeting". Baffled, James could only turn to the hated Dissenters. In April 1687 he issued his Edict of Toleration, suspending the penal laws, the Clarendon Code and the first Test Act, and at the same time he embarked on a long and bitter struggle to force a Catholic President on Magdalen College, Oxford. In May d'Adda was publicly consecrated Archbishop of Amasia *in partibus infidelium* at St James's Chapel, and in July he made his formal "Entry" as papal nuncio, at Windsor. James explained to his horrified Protestant friends that he knelt before d'Adda as archbishop, not as nuncio; the fact that he considered this a sufficient explanation is eloquent of his mentality. Finally he dissolved parliament with a burst of godly vigour, announcing to the council in July that the inconveniences arising from this decision were far outweighed by its contribution to "his principal aim, which was the advancement of the Catholic religion".

But an alliance with the Dissenters was still a huge pill for James to swallow. He dissolved parliament in the hope that an alternative policy would suggest itself, but none did. He was fifty-four now, still without a son, and half-estranged from the queen, who bitterly resented his furtive dalliance with heretic drabs. In desperation he requested Anne to receive instruction; her answer was to flee from Windsor to Hampton Court. The moderate Catholics were in a state of near mutiny and his Protestant ministers "regarded the Prince of Orange as if he were at the very gates of London, ready to call them to account for the damage they had done to the laws of England and the [powers of the] crown".

But in August, on a progress through the west of England, James made a detour to the shrine of St Winifred in Wales, where he prayed for a son, while the queen sought more mundane assistance to the same end in the curative waters of Bath. Reunited in the first week of September, they effected the longed-for miracle. Mary Beatrice herself was so incredulous that she waited until the end of her second month, but early in November she was able to publish the joyous news of her pregnancy to the world.

The expected child might be another daughter, of course, to take precedence in the succession after Mary and Anne, but James and William must each base his plans on the assumption that it would be a son. Transported by godly optimism, James at once embarked on a preliminary purge of the London city government, the municipal corporations, the county lord lieutenancies, deputy lieutenancies and magistracies, replacing the recalcitrant Anglicans with papists, whigs and "enthusiasts". He and his less pessimistic advisers contemplated a "general election" early in 1688. William at once despatched Henry Sydney to England, to sift the truth of the pregnancy and contact the dissident nobility; with him came a number of intelligence agents recruited from amongst the exiles in the Netherlands. Whether the prince at this stage seriously contemplated an invasion of England is open to discussion. There was no lack of firebrands like Charles, Lord Mordaunt, or the young Earl of Shrewsbury, to encourage such ideas, and since William's was a logical, tidy mind, with a breadth of vision that embraced every possibility, such a scheme must have existed in some back compartment or other of his brain. But he was a fatalist, his political attitude deeply tinctured by his Calvinistic beliefs. Like that other great predestinarian, Oliver Cromwell, he could usually identify his own best interests with the will of God, but in difficult cases such tortured reconciliations could only be accomplished after prayerful procrastination and intent examination of the available omens. In most cases he played the cards as they fell. Moreover, he was primarily interested in England's foreign relations. If James had six popish sons, it would be unfortunate, but God's will; if the English episcopate went to the stake *en masse* with the House of Lords, in some Whitehall *auto-da-fé*, it would be tragic, but foreordained. But if James abandoned his present neutrality, and swung decisively into the French orbit, then his operations would impinge directly on William's, and the prince would be entitled, and by his own standards compelled, to act.

James's own concept of foreign policy was antique. In 1687 he was still pathetically obsessed by the fear of a War of Religion, undertaken by a Protestant League—

though a glance at the efforts of Gustavus Adolphus and Cromwell in that direction would have set his mind at rest. A generation after the Thirty Years' War, he still could not conceive of political interests transcending religious differences, whether between Catholic and Protestant or Christian and Muslim. (He was the only ruler in Europe who declined to believe that His Most Christian Majesty of France was in alliance with the Turkish Sultan against the Holy Roman Empire.) He had forgotten Spain's traditional rivalry with France; he could not appreciate the anger of the Emperor and the German princes at Louis XIV's constant interference in Germany, his claims on the Palatinate now, and his infiltration into the Rhine archbishoprics of Cologne, Trèves and Mayence; he could not conceive that the bitter squabble between the Pope and the King of France was not just a question of diplomatic franchises or the status of the Gallican church, but a matter of international power politics.

Yet by 1688 the Catholic powers, Spain, Bavaria and the Empire, were already bound to their Protestant neighbours—Holland, Prussia and Sweden—in a tangle of loose but sufficient alliances; all they were waiting for was Louis's next false step, the next international incident that would give them an excuse to fall on France; while over all, and knowing all, brooded the Odescalchi pope. Of all the European states only England's allegiance was in doubt; all this century she had been the joker in the diplomatic pack. But James II was apparently unaware that he had determined that allegiance when he abruptly demanded the return of the English and Scots regiments from Holland in January 1688.

James would have recalled these seasoned troops as early as 1686 had he been able to pay them, but the expansion of his own army and navy had exhausted even the lavish provision made by parliament in 1685. But the queen's pregnancy at once increased his suspicion of his own subjects, and the more troops available to quell revolt the better. A solution was found at the end of 1687, when Louis XIV agreed to pay the regiments if they were recalled. James does not seem to have doubted his son-in-law's compliance, but William took refuge behind the States General's refusal, while he instructed the Pensionary Fagel to publish the *Fagel-Stewart Letters*, embodying his and his wife's considered rejection of James's whole policy.

Maddened by this *démarche*, James ordered the officers of the disputed regiments (who held his commission) to return individually, and a further proclamation authorising his warships to take English seamen off Dutch vessels brought the two countries to the verge of war in March. William's agents in England, and his Dutch scribes, joined the Anglicans in a vigorous propaganda campaign to prevent the Dissenters drifting into the king's camp, while in the first three months of 1688 James intensified his efforts to win over the county electorate and the borough corporations.

He was finally obliged to postpone the elections to the late autumn, but in May 1688 two decisive events set in train that slow, halting process known as the English "Revolution". One occurred in Cologne, where the chapter chose as the new archbishop-elector Louis XIV's candidate, Cardinal Fürstenberg; the other in London, where James ordered the Anglican clergy to read his Edict of Toleration from their pulpits. The Archbishop of Canterbury and six of his bishops presented a petition against this order; it was published, and they found themselves arraigned on a charge of seditious libel.

The Cologne election set the European scene. Innocent XI's inevitable refusal to invest Fürstenberg with the archbishopric would be the signal for a general war. No one but the English king and his advisers believed he could stay neutral, and his relations with Holland were so bad that he could only come down on France's side. William's first concern, then, was to blanket the royal navy and immobilise the English army. James, of course, was blissfully ignorant of such newfangled subtleties; he told the nuncio in March "that he had been assured by a reliable source that all the prince's measures were directed towards a war of religion", and he added that "if the Spaniards wanted to do good, here was their opportunity to strike a great blow for Christianity ". By now, unfortunately, he was the only ruler in Europe, not excepting the Pope, who thought that Christianity had any necessary connexion with politics or war.

As for the trial of the Seven Bishops, it neatly offset any advantage that James might have reaped from the birth of James Francis Edward, Prince of Wales, on 10 June. The prospect of a Catholic dynasty in perpetuity must in any case put a strain on his new alliance with the Dissenters, but conciliation and care might have prevented its fracture; as it was, they were treated to a gratuitous demonstration of mean revenge perpetrated on the highest Protestant dignitaries in the land, not long since the king's cosseted favourites. The weakness that lay behind the action was made ludicrously apparent by the acquittal of the bishops on 30 June, and the resultant confusion in the royal counsels. That evening the " Immortal Seven "—the Earls of Danby, Shrewsbury and Devonshire, Lord Lumley, Henry Sydney, Edward Russell and the Bishop of London—put their signatures to the famous letter inviting William to come over, suitably supported, and investigate the complaints of James's electoral activities and the rumours concerning the birth of the Prince of Wales.

There is no greater misconception in the mythology of whiggism than that the Revolution was a national movement. In fact, the greater part of the nation, Anglican and Dissenter, Protestant and Catholic, whig and tory, stood aside, in anguished expectation of civil war, while the vital decisions were taken, almost at random, by a few noblemen and their friends. The nobility were fast emerging as the most powerful political class; and they had suffered most from James's policy. Their lord lieutenancies had been stripped from them, their boroughs undermined, their places at court granted away to papists, francophil timeservers like Godolphin and Sunderland, or Celts like Melfort and Tyrconnel. Many had received sharper punishment: like the Earl of Devonshire, subjected to a punitive fine for a minor fracas at Whitehall, and forced to spend most of the reign rebuilding Chatsworth;

or at the other extreme Lord Lovelace, admonished by the
council and threatened with prosecution for ostentatiously
using as toilet paper a writ sent him by a popish magistrate.
(The brooding solemnity with which James pursued this
rabelaisian peccadillo confirms his lack of any sense of
humour, or much sense at all.) The signatories of the invitation to William were all noblemen or members of great
noble houses—Sydney was related to the Earls of Leicester,
Russell to the great Bedford clan, Bishop Compton to the
Earls of Northampton. Behind them were Nottingham and
Halifax, in regular correspondence with William, and behind
them even such devoted followers of James as the Duke of
Beaufort, the Earls of Clarendon and Bath, and John, Lord
Churchill. It was the inactivity, as well as the activity, of
such men that decided the issue in 1688, and the Earl of
Bath's failure to hold Cornwall was as important in the
long run as Danby's raising of the north.

On the other hand, William's decision to accept the invitation was little short of mad. True, the *lèse-majesté*, the
parricidal implications of his expedition could be excused by
reference to the doubts concerning the Prince of Wales.
Anne, whose own pregnancies had been an unrelieved disaster,
hated her lovely Italian stepmother with all the viciousness
of her mean spirit. She told Mary of Orange as early as
March—without a shred of evidence—that the queen was
not pregnant at all. After the event they exchanged scabrous
gynaecological chit-chat as only women can, while the circumstances of the delivery encouraged wild rumours that
the new prince was some varlet's brat, smuggled into the
palace in a warming-pan.[2] Only this could have led Mary,

---

[2] Clearly Mary Beatrice conceived early in September 1687, but,
unable to believe her good fortune, she waited until the second
interruption of the menstrual flow before definitely announcing
it. This, and her reluctance to discuss such matters in detail, misled
her English physicians into expecting the delivery in the first week of
July 1688. Hence the confusion on 10 June, and the unfortunate
absence of Anne or any notable Protestant. Even to the charitable it
looked as though Mary Beatrice had been delivered of an eight months'
child, and such a baby's chances of survival in the seventeenth
century were very slim indeed. See Kenyon, " The Birth of the Old
Pretender ", *History Today*, June 1963.

strictly pious and conventional as she was, to countenance her husband's impious and unconventional policy. And because the warming-pan legend has been so thoroughly discredited by posterity, its influence on the credulous majority in 1688 should not be underestimated. To many it was an excuse, to some a complete justification, for all that followed.

But, moral considerations apart, William's task was manifestly hopeless. He could not denude the Netherlands of troops, and he could not raise and equip fresh forces before the end of the campaigning season, in October, when the weather conditions in the Channel would be worsening fast, and the Continental war would be under way, perhaps across the Dutch frontier. As one modern historian has put it : " Only the direst necessity, or complete confidence that no resistance was to be anticipated, could have justified such an enterprise at all."[3] But William could anticipate strong resistance. As his agents warned him, the greater part of the nation was uncommitted and likely to remain so, and while the army and navy were restless and disaffected no one doubted that the first clash with Dutch warships or with William's mercenaries would reanimate them with patriotic hostility. The prince was faced with the prospect of a sanguinary civil war which—assuming that he won it— would only be the prologue to an interminable constitutional debate of the kind to which the loquacious and excitable English were peculiarly addicted. Meanwhile the fate of the Netherlands would hang in the balance of the Continental struggle.

Such arguments naturally convinced James II and Louis XIV that William did not contemplate an invasion of England for dynastic motives. But that does not mean that James lounged away the summer in supine negligence, as some historians would have us believe. As early as May it was clear that if war broke out William would attack the English fleet, perhaps even land an expeditionary force to pin down the English army, and James had taken prompt measures to meet such a threat. He could not increase his

---

[3] Andrew Browning, *English Historical Documents 1660-1714*, p. 19.

army further (and the transfer of troops from Ireland in October did him more harm than good), nor could he look to France. It was an article of faith with James's opponents that he had a secret treaty with France; the overt acceptance of French military aid would have confirmed this, alienated many of his moderate supporters, and given William what he so manifestly lacked—a cast-iron excuse for meddling in his uncle's affairs. So, in June 1688, James refused offers of French naval assistance, and when Louis tried to bring diplomatic pressure to bear at the Hague on his behalf he at once disowned him and recalled his envoy from Paris. When he was finally convinced that William did intend to invade England, all he requested from Louis was a small amount of silver to offset his shortage of ready money. As for Louis, he could not throw troops into England against James's expressed wish, and the only alternative—a direct attack on Holland—was far from attractive. It would weaken his main war effort, it was not likely to be effective in time, and he had not forgotten his harrowing experience in the seventies, when (to his mind) William had held him by the throat while Charles II stabbed him in the back. Moreover, there were no real grounds for pessimism; James had a confidence in his army and navy that was exaggerated, but not wildly so; certainly he seemed quite capable of holding William down until the following spring, when the whole situation could be reviewed. So, in September 1688, Louis launched his armies against the middle Rhine.

William sailed at the end of October, and succeeded in evading the English fleet, which was waiting for him off the Essex coast in the expectation that he would head for Yorkshire. Instead he passed unmolested down the south coast, rejecting any harbour that would make an easy jumping-off place for London, and finally landed at Torbay in Devon on 5 November. He at once issued a proclamation announcing that he had come on the invitation of certain prominent Englishmen, for the purpose of calling a " free " parliament, establishing liberty of conscience and worship for all, safeguarding the rights of the established church, and investigating the " legitimacy " of the Prince of Wales.

He then started slowly, almost lethargically, on the long march to London.

William's course of action, on the face of it so improvident, was dictated by his usual astuteness. It was designed to keep him out of the clutches of the more powerful English politicians as long as possible, and to put the king to the onus of provoking civil war. So he avoided Danby, who had seized York and Hull and raised the north against James, and he landed in the one part of the country which could be trusted not to rise in his favour, harrowed as it had been after Monmouth's rebellion. He advanced deep into England still uncommitted, and such nobility and gentry as came to join him did so of their own volition, and were welcomed not on their terms but on his. (Danby, arriving late to the feast, found that his signal services in the north had merely deprived him of the first two or three courses.)

Moreover, the slow march on London, taking over a month, compelled the royal army to fight, and accept the responsibility for civil war, or retreat before him for more than a hundred miles, a process that sapped its discipline and morale. When it reached Salisbury it began to crumble at the top; after Salisbury it was simply incapable of standing in its tracks and fighting a pitched battle. Meanwhile the whig government of London, and the dissenting mobs, had come to a difficult decision. If William had disembarked his Dutch-Swedish-German-Anglo-Scots army in Kent or Sussex they might well have identified self-interest with nationalist emotion and rallied to the king who had granted them religious toleration; as it was they had more than two weeks to make up their minds, and by the time William reached Salisbury their duty lay clear before them.

Most important—though it is unlikely that William foresaw this—this long retreat sapped what was left of James's nerve. It had already been undermined by his nephew's brazen effrontery in coming to England at all, and in November he had fallen back increasingly on his wife and the priests. As Jeffreys profanely but accurately remarked, "The Virgin Mary is to do all." The very strength of his legal and constitutional position enhanced James's fears for his own safety; he was obsessed not only by his father's fate but that of remoter ancestors. A fortnight before William landed he told the nuncio " that he had read in the history of England of two events applicable to his present case, and he recounted at length the tragic end of two kings . . . , the second Richard and a Henry [VI], who were each despoiled of life and estate by the aggression of their nearest relatives; he added with heat that he feared those at Whitehall more than his foreign enemies ". He ended with the pessimistic assertion " that he would defend the Catholic religion even unto death ".

On a mind in this state the defection of the Anglicans had the worst possible effect. Some indeed, like Feversham, Preston and Dartmouth, justified his faith in their personal loyalty. The rest did not. The blank refusal of Rochester to take the Lord Stewardship was a particularly bitter blow —Rochester, his friend and brother-in-law, who still enjoyed the huge pension granted him on his dismissal in 1687. James joined the army at Salisbury on 20 November sick at heart, and found its morale even lower than his. Had he been called upon to lead it into action no doubt he would have displayed his usual brute courage; but the present emergency called for qualities of a different order, guided by an intellect he did not possess. His mind was made up for him on the 23rd, when Churchill, one of his oldest and most trusted servants, deserted to William. Broken in spirit, he left Salisbury next day and returned to Whitehall, only to find his daughter Anne missing. She had fled the day before with her bosom friend Lady Churchill and joined the rebellious Midlands gentry assembling at Nottingham. Pathetically enough, he was forced back on the counsel of Lord Halifax, the man in England he most disliked.

His isolation heightened his terror of assassination. The refusal of Dartmouth to carry the Prince of Wales to France, though conceived in the king's best interests, finally convinced him that no Protestant was to be trusted, and the Catholics were slipping down to the coasts or seeking their estates. On 10 December the queen fled with her son, making it ever after impossible to clear up the mystery of his birth, and the king followed separately on the 11th. His detention by some fishermen at Faversham in Kent was the last shock that finally unmanned him. The posse of lords that came to bring him back found a dull-eyed, incoherent, broken-down old gentleman, whose link with reality was not over strong.

To William, who had ridden on ahead to Windsor, the king's flight had been a triumph, his return a disaster. James, uncomprehending, thought himself in a cage; all William wanted was for him to fly out of the open door. William was playing for the highest stakes, and he was not above conniving at his uncle's death. But James's death, however accidental in appearance, would make him a martyr in England and would imperil the prince's relations with his wife, whose compliance was essential if he was to gain the throne. He had promised Mary that no harm would come to her father, and he took careful precautions to that end, now and during the Irish campaign of 1690.

But James could not reason this out. He was agreeably surprised when William at once yielded to his request that he be allowed to retire to Rochester. Tactfully enough, no guards were posted at the back of the house, and in the early morning of 23 December he slipped down to the river and was away. He landed at Ambleteuse on Christmas Day, and proceeded to Versailles. The unanimous verdict of the French court was: "When you listen to him you realise why he is here."

CHAPTER VI

WILLIAM III AND MARY II

1689-1702   1689-1694

By his flight James II delivered the leaders of English politics to William, bound hand and foot. Few of those who had invited him over or joined him after his landing had visualised him as more than Regent, Protector or Prince Consort. But the circumstances of James's going left William's mercenaries as the sole restraint on political anarchy and religious enthusiasm. Inevitably he was asked to assume responsibility for the collection of taxes and the administration of justice, and to summon a parliament, or "Convention", which assembled at Westminster in January 1689.

William soon made it clear to the Convention that he would accept the crown or nothing, and those like Danby who had hoped to play his wife off against him merely found that their political flair was better than their judgment of human nature. Outwardly, and from a distance, his relations with Mary were far from being ideally happy. She had miscarried twice in 1678 and was thereafter incapable of bearing the son they so much desired. His customary reserve gave their relationship an air of stiltedness that it retained to the end, while his lack of manners, her unhesitating obedience, gave him the appearance of a domestic tyrant. One day in 1689, for instance, she and her ladies dined with one Mrs. Graden, a London dressmaker of dubious reputation. William remarked publicly "that he heard she dined at a bawdy house, and desired the next time she went he might go too. She said, she had done nothing but what the late queen had done. He asked her, if she meant to make her her example?" "More was said on this occasion", we are told, "than was ever known before, but it was borne with all the submission of a good wife."

Her absolute devotion to him made her refusal of the undivided crown inevitable. She had always assumed that her husband would reign with her after her father's death, and she had been astonished when in 1686 Gilbert Burnet pointed out that this was not necessarily so. She at once sent for William, and " promised him he should always bear rule; and she asked only that he would obey the command of ' Husbands love your wives ', as she should do that, ' Wives, be obedient to your husbands in all things '." He carried out his part of the bargain less punctiliously than she hers, but certainly his one known liaison, with Elizabeth Villiers, was so discreetly conducted as to be almost impenetrable. Her constancy in 1689 left Lords and Commons with no alternative but to offer them the crown jointly, as king and queen regnant, and on 13 February they accepted.

But Mary's terrible apostasy to her father bore heavily on the conscience of a woman truly devout, who had hitherto, as she said, " lived the life of a nun ", and her unnatural predicament was brought home to her the moment she landed in England, on 12 February. Forewarned by William that any show of distress would strengthen his enemies, she displayed a gaiety and lightheartedness that many thought indecorous in the extreme. Even Burnet, her devoted champion, " thought a little more seriousness had done as well, when she came into her father's palace, and was to be set on his throne next day ". She was confirmed in her misery by a letter from James himself, disowning her utterly, and laying a father's curse upon her. Besides this, she had to settle down in a country she had almost forgotten and no longer liked—" The first thing that surprised me at my coming over," she observed later, " was to see so little devotion in a people so lately in such eminent danger." Of her reunion with William she wrote : " He could not restrain [himself, and] as soon as we were alone we both shed tears of joy to meet, and of sorrow for meeting in England, both wishing it might have been in Holland, both bewailing the loss of the liberty we had left behind and sensible we should never enjoy it here; and in that moment we found a beginning of the constraint we were to endure hereafter, for we durst not let ourselves go on with those reflections, but dried up our tears lest it should be perceived when we went out."

And if James's curse did nothing else it sundered his daughters. Anne disliked William personally, and came naturally to resent his intervention in the succession between Mary and herself. On the other hand, since she was not the queen, she could allow her conscience greater play, and display more sympathy towards their father. On her part Mary resented her sister's possession of a promising heir, William, Duke of Gloucester, born in 1689, and she shared her husband's dislike of Anne's favourite Churchill, now Earl of Marlborough, and his domineering wife Sarah. The disgrace of Marlborough in 1692 for treasonable correspondence with the Jacobite court precipitated an open breach between queen and princess; Anne left Whitehall for Sion House, and Mary foolishly and spitefully withdrew the royal guards. They were never reconciled.

The result is evident in Mary's last portrait: she was an old woman in her early thirties. Weighed down by affairs of state during her husband's frequent absences, she breathed into her letters a love that grew stronger still as all other wells of affection were one by one corrupted, poisoned or exhausted. It was, she wrote, " a passion that cannot end but with my life ". William gave her as much attention as he could spare from his life's work, which was wrecking him too, and she did not seriously question his devotion. As she lay dying, " he said during the whole course of their marriage he had never known one single fault in her; there was a worth in her nobody knew but himself ". Her political influence was entirely passive, but none the less important. Her very presence on the throne determined the wavering allegiance of many, like Rochester, Seymour and Nottingham, who must otherwise have left political life. Similarly, her devotion to and interest in the Anglican church tided it over the most difficult period in its career. In general, her sweetness and graciousness served to mask the chilling reserve that made her husband one of the least popular kings in English history.

For "Our Great Deliverer" owes much of his prestige to posterity, and even now, like Byron amongst the poets, his fame is greater in Europe than in England. He was thin, weak and solemn, with a "roman eagle nose", and piercing eyes. His constitution had been undermined by a severe attack of smallpox in early manhood, and his chronic asthma gave him "a constant deep cough". (Unable to bear the London smog, he set up his court at rural Kensington, a decision confirmed by the destruction of Whitehall by fire in 1698.) As a result few men expected him to survive his wife, but there they were grievously mistaken. Every aspect of William's life, his health included, is a demonstration of what tenacity and will-power can make of poor material. In war and politics he was an indifferent commander, but his obstinacy in defence, his courage in attack, his willingness to master accepted techniques, carried him through. There was something in him of his grandfather Charles I, that fountainhead of Stuart failings—his slowness of brain, for instance, and his withdrawn self-sufficiency—but he possessed an intellect strong enough to conquer his personal inclinations, and a sublime fixity of purpose imposed on him by his great inherited responsibility, the defence of the Dutch nation.

He hid his slow brain, his gnawing distrust of men, behind an impassive exterior. He heard his ministers out in chilling silence, chewed over their advice until they had almost forgotten it themselves, then acted, relying only on his powerful memory and his exact judgment of men in politics. All his emotions were carefully schooled, and not least his anger, which was the more terrible for its rarity. Those ministers who felt it, like Sunderland in 1697, were not anxious to feel it again. He could be markedly convivial, of course, and not always with his Dutch friends. (This is the usual Jacobite canard.) In 1697 his Secretary of State made a laconic entry in his diary: "Cabinet in the evening; King had dined at Lord Albemarle's and had drunk hard; Lord

Bradford carried in the [sedan] chair, without the poles, in[to] the entry at Whitehall, dead drunk."[1] But his sense of humour was unpredictable and not always explicable; his drunkenness a dark, moody thing. He was not the man to endear himself to an emotional, extrovert people, and even of his closest advisers few liked him. His gifts automatically exacted respect, and for him that was enough; a lonely childhood had left him with a limited capacity for giving affection or receiving it.

Nor did the atmosphere of England in the nineties do anything to break down his reserve. There were so few men he could really trust—even Sanderson, the captain of his personal yacht, was denounced as a Jacobite agent in 1694. He was well aware that with the exception of Danby and perhaps Nottingham all his closest ministers " looked one way and rowed another "; that if they were not in touch with James II it was because they despaired of his forgiveness. But he knew, like them, that his government might collapse in military defeat any time between 1689 and 1692, that his own death, or Mary's, within the next ten years might be fatal to the Revolution settlement; and he was sufficiently detached to see with their eyes, think with their brains, and rely on their self-interest rather than their loyalty.

But he had no patience with canting timeservers like Sir John Trenchard, and he detested above all soldiers like Marlborough, who had deserted in the face of the enemy and expected his favour as a reward. A reported conversation with Lord Mulgrave defines his attitude, and emphasises his dilemma. He asked Mulgrave what he would have done if one of the conspirators had approached him, a Privy Councillor, in 1688; Mulgrave replied, " I would have told it to the master I then served." " I could not have blamed you," said William. So it is scarcely surprising that he refused to give Marlborough the Garter, nor that he seized the first opportunity to put him away, though on the evidence he was no more deeply implicated with St Germain than a score of others. When Shrewsbury tried to intercede

[1] 22 Apr. 1697, Sir William Trumbull's papers at Easthampstead. By kind permission of the Marquess of Downshire.

for him in 1694 he elicited the chilling reply: "I do not think it for the good of my service to entrust him with the command of my troops." His jealous control of the army, and his preference for Dutch generals like de Solms, who exposed the English regiments to butchery at Steenkirk in 1692, did nothing to enhance his popularity.

In politics he always distrusted the whigs, and particularly those wealthy and electorally potent families headed by the Earls of Bedford, Devonshire and Clare, and their outriders in the Commons, Wharton and Edward Russell. He displayed a tactful deference to the pious Lady Russell, relict of the whig protomartyr, but he left no doubt of his aversion for Shaftesbury and all he stood for; he ignored his son and grandson, and he dashed any hope that he might reverse his bastard cousin's attainder by giving Charles Mordaunt the earldom of Monmouth. With some justice he regarded the whig magnates as proponents of a weak, limited monarchy; his acceptance of the crown from parliament had put him in an ambiguous position from the outset, and he could afford no further concessions. It was this lack of bargaining-power, the absence of room for manœuvre, that caused much of the tension between him and his ministers.

The Englishmen to whom he gave his trust, therefore, had certain characteristics in common. Shrewsbury and Danby had committed themselves openly to his cause in 1687; each of them possessed a group of Commons supporters—Danby's was quite considerable—but they were essentially individual magnates, not united in any such tenuous identity of purpose as linked the whig peers, communing in their elegant cups at Boughton, Welbeck, Chatsworth or Woburn. Similarly, by taking Nottingham and rejecting Rochester he not only broke up the Anglican leadership, he also showed preference for a man who had always opposed James II, yet had withdrawn his allegiance to him only after much genuine heart-searching. For the rest there were Godolphin, Halifax and Sunderland, the professional independents with minimal parliamentary followings and precious few friends. So, after some preliminary shuffling, elbowing and over-turning of chairs, it was Danby, Shrewsbury and Sunderland who emerged as his most trusted English advisers in the nineties, joined later by Somers.

William's advisers had to face many new problems. The imposition of annual sessions of parliament after 1689 made it impossible any longer to ignore the questions that had been central to every constitutional and political dispute of this century : to what extent was it permissible for the king's ministers to control or guide parliament? and, what share, if any, should parliament have in their appointment? The much-trumpeted Bill of Rights, accepted by the new sovereigns with the crown, left all things dark; the hasty compilation of a few days, it had been more concerned to register political *faits accomplis* than point the way to constitutional advance. It had even omitted to provide for the regular renewal of parliament by a Triennial Act.

What William had seen of the English parliament in the seventies and eighties caused him to regard it with some suspicion, as the radical, whiggish, "levelling" element in the constitution. His predecessors had never been anxious to identify themselves with any one parliamentary faction or group, he still less so; if only because he was not protected, like them, by the mystery of Hereditary Succession and Divine Right. So, his first essay in ministry-making produced an uneasy combination of great magnates, representing all factions and opinions : Halifax, Shrewsbury, Nottingham and Danby.[2] Unfortunately the ministers were hopelessly divided by personal jealousies and animosities, while the Convention parliament was dominated by the embittered remnant of the exclusionists, the "old whigs", who were expert in obstructionist tactics and little else. Their long-drawn-out investigation of the iniquities of the last two reigns was cut short by dissolution early in 1690, but not before they had forced Halifax to resign and nearly provoked William to abdication.

The elections of 1690 swamped the "old whigs", but otherwise they brought the king no relief. William's sec-

[2] I propose to ignore Danby's promotion to the marquessate of Carmarthen (1689) and the dukedom of Leeds (1694).

retive handling of war and foreign policy confirmed the great mass of the parliamentary gentry in their dislike of him and his Dutch advisers, and the fortunes of war gave him no answer to their insistent criticism, for each victory was neatly counterbalanced by some new defeat: the battle of the Boyne in 1690, which won back Ireland, by Beachy Head, which gave the French navy preponderance in the Channel; and Russell's victory off La Hogue in 1692, by Louis XIV's capture of Namur. Paralysed by the king's cautious indifference, the ministers largely abandoned the attempt to control parliament, which continued to finance the war for mere motives of self-interest. But the ministers' helplessness did not shield them from the accusation of deliberate corruption, as the sudden demands of world war violently expanded the army, navy and financial administration, multiplying the amount of patronage at the crown's disposal. By 1693 parliament was known as the "Officers'" or "pension" parliament, and alarm mounted with the discovery that there was nothing in the statute book to prevent William retaining it for ever. Opposition, ceasing to be merely destructive, began to agitate for a Triennial Act and a Place Act, to exclude the king's servants from the Commons.

The gentry Opposition was headed by two groups, whig and tory according to the post-1688 meaning of those terms, which distinguished those who welcomed the Revolution as a notable constitutional advance from those who grudgingly accepted it as a sinful and infinitely regrettable necessity. The "new whigs" under Paul Foley and Robert Harley were loosely allied with the Anglican tories, led by Sir Edward Seymour. Dominating the important committees, and the vital commission for auditing the public accounts, they adopted towards government an obstructive, xenophobic policy typical of the "Country" party in the seventies: exposure of court influence on parliament, violent criticism of foreign favourites (with Portland substituted for Portsmouth, Dutch for French), and sporadic demands for the restriction of monarchical power.

Meanwhile Shrewsbury followed Halifax into opposition,

leaving Danby and Nottingham in charge, assisted by that very dubious monarchist, Sidney, Lord Godolphin; Rochester was taken aboard in 1691. This rightward drift of government, reflected in its distribution of patronage, pushed into opposition a group of brilliant junior ministers, ambitious thrusters who had strong connexions with the whig lords: Admiral Edward Russell, Thomas Wharton, Comptroller of the Household, Charles Montague, a junior lord of the Treasury, and the career lawyers, Sir John Trenchard and Solicitor-General Somers. The variegated skills of the Junto[8] gave a new edge to Opposition, and with Shrewsbury's countenance and protection they joined in the agitation for a Triennial Act and the removal of the " prerogative men ".

In fact, it was the most notorious of James II's " prerogative men " who succeeded in imposing a temporary peace. The Earl of Sunderland had fled to Holland at the Revolution, but he returned in 1690, purged of his inconvenient romanism and a convinced supporter of parliamentary government, and two years later he assumed the position of William's informal adviser on English affairs. The king valued him because his loyalty was never seriously in doubt, and in their cold appraisal of men and things, their willingness to forsake principle for expediency, and their impatience with fools, they were not unlike. Sunderland's brazen rudeness also impressed a man who never had much room for flatterers.

Even Sunderland, however, found it difficult to wean the king from his blind trust in the tories: " The king said, he believed the whigs loved him best, but they did not love monarchy, and although the tories did not like him so well as the others, yet as they were zealous for monarchy he thought they would serve his government best; to which the Earl replied, that it was very true that the tories were better friends to monarchy than the whigs were, but then his majesty was to consider that he was not their monarch." William was never convinced by this argument, even in the last years of his reign, but in the spring of 1693 his parlia-

---

[8] Strictly speaking, an anachronistic use of the term, which appears to have come in towards the end of the reign.

mentary position was so weak that he agreed to appoint Sir John Somers Lord Keeper and Trenchard Secretary of State. A year later Russell was appointed First Lord of the Admiralty and Charles Montague, the chief architect of the Bank of England scheme, Chancellor of Exchequer.

These ministerial changes were consolidated by the enlistment of the magnates. Nottingham resigned in the autumn of 1693, and Shrewsbury was persuaded to accept the vacant Secretaryship of State six months later, on condition that a Triennial Act be passed next session. Sunderland bribed the Earl of Mulgrave into supporting the government, and in 1694 William came to terms with the whig lords by simultaneously promoting the earls of Bedford, Devonshire and Clare to dukedoms, with Danby and Shrewsbury. Finally, Sunderland argued that since William was being blamed for the manipulation of " placemen " anyway they might just as well be organised in earnest; and this task was allotted to Trenchard and two other doubtful characters left over from the previous reign : Henry Guy, the secretary of the Treasury, and the Speaker, Sir John Trevor.

As a result of this reorganisation William obtained much larger grants from parliament (though given no more graciously than before), and his prestige survived the disasters that followed in 1693, the costly and indecisive battle of Landen; in 1694, the French attack on the Smyrna Fleet and the abortive Lancashire " Jacobite " trials—a piece of " McCarthyism " provoked by Secretary Trenchard's obsession with " security ". Most important, he survived the queen's death in December 1694 with an ease that no one would have thought possible a year or two before.

Nevertheless, the country gentry as a whole resented being manipulated by Sunderland and his henchmen; the tories were restless at Mary's death; and the Junto were furious because Sunderland and the king forbad them to extend their numbers by the judicious redistribution of crown patronage, now so much more extensive and valuable. As a result early in 1695 Montague and Wharton placed themselves at the head of Opposition in a brisk campaign against corruption in high places. They removed Guy and Trevor, smeared Mulgrave, and impeached Danby for the third time in his career.

The Junto thus broke the government, but they were unable to take its place. The elections of 1695—the first under the Triennial Act—gave the "Country" element, better organised now under Harley, Foley and Seymour, another huge majority, pledged to give William general support in the conduct of the war. The recapture of Namur that summer, coming hard on Russell's successful naval campaign in the western Mediterranean, had strengthened the king's personal position, and he declined to give his countenance either to Shrewsbury and the Junto or to their rivals, the so-called tories, who were now under the general patronage of Sunderland and Godolphin. It seemed that the Jacobite plot to assassinate the king in February 1696 must tip the scales in favour of the Junto, and in the first flush of public alarm Somers pushed through an Act of Association acknowledging William as "rightful and lawful" king, which divided the Opposition. However, the financial crisis of the summer of 1696 brought both sides to heel.

Montague's scheme to remint the debased English coinage, while excellent in its long-term effects, left the King without the ready cash to pay the Flanders army; an appeal to the Opposition Land Bank precipitated its collapse, and recourse had to be had to the Bank of England. But the Junto scarcely had time to gloat before the Fenwick case broke, in October. Sir John Fenwick, arrested for his complicity in the Assassination Plot, turned in a "confession" implicating Shrewsbury, Russell, Marlborough and Godolphin in certain negotiations with St Germain early in the nineties. William had known or suspected all this for years, but he affected complete incredulity. Russell chose to brazen the matter out in parliament, but Shrewsbury, neurotic, introspective and hypochondriac, insisted on remaining in the country. His defection weakened the Junto and let Sunderland in again. Sunderland procured the resignation of Godolphin, the least popular of the accused, and jockeyed parliament into exonerating them all. The inconvenient and tactless Fenwick was convicted by act of attainder (the last example of its use), and executed in January 1697.

Out of the confused events of 1695 and 1696 a pattern was now emerging which would hold good for the rest of the reign. The Commons was dominated by a "Country" majority, profoundly suspicious of Government and by definition non-constructive. They produced few leaders of ministerial calibre, and those they did produce only took office at the risk of forfeiting their support. After Foley's death in 1699 Harley began to break with this crippling tradition, but even he, one of the most able parliamentarians of his generation, dare not accept cabinet office until 1704. The small, well-organised band of Anglican tories had able leaders, but by 1697 William knew better than to fall back on Seymour or Rochester, who patently hated him and were waiting for Anne's accession.

This left the Junto, who had a strong Commons following, led by Charles Montague, and could add debating skill to the government's numerical majority in the Lords.[4] Unfortunately William disliked and distrusted them; he regarded them as a sinister political combination designed to monopolise crown patronage and wrest from him his prerogative of making and unmaking ministries—to "engross" him, as he called it. From 1697 to 1700 he used them as a buffer hetween him and parliament, but he steadfastly denied them any share in his confidence.

Shrewsbury's refusal to stay in London forced him to assemble another "neutral" government round Sunderland, who was appointed Lord Chamberlain in April 1697. With peace in sight, and with it the laying-up of the navy, Orford and Wharton were both firmly penned in the Admiralty, and though he was obliged to make Montague First Lord of the Treasury, patronage remained with Sunderland. In December, when Sir William Trumbull resigned the Secretaryship of State, William ignored Wharton's claim and promoted the non-political Under-Secretary, James Vernon.

---

[4] Wharton succeeded to his father's peerage in 1696 and Russell was made Earl of Orford in 1697. (Trenchard had died in 1695.)

To the Junto Vernon's appointment was the last straw, and it came at a most unfortunate time. The war had ended in the peace of Ryswick, in September 1697, by which Louis XIV recognised William as King of England, and Anne as his successor, and, theoretically at least, withdrew his support from the exiled Stuarts. The king and his advisers expected that this handsome result would make parliament more manageable, but the opposite was the case. When the Commons reassembled in December, with the restraint of the war emergency removed, no one could control them. To William's rage the Junto allowed Sunderland to be driven from office by threat of impeachment, and, worse still, they proved unable or unwilling to prevent the drastic reduction of the army to the tiny establishment of 1680. William was sick unto death of the whole English nation, but particularly the Junto, who according to him had "a natural sourness, that makes them not to be lived with", and were intent only on "carrying on their own interest, . . . to which the concerns of the public must give way". He laid it down that he would only accept a ministry managed for him by Sunderland or Shrewsbury; but the Junto rejected Sunderland absolutely, and Shrewsbury would not come to town. In July 1698 he dissolved parliament and embarked for Holland, leaving his ministers to face the first peace-time elections of his reign without his countenance or support.

William had never concealed his natural preference for his homeland; he was "Stadtholder in England", ran the saying, and "King in Holland". He made a progress through the more important electoral districts of England (and the best hunting lands) in the autumn of 1695, but the experiment was not repeated. The death of the queen, of smallpox on 28 December 1694, inevitably lowered his popularity in the nation at large and soured that grudging acceptance that had been his only portion since 1689. It also inflicted a personal wound that never healed. He told Burnet as she lay dying "that from being the happiest he was now going to be the miserablest creature on earth", and at the end he gave way to a passion that astonished those who thought they knew him; weeping, praying and ejaculating out loud, and falling across her bed in a dead faint. For some weeks after his own life was thought to be in danger, and he did not recover for nearly two months. As soon as he decently could he married off his mistress, Elizabeth Villiers, to one of his regimental commanders and thereafter ignored her. He lived and died with a lock of Mary's hair and her wedding ring next to his heart.

In a lonely widowerhood he was forced back on the friendships of camp and bottle. During the war years a rhythm had been established: he departed for the Flanders front in the spring and returned in the late autumn for a parliamentary session lasting all winter. This practice was continued into the peace, except that his five months' absence each year was staggered, beginning now in July. He spent his time abroad mainly in foreign negotiations, against a background of masculine conviviality at Het Loo in the Netherlands.

But even in the company of his oldest friends he found no peace. He and Hans Willem Bentinck had been wedded in a David-Jonathan relationship even since youth, never apart in council or on the battlefield. Bentinck landed with William in 1688, and was made Earl of Portland and Groom of the Stole in 1689. He continued to follow his master to war, and was badly wounded at Landen in 1693; in England he was the king's agent in the most delicate and confidential political negotiations. But in 1697, feeling himself displaced in the King's affections by the young Arnoud van Keppel, Earl of Albemarle, he resigned his offices and left the court. He rendered invaluable services in the peace negotiations of 1697, and as ambassador to Paris the following year, but he insisted on retiring for good in 1699, despite William's anguish. This celebrated tiff generated an extraordinary amount of emotional heat, and was not made up until William's last illness.

Clearly there was a deep homosexual strain in this relationship, and it is not surprising that Jacobite muckrakers seized upon it and embellished it with the most obscene details.* However, it is highly unlikely that either man saw anything unnatural in it until near the end; still less likely that it had any physical basis. William regarded Portland with the possessive emotion of a man who had few friends, never dare have many, and used him as a substitute for the father he had never known, the mother he could scarcely remember, the son he had never had, the wife he had lost. That he was a man of strong, though firmly suppressed emotions is well enough known.

It is Portland's emotion that calls for explanation; ordinary, unbrilliant, stolid as he was, happily married with children, it is difficult to account for his mulish jealousy. Perhaps he did at last see something in his relationship with William that the king refused to see; his conduct after 1697 might well be that of a man horrified at his own emotions and his friend's, who deliberately withdrew from an intimacy neither could entirely control. As for Albemarle, he was an obvious son-substitute; handsome, merry and dashing, he amused and diverted an aging man whose own generation was aging with him. To speculate further is just possible, but quite pointless —and a trifle unjust, when we consider that Anne's passionate liaisons with her own sex are always assumed to be free of sexual taint.[5]

Meanwhile, from 1697 to 1701 William was almost continuously immersed in diplomatic negotiations of the utmost complexity. The childless Charles II of Spain had been dying for twenty years, but now the event had nearly overtaken a Europe divided and unprepared. There were three possible claimants to the Spanish Empire in Europe and America: Louis XIV, who had delegated his claims to his grandson, Anjou; the Emperor, who had resigned his claims to his younger son, Charles; and the electoral (or " crown ") prince of Bavaria. In October 1698, after long and arduous negotiation, William, Louis and the Dutch signed the first Partition Treaty, dividing the spoils between these three claimants, with the lion's share, including Spain, going to the Bavarian prince. The death of this young boy in January

[5] Except by A. L. Rowse, *The Early Churchills*, pp. 299-300. He is, of course, quite right.

1699 overturned the treaty, and a new one was signed twelve months later dividing the Spanish inheritance between the French and Imperial claimants.

But both treaties were undermined by the omission of the Emperor, who in fact claimed the whole inheritance for his son and would take nothing less, and by William's obvious inability to speak for England. The English ministers had received no warning of the first treaty until the negotiations were over, and Somers put the Great Seal to it with reluctance. The king returned in December to find the Junto seriously weakened in the elections, and he at once had to swallow a further reduction in the army, which deprived him of his Dutch guards. This was the last insult; according to one account he wildly exclaimed, " If I had a son, by God, these guards should not quit me!"; certainly he toyed with the idea of retiring to Holland for good, and was only dissuaded by Somers. After this the Junto began to cave in, under extreme pressure from a strengthened and better-organised Opposition. In May 1699 Orford resigned the Admiralty and Montague the Exchequer. Shrewsbury resigned the Secretaryship, too, and the opportunity was taken to dismiss his fellow absentee, Danby, who since 1695 had been Lord President of a Council he was forbidden to attend.

William still insisted on a government managed by Sunderland or Shrewsbury, and the latter spent most of the summer of 1699 trailing round the spas and country houses of England in an attempt to reunite the Junto. But it was too late, and he was too ill; in the autumn he accepted the Lord Chamberlainship but at once retired to the country. In November Montague resigned from the Treasury. (All these vacancies were filled by nonentities whom it would be tedious to enumerate.) The Commons were now completely divorced from the Lords, under Somers, and scarcely amenable to government leadership at all. Attempts to bring Harley into the ministry failed, and early in 1700 the Opposition demanded the sale of the extensive estates in Ireland granted to William's favourites. A measure to this end was tacked on to the Land Tax bill, provoking a violent squabble between

Lords and Commons and raising London to a pitch of excitement not seen since 1680. In April William requested the Lords to give way, and the bill received his assent. But his next step was to dismiss Somers, leaving himself with only the rags and tatters of a government.

However, this was a turning-point; the king was absolutely obliged to find a new government. After making ineffectual attempts to repair the damage Sunderland retired to the country and refused to come back, while Shrewsbury left for the Continent, where he stayed until 1708. The king was brought to a final decision by the death of Anne's only child, the Duke of Gloucester, in July 1700. Anne was past child-bearing, so the succession after her must be vested in the Electress Sophia of Hanover, the last surviving grandchild of James I, and her eldest son George, and for obvious reasons it would be best if this were done by a strong ministry with an indisputable Commons majority, preferably Anglican tory in complexion. William, typically enough, took four months to reach a decision, but once it was reached he moved fast. Returning in December, he at once sent for Harley and Godolphin and offered them a dissolution. They accepted, and the result of the new elections was a " Country " majority sufficient to support a government led by Godolphin and the moderate tories, with Harley Speaker. Seymour was excluded, and Rochester sent to Ireland.

The parliament of 1701 duly placed the Hanoverian Succession on a statutory basis, but it made the Act of Settlement a gentry charter. It laid down that after Anne's death servants of the crown should not be eligible for election to the Commons, the culmination of the movement to transform the House from an instrument of government into a squirearchal talking-shop. It also neutered the cabinet by decreeing that all policy decisions must be taken in the Privy Council. Such demands were symptomatic of the fact that the gentry were rapidly losing the political influence they had exercised in the first half of the century. Power was passing to the electoral magnates in the Lords, the Somersets, Newcastles and Whartons, if not to the Upper House itself;

but the issue was still uncertain, and the gentry had yet to be reconciled to their diminished status. Thus their restlessness, and the bickering between the two houses, which reached deadlock in 1700 and 1701, and again in 1704 and 1712.

William could ignore changes due to take place long after his death, and he was only mildly annoyed at the provisions of the Act of Settlement which were clearly directed at him (that the Hanoverians should not leave the country without parliament's consent, for instance, or appoint Germans to offices under the crown). What did worry him was the Commons' refusal to take cognisance of a European situation growing daily more menacing. Charles II had died in November 1700, willing his undivided inheritance to the French or the Imperial claimant. Louis XIV had accepted on his grandson's behalf, and William had grudgingly recognised Philip V of Spain. But the Emperor was preparing to contest the will by force, and William and the Dutch were alarmed at France's new preponderance in the Mediterranean and Western Europe. However, instead of rearming as he demanded, the English Commons proceeded to examine those two dead letters the Partition treaties, and used them as an excuse to impeach the Junto lords, Somers, Orford and Montague (now Lord Halifax). Despite the public alarm and exasperation voiced in the Kentish Petition and Defoe's Legion Memorial they threw themselves into a struggle with the Lords that brought the session to a turbulent end in June.

William's position was unenviable, but the Lords had redeemed the honour of parliament by passing a unilateral resolution requesting him to negotiate an alliance with the Dutch and the Emperor. When he left for the Hague in July to implement this request, Marlborough went with him. Since 1695 William had gradually reconciled himself to a man whose abilities in war and diplomacy he had always recognised, and whose favour with Anne must make him the leading personality of her reign. He appointed him Governor to the Duke of Gloucester in 1698 and readmitted him to the Privy Council; henceforward he was always one of the Lords Justices (regents) of the kingdom during his absences abroad. In 1701 he was appointed commander-in-chief of the army and ambassador-extraordinary to the Netherlands.

As soon as the Grand Alliance was signed, in August, William was in search of a new ministry. He had been in touch with Somers during the previous session, and he had corresponded with him since through Sunderland. Somers pledged the Junto not to revive faction squabbles, and in return William promised them his full support. The turning-point came on 5 September, when James II died at St Germain and Louis XIV impulsively recognised his son, " The Old Pretender ", as James III, in flagrant violation of the peace of Ryswick. At the same time he prohibited English imports into France and requested Philip V to do the same for Spain. When William landed in England in November public opinion was behind the Grand Alliance, and he dissolved parliament, accepted Godolphin's resignation, and asked Somers to suggest names for a new ministry. Rochester was dismissed, but Somers and Marlborough's moderating influence prevented a violent swing to the left; similarly, the new parliament that assembled on the last day of the year was not so different in composition from the old, and it re-elected Harley Speaker by two votes. But even Seymour was now in favour of a war that would establish the Protestant Succession, ensure the separation of the French and Spanish crowns, and satisfy the Emperor's " just claims ".

But at this promising moment, the culmination of his life-long struggle against Louis XIV, William was struck down. On 21 February 1702 his horse stumbled on a molehill and threw him. He only broke a collar-bone, but his wasted body could not take the shock, and he died on 8 March. His tremendous responsibilities in the world war just beginning devolved at once on Marlborough.

A perusal of most histories, military or otherwise, leaves one with the impression that William handed on to Marlborough a baton and a parchment treaty, nothing more. Yet this is to deny him the credit he would have valued most. His decisive share in the creation of the eighteenth-century navy, its material, organisation and strategy, has been handsomely acknowledged,[6] but the incense rising in clouds from churchillian altars still obscures the fact that the allied armies Marlborough led to victory were largely William's creation, too—the Dutch regiments entirely. In 1689 he inherited an English army which had an exiguous war experience and few traditions, and whose morale had been shattered by the "campaign" of 1688. In 1690 he led it to Ireland and in 1691 to the Continent, the first monarch since Henry VIII to do so. Lacking all strategic ability and tactical sense, he could not give it victory; but he blooded it and stiffened it on the half-forgotten fields of Landen and Steenkirk, and from the mill of these campaigns he ground out the able, experienced subordinate officers without which the greatest commander is all but helpless. Marlborough's Quartermaster-General, Cadogan, his artillery expert Halcroft Blood, and his best regimental commanders—Cutts, Orkney, Ingoldsby, even his own brother, Charles Churchill—were selected and promoted by William III. Discussing the conduct of Orkney and Abercromby at Blenheim, Trevelyan remarks: "The contrast between Marlborough and Tallard that day is hardly greater than the contrast between the subordinate officers by whom they were respectively served."[7] King William would have desired no finer epitaph.

[6] John Ehrman, *The Navy in the War of William III, its State and Direction* (1953).

[7] G. M. Trevelyan, *England under Queen Anne: Blenheim*, p. 392.

CHAPTER VII

ANNE

1702-1714

Like Victoria, whom she closely resembled, Queen Anne was the quintessence of ordinariness; she also had more than her fair share of small-mindedness, vulgarity and down-right meanness, which she displayed three days after her accession by openly reflecting on her Dutch predecessor in her first Speech from the Throne—" As I know myself to be entirely English," she said, " I can very sincerely assure you there is not anything you can expect or desire from me, which I shall not be ready to do for the happi-ness and prosperity of England."

Despite a superficial reconciliation in 1695, Anne had always hated " Mr. Caliban " for his aversion to her beloved confidante Sarah Churchill and his failure to appreciate the abilities of her husband, Prince George of Denmark. William's blindness is forgivable, and was shared by Charles II and James. George's impenetrable stupidity was confirmed by his inability to express himself idiomatically in the English language after twenty years' residence, and offset only by a vast appetite, an almost unlimited capacity for hard liquor, and the fading reputation, earned before marriage, of a competent if unimaginative soldier. But an intelligent mate, lacking Albert of Saxe-Coburg's tact, could only have been an embarrassment to Anne, whereas George's kindness, devo-tion and absolute faithfulness (so rare when she looked round the rest of her family) converted into lifelong affection the teen-age infatuation with which she had first beheld his fair hair, blue eyes and manly figure back in 1683.

They had grown corpulent and prematurely middle-aged together. Even in youth it needed a skilful portrait painter to give Anne anything of that beauty usual in the daughters and granddaughters of Henrietta Maria. She took after her mother Anne Hyde, plain and predatory like the thrusting gentry stock from which she sprang, and a body never more than graceful had been battered into shapelessness by an unrelenting succession of pregnancies—one a year from 1683 to 1700—and by the dropsical infection that brought them all to frustrating, heart-tearing failure. She had twelve miscarriages; of her six children one was still-born and the other five, like the Duke of Gloucester, died at an early age of hydrocephalus.

A deeply-religious woman, she naturally accepted her tragic fecundity as a visitation from an avenging God, for her parricidal sin was all too evident. Not only had she abandoned her father in his agony, she more than anyone else had convinced Mary that their half-brother was a supposititious child, though her attitude towards him later makes it clear that she was swayed only by mean stupidity and petty-minded jealousy. Her father's anathemas had as great an effect as they possibly could on one of her selfish and unimaginative temperament; her remorse was confirmed by Gloucester's death in 1700; and deepened after her accession by the realisation that she could never right the wrong she had done without prejudicing the religion which was now her only consolation.

This guilt-complex dominated her attitude to politics, and she hated William not only as a man but as a symbol of her cruel dilemma. Her last quarrel with him arose from her desire to go into mourning for James II; yet the rapturous address of welcome she received from her first parliament referred to William as " our great Deliverer from Popery and Slavery ". In the beginning, at least, she automatically distrusted all the men William had trusted, reserving her particular dislike for those who regarded the Revolution as a happy event, or, worse still, divinely-inspired. Her anticipated reaction against the Junto lords was intensified by her horror at the disorder of their private lives and the dubiety of their religious principles, while her approval of the tories was sealed by her close relationship with their leader, her uncle Rochester, and their much-trumpeted devotion to the established church.

The truth is, all her politics hinged on personalities. William III disliked Lord Wharton as a powerful electioneer, an ambitious and able faction leader greedy for power; Anne loathed him because he was a lecher after other men's women, and had once (it was whispered) defecated in a church pulpit. William conquered his intense personal dislike of Marlborough because he recognised his qualities; Anne employed him gladly, but only because chance had married him to her female favourite. It has been suggested[1] that her aversion to the Hanoverians, which caused her to forbid them entry to the country during her lifetime, and so made their succession so much more hazardous than it need have been, arose from the fact that George, then electoral prince, had come to England in 1680 to seek her hand, then backed out. It would have been perfectly in character.

So Anne's accession was the signal for the re-emergence of the irreconcilables, like Normanby, who had refused the Oath of Association in 1696, and Weymouth, who had spent the last reign in retirement at Longleat. They at once entered the ministry, together with Rochester and Nottingham, and Anne took great satisfaction in accepting from Wharton his staff as Comptroller of the Household, which he had retained through all the vicissitudes of William's reign, and handing it in his presence to his worst enemy, Seymour.

But, whatever the faction colour of the moment, Sarah Churchill's overwhelming influence ensured that Marlborough would be the queen's chief executant, in politics, diplomacy and war, and his appointment as captain-general of the allied armies in Flanders was matched by a dukedom and the Garter. And Marlborough made it clear from the beginning that war was too serious a business to be entrusted to party politicians. (He wrote: "We are bound not to wish for anybody's death, but if Sir Edward Seymour should die I am convinced it would be no great loss to the queen nor

[1] A. L. Rowse, *The Early Churchills*, p. 171.

the nation.") He transmitted to Anne William's maxims of government : that the monarch must retain her powers of appointment, and must administer patronage and finance through a non-faction manager. The ideal manager was at hand, in the person of Godolphin, who was at once appointed Lord Treasurer, the first since 1686.[2] Beneath Godolphin was a financial hierarchy allied with faction but largely independent of it : William Lowndes, Secretary to the Treasury, Harley as Speaker, and Harley's friend Henry Boyle as Chancellor of Exchequer. William Blathwayt remained Secretary at War, a post he had held without a break since 1683, and the navy was put under Prince George as Lord High Admiral. It was Marlborough and Godolphin's aim to preserve the independence of this focal centre of government.

Anne bowed to Marlborough's will, but it was not long before she embraced his advice out of conviction. For she found to her dismay that the Anglican tories, grown crazed with age and fruitless opposition, had surrendered the initiative to the radical demagogues amongst them.

The Revolution had split the Church of England wide open; the saintly Sancroft, Archbishop of Canterbury, and some of his most respected suffragans, had refused the oaths to William and Mary and had been deprived of their sees. The existence of these " non-jurors " was a perpetual reproach to the consciences of sensitive Anglicans, and it led at the end of the nineties to a revolt within the church, directed equally against the " moderating " prelates installed by William—like Tenison of Canterbury, Sharp of York and the hated Burnet of Salisbury—and the Dissenters, who had been granted freedom of worship by the Toleration Act of 1689. This so-called " High Church " movement had nothing to do with doctrine or liturgy, nor has it any connexion with the " high " Anglicanism of today; it was essentially a political

---

[2] Godolphin was, and is, often described as a tory, just as Shrewsbury is labelled a whig. Both men were in fact independent magnates, survivors of an era in which party labels were only an embarrassment to an aspiring politician.

phenomenon—a rising of the lower orders in the church against the hierarchy. It dragged in its train a large body of radical gentry, sons and grandsons of the exclusionists, who were disillusioned at the outcome of the Revolution, alarmed at the revival of court and ministerial power typified by the rise of the Junto, and willing to take a tilt with constituted authority in church as well as state.

The leader of the high-flying divines was the factious and power-crazy Francis Atterbury, who began the agitation in 1697 for the sitting of the Convocation of Canterbury, which had only been permitted to meet once since 1664. Rochester and Seymour, sensing his value as a sanctified muck-raker, took him into alliance, in the hope that by diverting public hostility from papists to dissenters they might undermine the Junto's electoral strength. In 1701 they persuaded William III to allow Convocation to resume its sittings coterminously with parliament; with the result that the bishops of the Upper House were at once engaged in a furious conflict with the high-flyers in the Lower House which lasted until George I prorogued them *sine die* in 1717. At the very least, this gave the High Church movement an excellent platform for propaganda, and diverted the bishops from their important voting duties in the House of Lords.

It was only natural that Anne, ignorant and pious, should be deceived by the high-flyers' claim to represent all that was good in the Anglican church. Like them, she loathed dissenters and papists impartially, and of course she had an aversion to most of William's bishops, particularly Burnet, that aggressive champion of the Revolution. But she was only the more disillusioned when she realised that their loyalty was not to a church but a faction, and that the politics of that faction ran clean counter to hers.

For Nottingham and Rochester, with Admiral George Rooke their specialist adviser, were bitterly opposed to Marlborough's concept of the war, and in particular his assumption that the Archduke Charles must be imposed on the reluctant Spaniards as their king and that the main issue would be decided in Flanders. Instead, they and the tories insisted that England should concentrate her resources on a maritime and

colonial war, subsidising other nations to represent her in the
Continental campaigns. This "blue-water" policy was essentially "Country", "gentry" or "little-England" in character,
as opposed to the whiggish, cosmopolitan views imbibed by
Marlborough and the Junto from William, but it was neither
stupid nor irresponsible. After all, it was adopted in its
essentials by Chatham and his son in the later eighteenth
century. But Marlborough's policy was wholeheartedly the
queen's, and she was enough of her father's daughter deeply
to resent criticism of her published decisions. Most of all
she resented the tories' battle cry of "Church in Danger!",
which she took as a personal reflection on her capacity or
sincerity as its Supreme Governor.

Uncle Rochester was the first to feel the weight of her
anger. But his dismissal, in February 1703, merely intensified the faction conflict in parliament. The tories' answer
was to bring forward an Occasional Conformity Bill, designed
to kill the Dissenters' practice of qualifying for office by
taking the Anglican sacrament at long intervals. It was a
measure after Anne's own heart, and she even ordered her
Lutheran husband to vote for it in the Lords; but Marlborough and Godolphin, conscience-less, voted for it too,
leaving the Junto to amend it to rags.

The Junto were squarely behind Marlborough, as William's
political heir, and their decisive influence in the Lords,
supported by court peers like Devonshire, Kent, Somerset and
Newcastle, is a factor often neglected in the study of Anne's
parliaments. It led to a bitter quarrel between the two houses
in 1703, beginning with the tories' revival of the faction
questions of 1701, the partition treaties in particular, and
culminating in the celebrated case of *Ashby v. White,* which
arose from an election dispute in Wharton's borough of
Aylesbury. Industriously fanned by the great man himself,
this controversy was only halted by a prorogation in April
1704. The following month Nottingham resigned the Secretaryship of State and was replaced by Robert Harley, and
the queen dismissed Seymour, who soon afterwards died,
universally unlamented.

Hitherto the government's conduct of the war had been

wide open to attack. Rooke's expedition to Cadiz was a failure, and in 1702 and 1703 Marlborough was paralysed by the caution of the Dutch. But in the spring of 1704 the duke struck camp and marched his allied army, Dutch, English and German, halfway across Europe to Blenheim on the Danube. There he was joined by the Austrians under Prince Eugene, and together they destroyed the Franco-Bavarian army of Germany in one of the most famous of English military victories. As night fell on 13 August Marlborough, still astride his horse, pencilled a note to Sarah on the back of a tavern bill : " I have not time to say more, but to beg you will give my duty to the queen, and let her know her army has had a glorious victory. Monsr. Tallard [the French commander] and two other generals are in my coach and I am following the rest."

Blenheim made it certain that France could not win the war, even if she did not lose it; strengthened the ministers immeasurably in Lords and Commons, and it wedded the queen more indissolubly than ever to her faithful John and Sarah—or " Mr and Mrs Freeman ", as she jovially called them.[8] Parliament met that autumn with the tories in despair, so much so that Rochester and Nottingham took the disastrous step of " tacking " the Occasional Conformity Bill on to the Supply Bill (the convention being that the Lords could not amend a financial measure). The only result was to split their own faction into " tackers " and " sneakers ", the latter having behind them some of the most respected Anglican magnates, notably the old Duke of Leeds (Danby) and his Bertie in-laws, the Earls of Abingdon and Berkshire. The court and the Junto group stood firm, and the tack was removed in the Commons by 251 votes to 134. This split in the tory ranks was never entirely healed, and it drove the more radical faction further to the left. In January 1705 an alliance of " tackers " with backwoods gentry produced another Place Bill, to exclude office-holders from the Commons at once. It was thrown out, but Anne was incensed at this attempt to apply to her a clause in the Act of Settlement

[8] She and the prince were " Mr and Mrs Morley " and Godolphin was " Mr Montgomery ".

designed as a restriction on her German successors and an implied criticism of her Dutch predecessor. In April 1705 she dissolved parliament and made a clean sweep of her tory ministers. With them went Admiral Rooke, his battle honours at Gibraltar and Malaga smeared by a politically-slanted naval enquiry held under the auspices of the Junto peers.

Now that war was a branch of politics, or vice-versa, and the Lords the chief policy-making and investigating body, the tactical skill and debating ability of Somers, Wharton and Halifax was more than ever essential to Godolphin and Marlborough. Moreover, the elections of 1705 confirmed the Junto's followers as the largest single group in the Commons, led by the young Robert Walpole. Yet Anne's aversion to faction in general and whig faction in particular could not be overcome in a day, and she implored Godolphin to keep her out of the hands of " the merciless men of both parties ". Nor was Godolphin himself precisely enamoured of the Junto—he described the queen's aversion to them as " natural, but very inconvenient "—and there was no fear of their abandoning their support for his war policy. So the only whig to achieve cabinet office in 1705 was the moderate William Cowper, as Lord Chancellor.

But the first session of the new parliament was largely taken up by a piece of subtle party manœuvring that demonstrated once again the Junto's versatility and indispensability. Rochester and Nottingham, apparently gambling on Anne's ill-health, proposed that the Electress Sophia be invited over to England—giving the ministers the choice of offending her by refusing or outraging Anne by accepting. But Somers and Wharton caught the missile, adroitly changed hands, and sent it winging back to score a direct hit. Refusing the suggested visit on the grounds that the moment was " inopportune ", they riposted with a Regency Act which laid down a complex but virtually foolproof machinery to ensure the succession of the Hanoverian heir should he or she be abroad when Anne died. It passed in February 1706, and for their services in this emergency the Junto peers were appointed *en bloc* to the commission for negotiating a treaty

S.   G of union with Scotland. But such short-term compromises only had a cumulative effect. The successful conclusion of the union treaty later that year entitled the Junto to still further favours, and without their continued help Godolphin could not hope to push the treaty through the English parliament. In December 1706 agreement was reached; Wharton's pre-eminent claims were acknowledged by the grant of an earldom, but it was his young ally Lord Sunderland who took office.[4] "Driving the nail that would go", the Junto called it, for Sunderland, as Marlborough's son-in-law, had special claims on the queen's favour. He was appointed Secretary of State to the Northern Department to keep a watching brief on foreign policy in general and Hanover in particular while his colleague Robert Harley handled domestic affairs.

But Harley was restless and discontented. "Honest Robin", that bluff, candid, rather beery squire so beloved of the Commons gentry, had travelled far in the last ten years, accumulating new friends, new wealth; his dissenting past was far behind, his Anglican past slipping away. In 1704 he had taken the decisive step of accepting cabinet office. His aims were daring, but not impossible of achievement, given luck. He hoped to use his great influence in the Commons to emancipate himself from the "Country" interest while continuing to guide it, and so succeed to the rôle of the great neutral magnates, like Shrewsbury and the elder Sunderland, Marlborough and Godolphin. (He was very like Robert Walpole, and Walpole's career, staggered ten years, was to show what Harley's might have been.)

The ministry he served was growing less popular daily. The war had been on four years, and its end still could not be forecast. Another great victory by Marlborough, at Ramillies in 1706, brought him to Brussels, but in 1707 the allied armies in Spain were smashed by his nephew, the Duke of Berwick,[5] at Almanza, and with them any hope of

---

[4] The 3rd Earl of Sunderland. His father, the servant of James II and William III, had died in 1702.

[5] The illegitimate son of James II by Marlborough's sister, Arabella Churchill, and one of Louis XIV's most valued marshals.

imposing the Austrian archduke on the Spaniards. The loss of Spain made nonsense of the Allies' war aims, and frustration deepened into general misery as Godolphin's taxation steadily rose, and prices with it. Harley knew that he would have public opinion behind him if he bid for a negotiated peace, or, failing that, the introduction of the "blue water" policy and the severance of England's crippling liaison with the Emperor.

As for the ministry, it still looked strong enough, but it had always been entirely dependent on the queen's favour, and after a twenty-year honeymoon Anne was beginning to tire of her beloved Sarah. Worldly success had not improved the Duchess of Marlborough; her forthrightness had grown strident, her energy vulgar; and qualities that had stimulated an active, discontented young princess only jarred on an ailing, prematurely-aged queen. Her management of Anne had become downright bullying, though neither was quick to realise it, and by 1707 the queen had begun to turn, quite naturally, to her woman of the bedchamber, Harley's cousin Abigail Masham, who was quiet, cool, self-effacing and a good listener. Anne's violent dislike of Sarah's son-in-law tipped the balance against her. Sunderland had inherited all his father's excitability and bad temper with none of his charm for women, his intelligence but not his cynical commonsense. His fault was not that he under-estimated Anne, but that he allowed her to see it. His bad manners complemented his mother-in-law's bad temper, while his doctrinaire whiggism reminded Anne too sharply and too often of the Marlboroughs' influence on her conduct in 1688.

Marlborough and Godolphin, aware of Harley's intrigues, demanded his dismissal on 30 January 1708. On the queen's refusal they at once resigned, and she asked Harley to form a ministry. He tried, but as Godolphin had calculated, he could not win over the great court peers like Dorset, Somerset, Devonshire and Newcastle; that handful of wealthy but otherwise unremarkable men who formed the ballast in every administration between the Revolution and the Reform Act. Within a day or two the Treasurer and the Captain-General

were back. Harley was swept away, and with him his friend
Henry St John, who had succeeded Blathwayt as Secretary at
War in 1704. Walpole took St John's place, but Godolphin
was canny enough to go to the country before concluding the
inevitable alliance with the Junto. The advent of the Scots
Members to the first parliament of Great Britain the previous year had strengthened the whigs, but in the elections of
1708 they barely held their own, the mounting unpopularity
of the war being luckily offset by the Old Pretender, who
chose this moment to launch an abortive invasion of Scotland.
The death of Prince George in November not only destroyed
the queen's powers of resistance but conveniently made room
for the Junto leaders. The Earl of Pembroke was shuffled
into George's place as Lord High Admiral, and his offices
of Lord President of the Council and Lord Lieutenant in
Ireland allotted to Somers and Wharton respectively.

Somers's suavity and perfect manners soon won him Anne's
rather fickle regard, but nothing could reconcile her to
Sunderland, and the whole ministry rested on the uneasy
foundation of the Duchess of Marlborough's influence, still
being steadily undermined by Mrs Masham, and its majority
in the Commons, which was good enough for the present
but could not survive the next election unless the war took
a decisive turn for the better. Anne's comparative indifference
to Godolphin was sharpened to active dislike by his ill-
advised interference with episcopal appointments in 1708.
His intervention was inspired merely by political motives,
and resented accordingly; worse still, he aimed to promote
Bishop Trelawney of Exeter, the head of the great Cornish
electioneering family, and, other defects apart, a noted defender of the Glorious Revolution. Prince George's death
forced Anne to compromise, but it did not bring her to
complete surrender; Trelawney had to wait, and in the general
post Sunderland's old chaplain and friend, Charles Trimnell,
went to the see of Norwich—yet another count against the
young earl.

Harley was only waiting his opportunity to try again, and
this time he would succeed. For the Duke of Shrewsbury
had returned from abroad at last and, spurned by his whig

friends, had offered his services to the queen. His adhesion
to a new ministry would bring over the other court peers
who had failed Harley in 1708.

As for the ministry's strength in the Commons, that reflected the unnatural and unrepeatable conditions of 1708.
With every month of war the ministers' public credit
dwindled, and by 1709 even Godolphin was finding it
difficult to extract £13 million a year from an exhausted
country. It was clearly impossible to eject the Bourbons from
Spain, yet Marlborough and the Junto felt unable to go
back on their undertakings to the Emperor, the Grand
Alliance that had been William's last bequest—nor could
they do so without admitting that the greater part of England's
crippling war expenditure to date had been wasted. Louis
XIV refused to join them in driving his grandson out of
Spain as the price of peace, and " the last army of France "
foiled Marlborough's desperate bid to reach Paris in 1709
or at least secure a victory which would restore the ministry's
credit. The bloodbath of Malplaquet, where the allies lost
17,000 men to the French 11,000, was not that kind of
victory. In October Townshend pressed whig policy to a
logical conclusion when he negotiated the Barrier Treaty,
which kept the Dutch in the war at the cost of staggering
trade concessions in the Mediterranean, the Indies and
America.

War weariness was now finding violent expression in the
propaganda of faction, which reached its climax in this
reign. Over 8,000 political pamphlets alone—not counting
books or broadsides—were published in the years 1701-14;
and if the Junto could command Addison and Steele, Harley
had Defoe. All the hate and blood lust spawned by the
civil war *manqué* of 1688 and 1689, the terrible division
of allegiance between Jacobites and Williamites in the nineties,
the almost continuous fear of treason, assassination and rebellion, plus two dragging, lacerating wars in twenty years,
had poisoned men's minds and pens. Always a brilliant,
violent, unstable, voluble race, the English were lashed to
a foaming hysteria now; and so insatiable was the demand
for the mimic bloodshed of satire and polemic that playing

cards, ladies' fans, even printed handkerchiefs and napkins
were pressed into service to justify the Glorious Revolution,
damn Dutch William, revile the Pretender, or applaud the
party champions in the field, Marlborough, Peterborough,
Galway and Rooke. By the end of 1709 the mixture had
reached flashpoint; Henry Sacheverell, D.D., was the spark
that ignited it and blew up the ministry.

Sacheverell was one of the most notorious of the high-flying
clergy, and the chief public exponent of the doctrine that
the Revolution had involved the nation in the sin of resistance
to the Lord's anointed—so much so that even his allies could
not explain how he had swallowed the oaths of allegiance.
His handsome face, well-hung figure and rich, flowing utter-
ance made him the leader of those clergymen whose *métier*
(according to the whigs) lay in " working upon the ductile and
pliant fancies of the women, and watching all the unguarded
minutes, when the vapours were at the height, and the spirits
were under the most violent confusion ". This was the
fly that Godolphin and the Junto decided to squash with
the weighty instrument of impeachment.

On 5 November 1709 the Lord Mayor and Aldermen of
London, dabbling as usual with the most radical movement of
the day—exclusion in 1680, popery in 1688, and now toryism—chose Sacheverell to preach before them the annual
sermon commemorating the failure of Gunpowder Plot and the
success of William III's landing at Torbay. In a wild dis-
course, subsequently printed in large editions, he poured
scorn upon the Dissenters, denounced the Toleration Act,
characterised the bishops and the ministers as " false brethren "
in church and state, and declared that the Revolution had
" nothing of resistance in it ". Godolphin, a sincere Anglican,
was more resentful of attacks from his own clergy than
the Junto, and less accustomed to them. However, when he
proposed Sacheverell's impeachment they at once seized upon
the opportunity to justify the principles behind the Revolution, clear William's name, and embody in political terms
the theories of John Locke concerning the Original Contract

between king and people; and the majestic prologue to the charge read like a whig *credo*: "Whereas his late Majesty King William the Third, then Prince of Orange, did with an armed force undertake a glorious enterprise for delivering this kingdom from popery and arbitrary power; and divers subjects of this realm, well affected to their country, joined with him and assisted his late Majesty in the said enterprise; and, it having pleased Almighty God to crown the same with success, the late happy Revolution did take effect, and was established . . . , the happy and blessed consequences of the said Revolution are, the enjoyment of the light of God's true religion established amongst us, and of the laws and liberties of the kingdom, the uniting of her Majesty's Protestant subjects in interest and affection, . . . the preservation of her Majesty's sacred person, the many and continual benefits arising from her Majesty's wise and glorious administration, and the prospect of happiness for future ages by the settlement of the crown in the Protestant line."

But in the course of the trial the whig managers went much further than this. They swept aside the convenient fiction that James II had abdicated, and insisted instead that he had been deposed for breaking the implied contract between him and his people. Wharton even rejected the soothing belief that the Old Pretender was not James's son. But the substitution of a "contractual" fiction for a "non-resistance" myth was not popular, especially since it removed the last pretence of hereditary Divine Right and made the crown quasi-elective. Understandably, Anne showed by words and deeds that her sympathies did not lie with her ministers, and even the moderate whigs were alarmed. The two archbishops cannily absented themselves, and of the thirteen bishops present six voted for Sacheverell. Hooper of Bath and Wells voiced the queen's feelings when he said that, "The Revolution was not to be boasted of, to make a precedent, but we ought to throw a mantle over it, and rather call it a Vacancy or Abdication; and the Original Compact were two very dangerous words, not to be mentioned without a great deal of caution; that they who examined the Revolution too nicely [i.e., closely] were no friends to it, for at that rate the crown would roll like a ball, and never be fixed."

The mob, meanwhile, were unconcerned with such high matters; the passions, intellectual and political, that divided the electorate and the court communicated themselves to the London poor as a violent anti-clericalism, engendered as in 1641 and 1679 by economic hardship. This time their rage was directed against dissenters, not papists, and on the night of 1 March, when the mobs seized control, the Nonconformist meeting-houses went up in flames all over London; and the Bank of England, the citadel of whiggish capitalism, was saved only by a gamble that left St James's Palace denuded of troops. The Sacheverell Riots might be expected to sway the Lords against him, and in any case a verdict of guilty was the only one possible on the evidence; the ministry's weakness was revealed by the large minority in the Doctor's favour—52 against 69—and the mildness of his sentence. His sermon was burned by the common hangman (a meaningless ceremony), and he was forbidden to preach for three years. His journey through Oxford and Worcester to take up a rich living offered him in north Wales was a triumphal progress.

A majority of the electorate was now clearly in favour of "Sacheverell and Peace", and an election held on this rallying cry would certainly produce a majority against the ministry. More important, the Duke of Somerset and the Duke of Argyll had come out against the Junto. Harley and Shrewsbury now advised Anne to dismantle the ministry piecemeal, isolating and weakening the survivors without driving them to the joint resignation that had defeated her in 1708.

The breach between Anne and Sarah was now final. The duchess insisted on a last meeting, on 6 April 1710, but she lost her head completely, and to her hectoring, self-pitying tirade the queen could only reply, again and again, "You may put it in writing", or, "You desired no answer and you shall have none." Sarah retired in hysterics and never saw her mistress again, but she was not dismissed her

office of Mistress of the Robes until the following January,
1711.

The first blow against the ministry, in April 1710,
was apparently innocuous enough. Whatever their suspicions,
the ministers could not easily object when Anne suddenly
requested her Lord Chamberlain, the Marquess of Kent,
to resign (with a dukedom in recompense) and gave his
office to Shrewsbury. Nor did they feel disposed to rally
round Sunderland, who fell exactly two months later, on
14 June. Not content with making himself odious to the queen,
he had quarrelled with his father-in-law and all his chief
colleagues, and their alarm at his sudden replacement by the
tory Dartmouth was tempered by relief. Once Sunderland was
gone, however, the rest was easy. Another two months, then
Godolphin went, on 8 August, and all Somers could think
of was saving his own skin. But he went with the rest—
Walpole, Cowper and Wharton—before the end of the
year.

Anne showed the worst side of her character in the dismissal of her two greatest servants, who between them gave
her reign such glory as it possesses. She declined to give
Godolphin an audience, nor did she send him any message
of good will or gratitude or even conventional regret—just
a verbal order to break his white staff and leave the premises.
She was a Stuart through and through. When she dismissed
the greatest captain of the age, at the end of 1711, her
letter was so offensive that Marlborough tossed it on the fire
and never mentioned it again.

On the other hand, she had no intention of allying with
Marlborough and Godolphin's enemies. Her antipathy to
the high-flyers was lasting, and was reflected in her ecclesiastical appointments to the end of the reign. Most of them
were recommended by those two terrible old archbishops,
Tenison and Sharp; appointed in the early nineties, one
of them outlived the queen, the other did not die until
1714. She declined to give Jonathan Swift a bishopric,
or Sacheverell even a deanery, and she only sent Atterbury
to Rochester on the repeated importunity of Lord Chancellor
Harcourt, in whose integrity she trusted.

A similar attitude informed her political appointments:
as Godolphin and Marlborough had managed her business
with the assistance of the whigs, so Harley and Shrewsbury
would manage it with the assistance of the tories. Harley
told Newcastle: "The queen is assured you will approve
her proceedings, which are directed to the sole aim of making
an honourable and safe peace, securing her allies, preserving
the liberty and property of the subject, and the indulgence
to Dissenters in particular, and to perpetuate this by really
securing the succession of the House of Hanover." He did
his best to enrol Lord Cowper's support, too, pleading that
" a whig game is intended at bottom ".

But the decision of the remaining whigs to resign rather
than support the peace left Harley naked to the storm he
had done so much to raise. The elections of 1710, held in an
atmosphere of febrile excitement reminiscent of the Popish
Plot, produced, as in 1679, a House of Commons dominated
by backwoods country gentry, jealous of the court, jealous
of the whig magnates, and determined to castrate parliament
as an instrument of administration and restore it to the
limited rôle of High Court or Grand Legislature. They
took their religious affiliations, their faction colour, not from
Harley but from the violently ambitious St John, now
Secretary of State, who placed himself at the head of the
tory high-flyers in the October Club, who at once demanded a
clean sweep of the Junto's nominees in the Treasury, Customs
and Excise administration.

This is what Harley most feared. In 1705, as he slid
gingerly over into a more independent political position,
he had written: "If the gentlemen of England are made
sensible that the queen is the head, and not a party, everything will be easy. The embodying of gentlemen (country
gentlemen, I mean) against the queen's service is what is to
be avoided." But the defection of the Junto, Shrewsbury's
accustomed idleness and ineffectiveness, the growing aversion
of whiggish peers like Somerset, left him to fight a rear-
guard action alone. In May 1711 an attempt on his life by
a French spy swung parliamentary opinion momentarily

in his favour, and Anne took the opportunity to make him
Lord Treasurer and Earl of Oxford. Through the next two
years he steadily defended crown patronage against the en-
croachment of a faction-crazed House of Commons, and in
the face of an unsympathetic House of Lords struggled to
preserve the moderate policy to which he stood committed,
and make peace. His art collections, his mansions, his patronage of literature, proclaimed tastes worthy of the *grands
seigneurs* he emulated. But the overwhelming burden of
office slowly wore him down—or seemed to. He drank more
and more, grew stouter and stouter, more and more evasive;
but Anne's tolerance of his almost continuous drunkenness
suggests that it was, in part at least, a pose. Behind the obese,
mumbling, lethargic bulk of the Earl of Oxford lurked
cunning, weasel-toothed, sharp-sighted Robert Harley, watching
patiently, taking his decisions suddenly, incisively and craftily.

The embattled gentry could not wait to implement their
charter. They started in 1710 with an abortive Place Bill,
which St John opposed. But he supported the Landed
Property Qualification Bill, designed to exclude from parliament landless " carpet-baggers " and the sons of peers,
and he voiced all the atavistic terror of the average squireen
when he declared that without this bill " we might see a time
when the moneyed men might bid fair to keep out of the
House all the landed men ". The older generation of politicians was dying off: Rochester in 1711, Leeds and Godolphin
in 1712. Harley made approaches to the Junto, but the issue
of the Peace came between them, and they suspected his
soundness on the Succession. So did the Earl of Nottingham,
the surviving elder statesman of toryism, who held off from
the ministry in 1710 and the following year made his peace
with the Junto. Cynically abandoning their much-advertised
principles of toleration, they agreed to push his Occasional
Conformity bill if he would oppose the Peace of Utrecht.
So the Occasional Conformity Act passed into law, and the
peace treaty was about to fail in the Lords when Anne, on
Harley's advice, created twelve new peers and secured a bare

majority. In the Commons open war broke out, and Walpole was sent to the Tower on charges of corruption; Marlborough, faced with similar accusations, went abroad.

At this stage St John's services as the leader of the Commons and as chief negotiator of the peace called for some signal reward. But Anne was alienated by the faction violence of his supporters and his notorious sexual profligacy. In July 1712 she refused him the earldom he had a right to expect, and created him Viscount Bolingbroke instead. He blamed Harley for this reverse, and henceforward the enmity between the two men was undisguised.

The elections of 1713, on the issue of the peace, returned a House of Commons substantially as before, and confirmed the authority of Bolingbroke's henchmen, Wyndham and Bromley. In August Bromley was made Secretary of State and Wyndham Chancellor of Exchequer, against Harley's wishes. But the queen's serious illness that Christmas underlined the fact that she had not long to live; her constitution was undermined by dropsy, and her heart was failing under the burden of her swelling body. The free-thinker Bolingbroke hung over her bed, praying, "God in his mercy to these kingdoms preserve her."

The queen's attitude to the succession was Harley's. Neither loved the Hanoverians, and it was clear that the accession of a German king would not be popular in the country at large; if James III would only turn Protestant, then a parliament could soon be found to repeal the Regency Act and amend the Act of Settlement, and Anne would willingly have eased her conscience at the last by helping her half-brother to the throne. As for the tories and their squirearchal allies, whether they realised it or not they were a faction in revolt against the established order; desiring a weak king with a weak title, they turned to James the Old Pretender as the exclusionist leaders had turned to James, Duke of Monmouth. But, like the exclusionists, the high-flyers could never force a tainted candidate on the bulk of their followers: a bastard would not do in 1680, nor would a papist in 1714.

The Peace of Utrecht gave Harley and Bolingbroke every

motive for Jacobitism, for the Elector of Hanover regarded
the treaty as a flagrant betrayal of the Emperor and the
German princes. Their iniquity in his eyes was only confirmed by Bolingbroke's restraining orders to the British
Army in 1712, forbidding it to advance with the Elector
and the Dutch against the last French positions barring the
road to Paris and a dictated peace. Already he was in touch
with the Junto lords, and what faint hopes Bolingbroke might
have had of some accommodation with the dowager Electress
were blasted by her death in April 1714; the first act of
the future King George I was to revise the secret list of
regents who would assume control at Anne's death so as to
give the Junto and their allies a decisive majority.

But if it was impossible for Harley and Bolingbroke to
make their peace with Hanover, it was not much easier to
reach a sensible accommodation with St Germain. The son
of James II and Mary of Modena would scarcely think London
worth the Anglican sacrament, and he made the great refusal
early in 1714. With this went the last hope of forming
a strong parliamentary Jacobite party, and the ministry drifted,
the tiller loose in Harley's hands, while the saner of the
tories—the " Whimsicals ", or Hanoverians—filtered through
into Nottingham's camp. Their leader, Sir Thomas Hanmer,
was elected Speaker in the new parliament, but his official
status did not prevent him leading his followers into the
Opposition lobbies in April 1714 on the motion that the
Protestant succession was not secure under the present
ministers. In the Lords the same motion only failed by twelve
votes—the exact number, it was noted, that Anne had created
to pass the tory Peace. The death of the Archbishop of York
was another test of Bolingbroke's influence at court, and
again he failed. The last kick of faction was the Schism
Act, passed in June 1714; it made illegal those dissenting
academies one of which had educated the young Robert
Harley. On 8 July parliament was prorogued and the crisis
was re-focused on the queen, slowly dying at Kensington.

Harley's passivity, drunkenness and inattention to business
were at last growing too much for Anne, and Bolingbroke

had secured the invaluable aid of Lady Masham. His only hope was that as the queen's physical powers declined so might her Protestant scruples weaken, until she was ready to salve her conscience at death by making some decisive gesture in the Pretender's favour. The symbolic approval of an anointed queen, the Supreme Governor of the Anglican church (to which all rational men knew she was unswervingly loyal), might just work the miracle; for the next ten years were to show that if the country was not Jacobite it was certainly not Hanoverian, and while the Stuarts were the devil men knew the Guelphs were an unknown quantity. The Elector's Lutheranism made the archpriests of Anglicanism tremble, while his fierce opposition to the Peace of Utrecht, his deep involvement in German and Scandinavian politics, worried more perceptive men.

But in this final crisis Anne was true to the nation's interests, and the monarchy's. On 27 July she gave way and dismissed Harley, but she declined to appoint Bolingbroke to his place. As Secretary of State Bolingbroke could not act with that authority, that command of patronage, which possession of the Treasury would have given him; and behind his shoulder now was the enigmatic Duke of Shrewsbury, who had been watching the events of the past year from the secure vantage point of Dublin Castle.

That last desperate scene in the council chamber on the 27th, when Harley and Bolingbroke had leaped to their feet and hurled insults and accusations at each other across her semi-recumbent body, had been the final blow to Anne's health. On the morning of the 30th she was so clearly sinking that a meeting of the Privy Council was summoned to Kensington. The whig lords who were still technically Privy Councillors—Somers, Cowper and Sunderland—were canny enough to stay away, but they had come to an understanding with the Dukes of Argyll and Somerset, and Shrewsbury's line of conduct was not in doubt. Lord Dartmouth was also a staunch Hanoverian, and so was the Lord Privy Seal, Bishop Robinson of London. The authority of these men carried the day against the majority of the Council. Unstrung by the imminence of the queen's death, and fearing the

return of a vengeful Harley more than anything, Bolingbroke and his followers agreed to recommend Shrewsbury's
appointment as Lord Treasurer. Bolingbroke himself led
the deputation into the bedchamber, and the white staff
was brought in to the queen, who at once handed it to
Shrewsbury. Under his leadership they spent the rest of
that day and all the next issuing a stream of orders that
secured the country against a Jacobite invasion or *coup d'état*.
They were soon joined by Harley and the whig peers, and
the Elector was summoned from Hanover.

They had almost forgotten their titular mistress. Lying
widowed and friendless in the great sweltering bed at Kensington, without son, daughter, brother or sister, the last
crowned and anointed monarch of the Stuart race inched her
way across the frontier into death. There was no last
reconciliation with Sarah, as between William and Portland,
and even Abigail Masham had gone.

Her death, at half past seven on the morning of 1 August,
was an anticlimax. The council, hastily reconvened, proclaimed the new king almost absentmindedly, then turned
to the secret list that would tell them who had won the
draw for the council of regency. That same morning, long
before the news reached Oxford, the "trimming" President
of St John's ordered King George to be prayed for in the
college chapel. The horrified Fellows pointed out that the
queen was not yet dead. "Dead!" he replied, "she is as
dead as Julius Caesar."[6]

6 W. R. Ward, *Georgian Oxford*, pp. 50-51.

SUGGESTIONS FOR FURTHER READING[1]

The seventeenth century is covered by two workmanlike volumes in the Oxford History of England: *The Early Stuarts 1603-1660*, by Godfrey Davies (2nd ed., 1959), and *The Later Stuarts 1660-1714*, by Sir George Clark (2nd ed., 1955). The best one-volume account is Christopher Hill's *Century of Revolution 1603-1714* (1961), though it is not for the beginner. Charles Wilson deals with the economic history of the period in *England's Apprenticeship 1603-1763* (1965).

Contemporaneous events in Europe are recounted by David Ogg, in *Europe in the Seventeenth Century* (rev. ed., 1954). Sir George Clark's *The Seventeenth Century* (2nd ed., 1945) is a book quite on its own, a brilliant comparative study of institutions, administration and ideas. *The Crisis in Europe 1560-1660*, ed. Trevor Aston (1965) is a collection of stimulating essays, many of which are directly applicable to English history.

D. H. Willson's *King James VI and I* (1956) superseded all previous biographies, and nothing has appeared to match it since; it is consistently interesting, though a trifle old-fashioned in its treatment of constitutional and economic issues. It contains a good short sketch of James's career in Scotland. In many ways the most perceptive observer of court and government between 1603 and 1642 is David Mathew, and his *Jacobean Age* (1938), *Age of Charles I* (1951) and *Social Structure in Caroline England* (1948) are all recommended. *The King's Servants* (1961) is an exact and detailed study of the court and the royal household on the eve of the Great Rebellion, by G. E. Aylmer. However, the only full portrait of Charles I is that of Samuel Rawson Gardiner, in the relevant volumes of his great *History of England 1603-1642* (10v., 1883-4), and its sequel, *The History*

---

[1] Unless otherwise stated all the books mentioned are or were published in Great Britain.

of the Great Civil War 1642-1649 (4v. 1893). Gardiner is the starting point for any serious study of this period; C. V. Wedgwood has embarked on a new history of the Great Rebellion, but if her intention was to displace Gardiner she has not yet succeeded. Two volumes of Miss Wedgwood's history have so far appeared, *The King's Peace 1637-1641* (1955) and *The King's War 1641-47* (1958), plus an additional volume, not part of the series, on *The Trial of Charles I* (1964).

Clarendon's *History of the Rebellion* enshrines the classic contemporary view, and for those who cannot face the six volumes of the standard edition (ed. W. D. Macray, 1888) there is an admirable anthology in the World's Classics series, *Selections from Clarendon*, by G. Huehns (1955). Two of Charles I's leading ministers have been well served by biographers: see *Strafford: a Revaluation*, by C. V. Wedgwood (1961), and *Archbishop Laud*, by H. R. Trevor-Roper (2nd ed., 1962). M. A. Gibb's *Buckingham* (1935) is also worth a mention. Carola Oman's *Henrietta Maria* (1936) is that rarity, a good biography of a queen consort.

The fortunes of Charles II in exile are recounted by Hester Chapman in *The Tragedy of Charles II* (1964); for his reign proper David Ogg's *England in the reign of Charles II* (2nd ed., 1955) is essential. Sir Arthur Bryant's *King Charles II* (2nd ed., 1955) is the best biography, though this is faint praise; it is very readable and packed with information, but it is essentially a piece of special pleading. Lord Halifax's "Character of King Charles II", a masterpiece of wit and fine observation, can be found in his *Complete Works*, ed. J. P. Kenyon (Pelican 1969). The complete contemporary account, extending to 1714, is Gilbert Burnet's *History of My Own Time*, a book which posterity has been inclined to underrate. This is perhaps why there is no good modern edition, and why the useful Everyman abridgement is out of print.

Charles II's private life has been treated in a multitude of books, most of them ineffably dreary. Honourable exceptions are *The Vagabond Duchess* [of Mazarin], by Cyril Hughes Hartmann (1926), and *Nell Gwynne*, by Arthur

Irwin Dasent (1924). For court life in the sixties Samuel Pepys's *Diary*, the racy and amusing *Memoirs of Count Grammont*, by Anthony Hamilton, and Rochester's *Poems* are invaluable. The standard edition of Pepys is by H. B. Wheatley (10v., 1893-9, 8v., 1904), and of Rochester by V. de Sola Pinto (Muses' Library, 1953). Pinto's biographical study of *Rochester* (2nd ed., 1962) is useful, as is John H. Wilson's *Court Wits of the Restoration* (Princeton, 1948). George de Forest Lord is editing for Yale University Press a collection of political verse for the period, under the title *Poems on Affairs of State.* Four volumes have so far been published, up to 1688, and it should be mentioned here, though it is probably not easily or generally available.

I should also mention here the volumes of royal letters originally commissioned by Cassell in the 1930s and recently (1968) republished. The series includes volumes on *Charles I, Charles II* and *Queen Anne*, edited by Sir Charles Petrie, Sir Arthur Bryant and Beatrice Curtis Brown respectively. They make agreeable and instructive bedtime reading, and that on Charles I is particularly valuable.

F. C. Turner's *James II* (1949) is one of the best biographies of any Stuart sovereign, dispassionate without being dull. David Ogg's *England in the reigns of James II and William III* (1955) is sound and perceptive, and written to his usual high standards, though it could with advantage have been longer. Macaulay's *History of England* retains its interest and a great deal of its value, despite its pronounced Whig bias. The edition by Sir Charles Firth (6v., 1913-15) contains a wonderful collection of prints and drawings, but for ordinary reading purposes the Everyman edition is as good as anything. Firth also published a searching *Commentary on Macaulay's History* (new ed., 1964).

The task of amending Macaulay has been continued by Lucille Pinkham, in *William III and the Respectable Revolution* (Harvard 1954), by Maurice Ashley, in *The Glorious Revolution of 1688* (1966), and by John Carswell, *The Descent on England* (1969); but they are all consciously biassed towards the European aspects of the Revolution, and none of them pretend to be that full-scale study which is now very much needed. The definitive biography of William III is by Stephen B. Baxter (1966). There is no good biography of Anne, but G. M. Trevelyan has given us a colourful and essentially sound history of her reign, *England under Queen Anne*, in three volumes, *Blenheim* (1930), *Ramillies and the Union with Scotland* (1932), and *The Peace and the Protestant Succession* (1934).[2] Geoffrey Holmes has now edited an extremely interesting and valuable collection of essays by leading scholars on various aspects of William and Anne's reigns in *Britain after the Glorious Revolution* (1969).

The later seventeenth century is not rich in political biographies, but Louise Fargo Brown's *Shaftesbury* (New York, 1933), Andrew Browning's *Danby* (1951), J. P. Kenyon's *Sunderland* (1958), and the first volume of J. H. Plumb's *Sir Robert Walpole* (1956), should all be noted, and there is a good sketch of Wharton in *The Old Cause*, by John Carswell (1954). K. H. D. Haley's new life of *Shaftesbury* (1968) is particularly valuable, and Maurice Lee's *The Cabal* (Urbana 1965) is a successful essay in the difficult art of collective biography. G. W. Keeton's life of *Lord Chancellor Jeffreys* (1965) is clumsy and repetitive, but it contains a great deal of information, and there is not much else on the Stuart judiciary. Sir Winston Churchill's *Marlborough* (4v., 1933-8, re-issued in two, 1947) is a historical monument rather than a biography; but again, it contains much information, and those who enjoy Churchill's rhetorical prose will read it with pleasure and profit.

Wallace Notestein's *English People on the Eve of Colonisation* (1954) is a rather 'folksy' description of English society under James I. Much better analyses of the same society at the end of the century are provided by J. H. Plumb, in *Walpole*, and by David Ogg in his *James II and William III*. *The World we Have Lost*, by Peter Laslett (1965), is an attempt at a sociological picture of seventeenth-century society. This should be set against Trevelyan's more conventional *English Social History* (1944).[3] The great controversy

2 Available in the Fontana series.

3 The four volume edition, with many illustrations, is now available cheaply in the Pelican series; the second volume covers this period.

on the rise (or fall) of the gentry is summed up by Lawrence Stone in *Social Change and Revolution in England 1540-1640* (1965), which has a full bibliography. Stone's *Crisis of the Aristocracy 1558-1641* (1965), though of intimidating length and complexity, makes good reading; it is also the best study we have of the English nobility for any period. The history of politics at the end of the century is still in a state of flux. J. R. Jones's *The First Whigs: the politics of the Exclusion Crisis* (1961) is very good, and so is Keith Feiling's *History of the Tory Party 1640-1714* (1924), though it is now somewhat out of date and should be read in conjunction with Geoffrey Holmes's brilliant *British Politics in the Age of Anne* (1967). J. H. Plumb's *The Growth of Political Stability 1675-1725* (1967) is another major contribution to this subject. Finally, most of what Sir John Neale has to say in his brilliant analysis of *The Elizabethan House of Commons* (1949) is applicable to the seventeenth century, up to 1640, at least.

A few special topics. There is really nothing on the British Army in this period, but the Navy is well served by John Ehrman, whose *Navy in the War of William III* (1953) is a classic. Sir Arthur Bryant's three-volume life of *Samuel Pepys* (1934-8) has a great deal on the Restoration Navy, too. For naval strategy Admiral Sir Herbert Richmond's *The Navy as an Instrument of Policy 1558-1727* (1953) is the best introduction.

The coverage of religious history is patchy. There is scarcely anything on the established Church between 1603 and 1660 except for Christopher Hill's *Economic Problems of the Church* (1956) and Trevor-Roper's *Laud*, which is brilliant but unsympathetic. Puritanism, on the other hand, has been the subject of innumerable works, only a few of which can be mentioned here. The best examination of Puritanism as a religious and intellectual movement is by William Haller, in *The Rise of Puritanism* (New York, 1938); in *Society and Puritanism in pre-revolutionary England* (1964) Christopher Hill attempts to relate it to its social and economic background. The best single survey of Puritanism in all its aspects is *The Protestant Mind of the English Reformation*

1558-1640 (Princeton, 1961) by Charles and Katherine George; the best short introduction is by another American, Alan Simpson, *Puritanism in Old and New England* (Chicago, 1955). G. A. Cragg rounds off the story in *Puritanism in the Period of the Great Persecution 1660-88* (1957). A symposium published to celebrate the recent *rapprochement* between the Anglican and Free Churches contains some first-class essays on the Church under the later Stuarts: *From Uniformity to Unity 1662-1962*, ed. G. A. Nuttall and O. Chadwick (1962). Norman Sykes's brilliant study of *Church and State in the Eighteenth Century in England* (1934) also contains a great deal that is relevant to the earlier period. There are many biographies of Caroline and Williamite bishops, but most of them are by practising clergymen, devoted but ill-equipped; exceptions to note are G. V. Bennett's life of *White Kennett* (1957) and Norman Sykes's *Edmund Gibson* (1929) and *William Wake* (1957). A memorial tribute to Sykes published in 1968, *Essays in Modern Church History*, ed. G. V. Bennett and J. D. Walsh, also contains some very valuable material.

Basil Willey's *Seventeenth Century Background* (1934) is a good introduction to the intellectual movements of the time; Christopher Hill's *Intellectual Origins of the English Revolution* (1965) is more specific. In a century dominated by Hobbes and Locke it is disappointing to find no general study of political thought, except for two brief volumes in the Home University Library series; *Political Thought from Bacon to Halifax* (1914) by G. P. Gooch, and Harold Laski's *Political Thought from Locke to Bentham* (1920). There is a plethora of monographs on this subject, of course; here it is possible only to pick out a few which are especially important for political and constitutional history: J. W. Gough, *Fundamental Law in British History* (1955); J. G. A. Pocock, *The Ancient Constitution and the Feudal Law* (1957), W. H. Greenleaf's *Order, Empiricism and Politics 1500-1700* (1964), and J. N. Figgis's classic *The Divine Right of Kings* (repr. 1965 with an important introduction by G. R. Elton). The standard life of *Newton* is by L. T. More (1934); Frank Manuel's *Portrait of Isaac Newton* (Harvard 1968) is more stimulating, though a trifle eccentric. His impact on his contemporaries is discussed in *The Scientific Revolution 1500-1800* (1954) by A. R. Hall, and in Herbert Butterfield's *Origins of Modern Science* (2nd ed., 1957). Paul Hazard analyses the general ferment of ideas at the end of the century in *The European Mind 1680-1715* (1953).

Finally, the art and architecture of the period are covered by two volumes in the Pelican History of Art; Ellis Waterhouse, *Painting in Britain 1530-1790* (1953) and John Summerson, *Architecture in Britain 1530-1830* (2nd ed., 1955); and by two volumes in the Oxford History of English Art: Eric Mercer, *English Art 1553-1625* (1962) and Margaret Whinney and Oliver Millar, *English Art 1625-1714* (1957). All four are excellent works, containing full bibliographies; Mercer's book is especially interesting to the historian.

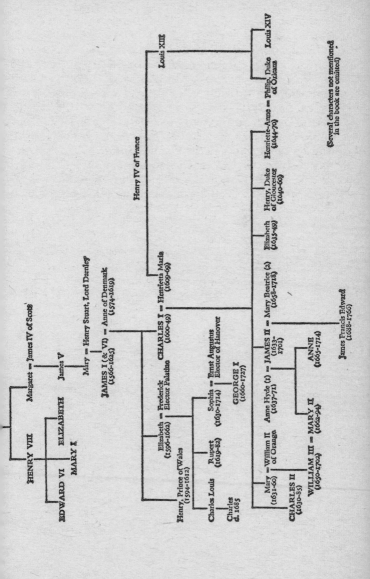

(Several characters not mentioned in the book are omitted)

INDEX

Abbott, George, Archbishop of Canterbury, 24

Abercromby, Sir James, 185

Adda, Count d', papal nuncio, 151, 155, 164

Addison, Joseph, 197

Adwalton, Moor, 91

Albemarle, Arnoud van Keppel, Earl of, 169, 179, 180

Albeville, Ignatius White, marquis d', 153, 154

Alibone, Sir Richard, 153

Almanza, 194

Andrewes, Lancelot, 30

Anne, Queen
  as princess, 112, 152, 154, 155, 160, 164, 168, 177, 178, 180, 182, 183,
  character, 160, 168, 186*ff*, 190
  and her father, 187, 191, 204
  death, 206-7

Anne of Denmark, Queen Consort, 39, 41, 46, 57

Argyll, Archibald Campbell, Earl of, 111, 117

Argyll, John Campbell, Duke of, 200, 206

Arlington, Henry Bennet, Earl of, 112, 116, 117, 119, 121-2, 123, 124

Arminianism, 75*n*

Army
  New Model, 74, 91*ff*, 107
  Under Charles II, 125
  Under William III, 183-4

Army Plot, First, 86

Arundel, Thomas Howard, Earl of, 46, 66, 69

Arundel of Wardour, Henry, Lord, 153

Ashley: *see* Shaftesbury

Assassination Plot, The, 176

Atterbury, Francis, 190, 201

Authorised Version of the Bible, 38

Bacon, Francis, 29, 32, 44, 45-6, 55, 56

Balcarres, Alexander Lindsay, Earl of, 100

Bancroft, Richard, Archbishop of Canterbury, 24, 38, 45

Bank of England, The, 175, 176, 200

Barillon, Paul de, French ambassador, 131, 135, 142, 149, 150

Barrier Treaty, The, 197

Bath, John Granville, Earl of, 160

Bayonne, Charles II at, 107

Beachey Head, 173

Beaufort, Henry Somerset, Duke of, 160

Beaumont, Mary, Dowager Duchess of Buckingham, 50, 55

Bedford, Francis Russell, 4th Earl of, 19-20

Bedford, William Russell, 5th Earl (later Duke) of, 171, 175

Belasyse, John, Lord, 153

Bennet, Sir Henry: *see* Arlington

Berkeley, Charles, 106

Berkeley, Sir John, 106

Bernini, 64*n*

Berwick, James Fitzjames, Duke of, 152, 194

Berwick, Peace of, 81

Bill of Rights, The, 172

Blathwayt, William, 189, 196

Blenheim, 185, 192

Blood, Col. Halcroft, 185

"Blue Water" Policy, The, 190-1, 195

Bolingbroke: *see* St John, Henry

Booth's Rising, 107

Bower, Edward, 64

Boyle, Henry, 189

Boyne, The, 173

Bradford, Francis Newport, Earl of, 169-70

Bradshaw, John, 96

Brent, Robert, 153

216